0064797

WITHDRAWN

DATE DUE

MAR 7 1994	

BAKER & TAYLOR BOOKS

Congressional
Careers

Congressional Careers

Contours of

Life in the

U.S. House of

Representatives

John R. Hibbing

The University of

North Carolina Press

Chapel Hill and London

© 1991 The University of North Carolina Press
All rights reserved

Library of Congress Cataloging-in-Publication Data

Hibbing, John R.
    Congressional careers : contours of life in the U.S.
House of Representatives / John R. Hibbing.
        p.   cm.
    Includes bibliographical references and index.
    ISBN 0-8078-1984-0 (cloth : alk. paper)
    ISBN 0-8078-4340-7 (paper : alk. paper)
    1. Legislators—United States—Biography.
    2. Legislators—United States—Longitudinal
studies.   3. United States. Congress. House—Term
of office.   I. Title.
JK1319.H53   1991
328.73′073′0922—dc20
    [B]   91-182
                                                          CIP

The paper in this book meets the guidelines for
permanence and durability of the Committee on
Production Guidelines for Book Longevity of the
Council on Library Resources.

Manufactured in the United States of America
95 94 93 92 91   5 4 3 2 1

To Anne

for everything

Contents

Tables and Figures

Tables

Figures

Preface

I have a knack. It is not a very good knack for a social scientist to have, and I try my best not to pass it on to any students with whom I come into contact, but it is a knack nonetheless. I frequently involve myself in research projects requiring prodigious amounts of data collection. Once the study for which the data were originally collected is completed, I move on to other things, apparently content to know these mounds of data are resting securely in my file cabinets and on my computer discs. As many of my graduate students will attest, I am among the world's least efficient data collectors. For example, in this manuscript, as was the case with my only other book-length effort to date, large and distinct data sets were required for each substantive chapter.

The reason I mention all this is that, as a result of the data requirements of this project, I have an unusual number of people and organizations whose assistance I want to recognize publicly. First, there are those who provided financial assistance. The University of Nebraska Foundation Fund for Research on the U.S. Congress has been an extremely valuable resource. I greatly appreciate the assistance of the anonymous benefactor of the fund and also the first executive director of the fund, Adam Breckenridge—whose Kentucky family, I might add, knows something about careers in Congress. The Dirksen Congressional Center supplied financial assistance at the crucial nascent stages of the project, and I am deeply appreciative of the center's support. And the National Science Foundation provided the major source of funding for this effort in the form of grant number SES-8619518. My sincere thanks to NSF.

Most of the data were collected quite recently, but the foundation for the data set used in chapter 2 was laid during the summer of 1980 when John Alford and I should have been studying for our comprehensive examinations. Instead, we did something even more tedious—we coded data on congressional elections (with an important assist from Sue Strickler). The fact that the data we coded that summer in Iowa City have been useful in more than one project is a clear indication I did not design that research project on my own. Some of the data utilized in chapters 4 and 6 come from the Inter-University Consortium for Social and Political Research. Neither that organization nor the original collectors of the data bear any responsibility for the analyses and interpretations contained in this document. In compiling the data for the remaining chapters, I was fortunate to have the opportunity to work with several very capable graduate assistants. My thanks to Zoltan Barany, Don Beahm, Chris Carney, Rebekah Herrick, Tim Howard, Mark Leeper, Ed Miller, Patty Moock, Jay Ovsiovitch, and Jiang Ren. But most of all I should thank Michael Moore and Jerry Stubben for the extra efforts they made. Without the organizational abilities and hard work of first Jerry and then Michael, I would have drowned in a sea of data. I am in their debt.

Early readers of this manuscript made invaluable contributions. Among their many other observations, Gary Jacobson and Susan Welch saved me from an important methodological error in chapter 7. Roger Davidson and Richard Fenno pushed me to do a better job of convincing readers that, beyond the fact that it has not been done before, there is an important reason to look at careers in a longitudinal fashion. On this particular project and on many others, John Alford's counsel has been occasionally unreliable but always indispensable. As usual, John's comments were novel and perceptive. And Paul Betz was everything a good editor should be: friend and foe, patient and impatient, supportive and critical. My thanks to them all.

More generally, I would be remiss if I did not mention my parents, Vernon and Ardyth Hibbing, whose strength during our family's real-life version of the 1980s farm crisis in America was an inspiration. They have been a great help to me through the years. Finally, my wife, Anne, has been of unfathomable assistance in all kinds of ways. I can't thank her enough. Even so, Anne almost needed to share the dedication page with Michael (age 10), Matthew (age 7), and Anthony (age 3). They certainly deserve a dedication, too, and I am not sure how many more times I will be able to collect all the data I seem to require for a book-length manuscript. But since Anne has put up with me longer, the children will have to bide their time. Of course, if for some unusual reason they are really hot to have a book dedicated to them, they can always sharpen their pencils and buy some coding sheets.

John R. Hibbing
Lincoln, Nebraska

Congressional
Careers

1 Introduction: Manny Celler Stayed Too Long

During most of his extraordinary career in the U.S. House of Representatives, Emanuel "Manny" Celler had been the envy of just about all his House colleagues. Despite numerous redistrictings, his Brooklyn constituents remained steadfastly supportive of him. He did not have to bother spending a lot of time doing service work or being "on display" in the district. His experience, wit, and excellent memory caused an unusual number of House members to seek his counsel on various policy and procedural matters. And his Judiciary Committee chairmanship made him one of the House's "movers and shakers," as illustrated by the pivotal role he played in the titanic struggles during the early 1960s to pass a civil rights bill. Manny Celler seemed to be living in a legislator's Nirvana.

But this idyllic situation also created a problem. Manny Celler's congressional world was too comfortable, and he did not know when or perhaps even how to leave that world. He stayed and he stayed. He stayed for fifty years. He stayed until the psychological distance between him and the people of the district became too great. He stayed until a movement he did not understand overtook him. He stayed until his district and party turned on him in the 1972 Democratic primary. He stayed until he was ignominiously removed from the seat he had held for half a century. He stayed so long that several near-retirement-age House members looked at a slightly befuddled Manny Celler and said they were not going to let "that" happen to them.

Manny Celler spent his entire adult life in the U.S. House of Representatives. Although the length of his stay is somewhat unusual, it is not greatly out of line with the tenure of others in the modern Congress. Carl

Vinson (D-Ga.), for example, actually spent a few more months in the House than Manny Celler. Sam Rayburn (D-Tex.) spent the last 47 years of his life in the House. Had not a heart attack cut him short, Rayburn may have made the same mistake as Manny Celler, since they both radiated identical "the House is my life" attitudes. George Mahon (D-Tex.) served 44 years; W. R. "Bob" Poage (D-Tex.), 41; Melvin Price (D-Ill.), 44; and Jamie Whitten (D-Miss.), 50 and still counting, as of early 1992 the holder of the record for longest House service. If the issue is length of a congressional rather than a House career, Carl Hayden makes Manny Celler, Carl Vinson, and Jamie Whitten look like veritable flashes in the pan. Hayden's 15 years in the House and 42 years in the Senate constitute the record for longest service in Congress. In fact, his retirement in 1968 at the age of 91 marked the first time since Arizona had become a state that it was not represented in the U.S. Congress by Carl Hayden.

Historical Trends in Congressional Careers

The congressional career of Manny Celler would appear much more remarkable in the context of the nineteenth-century Congress. The fact that all the lengthy careers just mentioned were logged by individuals serving well after 1950 is not a coincidence. The likelihood of a new member of Congress staying for an entire career has been much greater in the second half of the twentieth century than at any time previously. Since 1953 the average member of the House has stayed almost eleven years. One hundred years ago, an eleven-year career in the House would have been considered unusually long. As H. Douglas Price remarks, "Up until the 1890s only a handful of men had pursued substantial lifetime careers within the House, and they were often the occasion for puzzled comment" (1971, 16). Price goes on to note that William Holman (D-Ind.) was "one of the few really long-term nineteenth-century members" (1971, 21), yet Holman served barely thirty years, a record of longevity that is hardly impressive by modern standards.

Charles Bullock (1972) once defined a "careerist" in the House of Representatives as someone who had served at least ten terms. In the 92d Congress (1971–72) the number of careerists reached an astounding eighty-seven—indicating that fully one out of five representatives in the House at that time had served over twenty years in the body. The number of careerists has gone down some in the last fifteen years, but still approximately one out of eight members meets Bullock's criterion.

Information on nineteenth-century Congresses is not as tidy and complete, however there is no mistaking the contrast with modern congressional careers. According to Price's data (1977, 38), of the 242 House members in the 24th Congress (1835–36), 128 were not even in the 25th. If the analysis is restricted to members elected from districts outside the South, the high level of fluidity is even more apparent: 100 of the 166 nonsouthern members in the 24th Congress were not in the 25th—and 79 of these 100 left voluntarily (3 others died and 18 were defeated). In the 49th Congress (1885–86), there were 325 House members, and only 193 of these answered the call for the 50th. Again, voluntary retirement was the major source of turnover. Throughout most of the nineteenth century, members rarely made it into their second terms, let alone their tenth! Data on average career length have been collected by Stuart Rice (1928) and updated by Nelson Polsby (1968). They show quite clearly that House career length increased during Congress's 200 years.[1]

Why were congressional careers typically short back then? It is not hard to come up with reasonable explanations. At times during the 1800s turnover in many states was pushed higher by the tradition of congressional rotation (see Kernell 1977; Struble 1980; Dometrius and Sigelman 1989). Moreover, for a good deal of that century the nation's capital was not particularly dignified. Accounts abound of the swampy, mosquito-infested, rural-outpost nature of Washington's early days. The Congress itself was somewhat raucous. Price writes of "bitter and outrageous language, scathing ridicule, and sarcasm . . . outbreaks of physical violence, guns and knives on occasion being carried into the chamber" (1971, 18). Polsby (1968, 166–67) recounts in vivid detail some of the classic altercations of the nineteenth-century House, including those involving Charles Sumner's caning, Matthew Lyon's expectorating, John Randolph's hunting dogs, and a gunshot wound that was inflicted in the chamber of the House. Former Speaker Thomas B. Reed's simple description of life in Congress during this period seems an apt summation: "These were not pleasant days" (quoted in Polsby 1968, 167).

Finally, the Congress of that era did not possess a great deal of power. Morris Fiorina writes that it was not until 1890 that the U.S. Congress became more important than the Virginia state legislature (1977b, 6). Price notes that "in many respects the pre-1900 House was similar to the average current state assembly" (1971, 18). Congress was a part-time body with a part-time role in a limited federal government. During this period it was common for even the most powerful members of the House (including Speakers) to leave the body in order to take a chance at becoming a senator or a governor. In short, Congress was neither a pleasant nor a powerful place, so, unlike Manny Celler, most nineteenth-century members did not stay.

But all this is really nothing new. The growing professionalization of Congress over the years has been very well documented. In three separate articles, Price describes the trend (1971, 1975, 1977). Fiorina sets the stage for his indictment of the "Washington establishment" with a brief discussion of the early Congresses (1977b, 1989). Samuel Huntington (1965) sees careerism itself as a major reason Congress is in need of indictment (or at least was in need of indictment in 1965). The thesis of David Mayhew's (1974a) justifiably well-known essay on congressional structures and behavior is that an enormous amount of analytical leverage is obtained by assuming that members of Congress are interested in nothing except getting reelected, and his first step is to show that in the modern Congress most members do in fact seek and win reelection. Polsby (1968) puts the trend in larger perspective by calling it part of the "institutionalization of the House." T. Richard Wittmer (1964), Bullock (1972), and Fiorina, David Rohde, and Peter Wissel (1975), using slightly different measures, all provide important supportive evidence that, with the passage of the decades, congressional careers have become longer. Just about every textbook on Congress and even many general textbooks on American politics also note the fact that typical congressional careers are now much longer than they used to be and that these lengthy careers can be seen as an important part of the professionalization or institutionalization of Congress. Although some slightly peculiar things have happened to this trend since the early 1970s, there would be little benefit in providing additional evidence supporting the well-established basic fact that congressional careers have lengthened.

Some members may stay too long; others leave before it is too late; but the fact remains that, by historical standards, most modern members stay quite a long time. Lengthy modern congressional careers are now accepted as the norm. The puzzled comment that used to surround those unusual creatures who spent lifetime careers in the House is now reserved for those who turn their backs on further service in Congress. It is widely assumed that a politician who would do this must have ulterior motives. Why would anyone want to leave the House except to make a run for the Senate, and why would anyone voluntarily leave the Senate except to make a run for the presidency? Perhaps, besides seeking higher office, they might leave because of advanced age, poor health, or impending scandal revelation, but certainly not for any other reason. The incredulity with which many voluntary retirement announcements of members of Congress are greeted is perhaps the ultimate testimony to how far Congress and the congressional career have come in 200 years.

Where Research on Congressional Careers Is Lacking

No, we do not need another recitation of how congressional careers have evolved. The general changes are quite well-known and largely unsurprising to anyone who has spent time reflecting on the history of Congress and the United States. But what we do not know is how our national representatives change while they are in Congress. We know more (but not much) about the evolution of legislatures than we do about the evolution of legislators, and this is unfortunate.

Perhaps too many of us have been transfixed by the clarity of the trend toward longer congressional careers, for we have spent far too much time dreaming up new ways to document it. We have used percentage of members in their first term, percentage who have served five terms or more, percentage who have served ten terms or more, mean number of terms served, mean number of years served, average age of members, percentage seeking reelection, percentage replacements, Polsby-Rice percentage first-term, median terms served, and several other perfectly reasonable and relevant measures. We have almost as many ways of documenting the declining membership turnover in Congress and the increasing longevity of congressional careers as we have of measuring the increased electoral safety of incumbent House members!

What we are missing is actual knowledge of how the situations and behaviors of members of Congress change (or do not change) as these members move through what are now frequently lengthy careers. Numerous insights are likely to be generated if the extended congressional career is viewed as an opportunity to observe changes in individual legislative environment and behavior over a several-year period, not as something to discard as soon as we have proven that lengthy careers are in fact quite common in the modern Congress. Career-based research is difficult and meaningless when most members stay in Congress for only a few months. But when a large number of individuals are staying for several decades, career-based research becomes possible and potentially fruitful.

The major reason this research approach holds so much potential is that it reflects how members themselves view the situation—and if one of our goals is to understand congressional behavior, we must approximate as closely as possible the perspective of those doing the behaving. When queried about their electoral situation, members of Congress invariably respond by reciting the support they have received over the years, not by comparing their present electoral status with the other 434 members. When queried about their activities back in the district, they recount all they have done over the years. And when queried about their legislative positions or actions, perhaps on a specific issue, they are more likely to mention what they did on a similar issue years ago than to compare their current predilections with those of other members currently serving. Representatives, like most of us, utilize the past as a bench mark for understanding the present and perhaps the future.

The extent to which past behavior acts as a constraint on the subsequent behavior of representatives is an important piece of information for those prone to reflect upon the nature of Congress and the need for reform. To offer one example, pressure is mounting to pass a constitutional amendment limiting the length of congressional service. This is an issue that will not go away. It has been with us longer than the Constitution (the Articles of Confederation limited stays in the Confederate Congress). Seventy percent of the U.S. population support term limits for members of Congress (see Hook 1990, 567), interest groups now exist for the sole purpose of establishing the congressional equivalent of the Twenty-second Amendment, the popular press of late has bristled with debate on this issue, and some states have now limited the terms of state legislators. But the sad thing is that this debate is taking place at an incredibly low level. Proponents make their case by drawing attention to the length of congressional careers and by offering vague claims concerning the need for "new blood." Opponents, who are usually led by sitting representatives and senators themselves, counter by pointing out that even with long careers we still have reasonable levels of turnover (as of 1989, well over 50 percent of House members had begun their service in the 1980s) and by offering equally vague claims concerning the glories of legislative experience.

Both positions miss the point. The truth is that raw turnover levels do not say much at all about the extent to which Congress is innovative, activist, legislatively sharp and focused, sensitive to constituents, and more generally in tune with the country. To draw conclusions on these issues, we must pay closer attention to how members change throughout their careers. Do they change their roll call voting behavior during a career? Do they change with regard to non-Washington activity, such as taking trips back to the district, doing constituency service, delegating staffers to district rather than Washington offices, and communicating with constituents? If these behaviors do vary with career stage, why? Is it because of career-related variation in electoral support, in formal positions held within the body, or in something else?

In short, the debate on the advantages and disadvantages of legislative experience is taking place without any evidence on what exactly it is that this experience brings. Is there a learning curve? How much would be lost by mandating the removal of senior legislators? If longitudinal research discovers that member behavior is generally constant across a career, it seems to me that serious thought should be given to term limitations. If, however, there are signs that senior legislators are offering something that junior members are not, lengthy careers just may make Congress a better rather than a worse legislative assembly.

Despite the fact that the consequences of careerism should be the foundation for an understanding of the modern Congress, we know next to nothing about them. Most research on individual congressional environments and behaviors has been concerned with cross-sectional rather than longitudinal questions. Why do some representatives support their party more than others? Why do some incumbents attract more votes than others? Why do some representatives run for the Senate while others do not? Why do some members do more constituency service work than others?

On occasion, researchers have attempted to address questions about the effects of tenure on behavior. But often this research is not what it seems. For example, some recent attention has been given to the issue of whether senior members are less likely to do constituency service work than younger members. This may appear to be a tenure-based research question, but in many cases it turns out to be something else. Despite the longitudinal overtones to the issue, it is often tested with cross-sectional data. Typical research on this question may tell us that in a certain Congress members with ten terms of service were less likely to do constituency service work than members with two terms of service, but this really says nothing about tenure-based effects. It may be that those ten-termers have done relatively trivial amounts of constituency service work throughout their entire careers. It may be that those second-termers will continue to do incredible amounts of constituency service even when they are ten-termers. We do not know. The cross-sectional research design, even when it includes tenure as a variable, does not tell us much about change over the course of a career.

Using cross-sectional data to test longitudinal questions usually means it will be impossible to sort out generational, life-cycle, and, for that matter, period effects. In the example presented above, if the ten-termers did in fact always ignore constituency service work, the effect would seem to be generational—the newer generation simply is more likely to do constituency service work because it was socialized into congressional activities at a different time and in a different way. If the ten-termers used to do a lot of constituency service work but drifted away from it sometime during their careers, the effect would indeed be a life-cycle (or career-cycle) effect since the stage of the career is what makes the difference. A period effect is one in which all cohorts are moved to a different level by some force. In the case of constituency service, perhaps all cohorts of representatives began doing more of it when the resources to undertake this work—staffers, monetary allocations for trips home, etc.—were increased. But since we do not know how much constituency service work the ten-termers did before they became ten-termers or how much the second-termers did after their second term, data from a single Congress provide an insufficient basis for conclusions regarding the effects of career-cycle forces on congressional behavior.

There are also problems with taking the members of a single class and following them all the way through their careers. Setting aside the possibility that the particular class selected may be atypical of even the classes around it (see Loomis 1988a; Schneider 1989), the key problem with this kind of design is that it is unable to distinguish clearly between life-cycle and period effects. If a change appears somewhere in the course of the careers of many members of this class, is this change the result of a career cycle or is it something that affected everyone in Congress regardless of where they were in their own career cycle? This kind of question cannot be answered with single-cohort data. So even the small amount of research purporting to be interested in longitudinal questions is often much less than it claims.

In this study, I avoid such pitfalls by relying, with one exception, on data structured across individual congressional careers and by including data from numerous cohorts. The task of collecting and organizing the data in this manner confirmed suspicions regarding the virtual absence of previous career-centered approaches to the study of Congress and congressional behavior. Existing data on Congress seldom are structured along individual congressional careers. It is easy to find out what Representative Smith did in the 99th Congress, but generally what that same Representative Smith did in the 100th Congress is treated as an entirely different case, not as a continuation of what that member had done before. If the data do extend over time, more often than not they trace what changed within a congressional district. Again, the individual career fades to the background as several different members may have represented the district during the period in question.

All this is only to point out that relatively few analysts have used appropriate data to pursue questions concerning changes over the course of congressional careers. While there are countless references in the literature to the need to obtain more than just a cross-sectional "snapshot" of congressional behavior, most of these references are followed by research that does in fact present a cross-sectional snapshot. Much wailing and moaning can be heard, but only a scattering of researchers have attempted to obtain moving pictures of specific aspects of congressional careers, and certainly no one has assessed with appropriate data how these specific aspects fit together into the overall congressional career. Until this is done, little progress can be made in coming to grips with the advantages and disadvantages of careerism in the modern House.

Four Previous Works on Life-Cycle Effects

In the study of general political behavior, it is fairly common to take into consideration life-cycle effects. It is widely believed that the propensity of individuals to do some things and not to do others is dependent upon where they are in the life cycle. The degrees to which people participate in politics and are "set in their ways," to take but two examples, are commonly thought to be influenced by these life-cycle effects. It is a fact, to continue with one example, that people in the 18–25-year-old age category are less likely to vote than middle-aged individuals (see Verba and Nie 1972; Strate, Parrish, Elder, and Ford 1989; but also see Beck and Jennings 1979). And it is a fact that the rate of participation of the very elderly, for obvious reasons, is less than the rate of participation of those who are not quite so elderly. Indeed, it is probably safe to say that any treatment of a topic such as voting participation that did not at least address the possible effects of the life cycle would be considered woefully incomplete. Given the widespread assumption that life-cycle effects are important in the study of general political behavior, it is more than a little surprising that there has not been a concerted attempt to test for life-cycle effects in Congress. Instead, previous research, though promising, is quite sketchy and inconclusive. I illustrate this point by summarizing the four most relevant previous works.

Richard F. Fenno, Jr. (1978, chap. 6), insightfully suggests that members generally evolve from an "expansionist" to a "protectionist" career stage. While this observation has the clear ring of truth, Fenno applies these terms only to careers in the constituency and does not flesh out the concepts in full detail. Therefore, many questions remain regarding this fledgling typology. Can the progression from expansionist to protectionist stages be observed in other areas of the congressional career? Do legislative interests, for example, narrow after early, expansionistic forays into a variety of diverse policy areas? Are some members arrested in the expansionist stage? Is the movement from expansionist to protectionist stages driven by a progression from marginal to safe seat? Are there really only two stages, or might there be gradations of expansionism and protectionism? Is the progression from expansionism to protectionism evident only through the impressionistic observations of someone with the skilled ear and hard-earned access of Richard Fenno, or can this evolution be documented in traditional, objective measures of congressional behavior?

Glenn Parker (1986a) attempts to address this last question by employing an objective measure of congressional behavior. Moreover, Parker is directly concerned with whether or not this measure—the number of days members spend back in their districts rather than in Washington—fluctuates with changes in members' career stage. As will be discussed in more detail later, Parker's main conclusion is that the tendency to spend time back in the district changes very little throughout the course of a career: "A major attribute of home styles is their permanence; once established, the patterns that mark them tend to persist" (1986a, 35). If substantiated, this is an important contribution to our knowledge of congressional career evolution. Still, while going back to the district is an important activity, it is only one of many important activities in which members of Congress engage. In addition, if we study only a single type of behavior, it is impossible to analyze the interplay of various behavioral proclivities over the course of the years.

Charles Bullock and Burdett Loomis (1985) deal with the important question of whether or not modern members of Congress achieve positions of power more quickly than was the case a few decades ago. Despite the fact that most observers believe the movement to formal positions occurs more rapidly than it used to, Bullock and Loomis find the evidence to be uneven. They arrive at conclusions such as: there is "no clear trend for legislators to become their party's most senior member [chairman or ranking minority member] on a committee earlier in their careers" (75); "The survivors of earlier classes were more likely to be senior members of subcommittees after five terms than were the representatives elected in 1970" (76); and, "The Class of 1970 did not enjoy a marked advantage over earlier classes once five terms had elapsed" (76). To be sure, elsewhere they detect some evidence of the expected contour change (see also Loomis 1984), but support for conventional wisdom with regard to this element of congressional careers is anything but pristine. Part of the inconclusiveness here may be due to a reliance on scattered cohorts. Moreover, as with Parker's work, the focus of attention is on a single aspect of the congressional career; in this case, formal positions held. We would benefit from another look at the relationship of career cycle to the acquisition of formal positions as well as to other elements of the congressional career.

Herbert Asher and Herbert Weisberg (1978) make an important contribution to the study of congressional careers by analyzing the degree to which the roll call voting behavior of representatives changes over the course of the typical member's career. They conclude that most members enter their decision-making calculus on an upcoming vote with an established "voting history" and that remarkable consistency is evident across most careers. While this is a provocative conclusion, and one that ties in nicely with the well-developed literature holding that policy change in Congress generally comes by way of membership change rather than membership conversion (see, for example, Brady and Lynn 1973), the evidence is weak and the conclusion pertains only to one small aspect of the legislative career (roll call voting). A sense of the contours of the full array of legislative activities remains to be presented, as does a complete picture of the interrelationships of these legislative activities with other aspects of the general congressional career.

Thus, extant literature presents no broad-based, systematic description of how members of Congress evolve. We have some quality research on specific features of the modern congressional career but no integrated picture. And even on the specific features of the career we find uncertainty over what the findings actually mean and a disconcerting amount of disagreement with conventional wisdom. In truth, despite lengthy careers and lots of data, we do not know how members of Congress change over the course of their careers.

The Political Life Cycle and Modern Congressional Careers

What kinds of changes might we *expect* to occur during the congressional career? By far the most thorough set of expectations concerning career-based change in Congress can be found in Donald Matthews's classic work, *U.S. Senators and Their World* (1960). In this book, Matthews describes what he calls the political life cycle of senators. I quote from this work at length, using brackets to indicate how the passage would look if applied to the House, the focus of attention in my study.

> Once seated, a [U.S. representative] is hard to beat under most circumstances. . . . Aggressively pursued case work provides him with a larger circle of friends. He has the publicity edge on almost any challenger. His seniority and legislative know-how are valuable to his constituents, and many of them know it.
>
> If the [representative] survives [early challenges] to his position, then he becomes more secure than before. All the advantages he possessed in the first [few reelection bids are] even more compelling now. But with greater seniority and security go additional legislative responsibilities. [After a few terms], he is, in all likelihood, a senior member of major committees. He is well on his way to becoming an important national figure, increasingly concerned with pressing national and international problems. In the vocabulary of social psychology, his "reference groups" change, he becomes more concerned with [House], national, and perhaps international problems, and devotes less time and attention to the folks back home. The press of legislative duties becomes ever harder to escape. Advancing years make fence-mending trips increasingly onerous. Senility, real or apparent, may become a political problem. . . .
>
> Meanwhile, there have been changes in the character of his [dis-

trict,] and it is difficult to alter publicly staked-out positions and group relationships formed when circumstances were different. . . . [New generations of voters come along, and the representative does] not get back to the district as often as he used to. Thus, as a [representative's] power and prominence approaches a peak, his electoral support is crumbling. [After many terms], the senior [representative may become electorally vulnerable]. . . . The cycle reaches its bitter end when [the representative is denied reelection]. Not many survive to the end of this political life-cycle, but for those who do, defeat suffered at the peak of their careers provides a cruel reminder of the constituents' power. (241–42)

As can be seen in Matthews's words, this cyclical view of congressional careers is characterized by a definite rhythm, and it is assumed that this rhythm is driven primarily by the relationship between tenure and electoral security. Representatives start out in a precarious electoral position; they gradually improve and stabilize their hold over the district; but then, later in the career, they become so complacent that attentions turn elsewhere, energies wane, and the voters deliver the ultimate "cruel reminder of the constituents' power." The cyclical view clearly hypothesizes that diminishing constituency attention and diminishing electoral security accompany each other at the later stages of many careers.

Further, according to the cyclical view, one of the main reasons for the late-career decline of both electoral security and attention to the constituency is the late-career *increase* in attention to national policy matters (see also Davidson 1969, 103). Gary Jacobson describes it well: "Some opportunities to build support back in the district must be foregone if a member is to share in governing the country. And the longer a member is in office, the more opportunities arise to influence policy and to gain the respect of others in government. Members very soon find that they have to balance their desire for electoral security against their desire for a successful career in Washington" (1983, 37). Whether the representative is said to have "gone Washington" or to have contracted Potomac Fever, the concept is the same and ofttimes so is the result. Matters other than direct constituency concerns are perceived to have become more important to the representative. The representative's attention, agenda, and perhaps even voting record may have wandered from the district. So the constituency takes its revenge (remember Manny Celler).

But Matthews was writing about the 1950s Senate. His version of the political life cycle is presented at the end of a chapter and goes untested. But even if it had been punctiliously documented, there is no reason to assume it would necessarily apply to the modern House. In fact, the findings scattered throughout most recent research on the topic seem inconsistent with the political life-cycle view. More specifically, numerous contemporary studies emphasize features of the congressional career that appear to remain stable—or, if they do not remain perfectly stable, features that respond to idiosyncratic forces rather than some immutable natural cycle of congressional life. Electoral security/insecurity is still seen as a basic component of careers, but the thrust of recent research tends to be on the absence of change in feelings of electoral security over the course of lengthy stays in the House.

For example, Karl Kurtz (1972) and Albert Cover (1980) both claim that the relationship between seniority and marginality is limited and weak. Cover reports a correlation between seniority (I assume this to mean number of years in the House rather than true seniority rank) and marginality (I assume this to be percentage of the two-party vote rather than a dummy for whether the last race was marginal or not) of only .24, and most of this, Cover implies, is attributable to "an abrupt increase in electoral support following a member's first or second term" (1980, 129). Kurtz uses defeat rates rather than marginality and finds that between 1954 and 1968, 15 percent of incumbents seeking reelection for the first time were defeated; about 7 percent of those seeking reelection for the second time were defeated; and from the third reelection bid on only about 4 percent were defeated (1972, 90). After the first term or two, stability rather than cyclical variation seems to be the norm, according to more recent research.

And the relative electoral insecurity of first- and second-term representatives has even been called into question. Richard Born (1979), following his interpretation of Morris Fiorina (1977a, 1977b), claims that those seeking reelection for the first time—those he calls sophomores—are doing much better than they used to in improving their vote share over and above their initial victory. Jacobson notes that "first-term incumbents have been especially difficult to defeat in recent years" (1983, 45). Strong support for this belief is provided by events of the 1970s. In a horrible year for Republicans, 1974, first-term incumbent Republicans as a group "actually improved their position" over 1972 (Burnham 1975, 419). Moreover, in 1976, seventy-two of the seventy-four freshmen Democrats were able to hold their seats despite a "return to normality" after the events of 1974. Perhaps even more surprisingly, no freshmen Democrats elected in 1978 were defeated in the very good Republican year of 1980 (see Jacobson 1983, 36).

On the flip side, however, fourteen incumbent Democrats with ten or more years of service were defeated in 1980 (see Jacobson 1983, 46; Barone and Ujifusa 1981, 158–59). This peculiar situation led former representative Al Ullman (D-Oreg.) to state, "There's a rather open revolt against the guys who are in office and the more power they have, the more some people are likely to vote against them" (see "Congress" 1980, 28; Hibbing and Alford 1981, 437). Is it possible that freshmen are safer than upperclassmen? If so, the resulting pattern would represent an inversion of the political life cycle.

Further, even if, as the life-cycle view assumes, vote share increases with tenure (at least for a time), this may be meaningless since *all* members, regardless of margin, are thought to feel electorally insecure (see Mann 1978).[2] The idea here is that if we had a meter capable of measuring subjective feelings of electoral security, it would reveal that all members are electorally insecure, no matter where they happen to be on the congressional career cycle and regardless of their last victory margin. One reason for this situation may be that at some time in their electoral career most members have had a close race. David Mayhew reports that 77 percent of the members of the 93d Congress had in one election or another won with less than 60 percent of the total vote, although this finding is difficult to interpret since it appears that first-election in addition to first-*re*election margins may have been included in these calculations (see Mayhew 1974a, 33). Also, consider Jacobson's remark on a related reason for representatives to feel electorally insecure: "The few examples each election year of supposedly secure incumbents going down to defeat are sufficient lessons to the rest; they make most incumbents remarkably responsive to changing political forces" (1983, 46).

The larger point is that rampant, indiscriminate, electoral neurosis may leave little room for career cycles. This chronic electoral insecurity means it is unlikely other aspects of the congressional career—particularly aspects thought to attract votes—will display cyclical patterns. A reading of recent literature seems to suggest that members enter Congress doing constituency service work and leave Congress doing constituency service work (recall Parker's findings on the stability of constituency activity patterns). They quickly move into positions of influence in the House (see the expectations of Loomis 1984 and Bullock and Loomis 1985)—

perhaps a subcommittee chair after only a term or two—and then they stay there. But even when they acquire a somewhat better position, their attention to the district, contrary to the life-cycle view, may continue unabated (thanks to staff, resources, and sometimes unfathomable stamina).

According to these accounts, modern members rarely "convert" to a different modus operandi (see Fenno 1978; Parker 1986a, 1986b). Similarly, they rarely disrupt their established voting patterns on the issues (recall the Asher and Weisberg findings described earlier). New styles of activity and new policy proposals are generally thought to enter Congress by way of membership changes rather than changes on the part of the membership (see Fiorina 1977b, 54–55; Brady and Lynn 1973). Electoral insecurity leads members to want to do whatever they did last time, only perhaps a little better. Protectionist strategies, to use Fenno's words, are the rule of the day. As Mayhew notes, "Behavior of an innovative sort can yield vote gains, but it can also bring disaster. . . . For the most part, it makes sense for congressmen to follow conservative strategies" (1974a, 47). Seen through these lenses, change is rare; careers are characterized by stability.

Consistent with this thrust, recent congressional research holds that the apprenticeship norm has been mortally wounded and that the rewards of issue expertise have been badly hit as well. It does appear as though members are constantly pontificating and that, as a result, little time is left to acquire more than a superficial knowledge of public policy. At first blush, modern careers seem to contain no extensive period of quiet research on the issues of the day and meditation on the mores of the institution followed only then by the coming out of a fully flowered, honest-to-goodness legislator, equipped with issue expertise, a committee chair, and back-slapping, behind-the-scenes bargaining skills. There is only more of the same banal grandstanding, posturing, and gamesmanship, year after year, term after term. Stroke constituents, vote the same as you have in the past, gloss over the issues whenever possible, grab a position of authority early, milk it for as long as possible, and hope for the best in an unpredictable electoral climate. Members rarely strike out on a bold new course or even rock the boat in any way that is not absolutely necessary. Hill style and home style alike may not be frozen but they are altered grudgingly. As a result, concepts such as career-based change and the political life cycle are not featured prominently in much of the recent literature on Congress.

The Changing Modern
Congressional Career?

Thus, the only existing set of theoretical expectations concerning career-based change is at odds with a sizable chunk of modern congressional research. Is this because the political life-cycle view never applied to the House, even when Matthews observed it in the Senate? Or does the discrepancy stem from the fact that congressional careers changed between the 1950s and the 1980s? In many respects, the changing career contour explanation is appealing. It may be that while the nature and level of congressional activities still change over the course of a career in the House, the *degree* of change from early career to late career is now much more constrained than it was decades ago. House careers may have become increasingly static and decreasingly cyclical. The "throw" provided by additional House tenure may be more muted than in years past, suggesting that members are learning about congressional service more rapidly than they used to; that the pressure to be consistent over time is perceived by members to be more intense; that modern members are politically more cautious than they used to be; or some combination of these explanations.

Were it to be documented empirically, this flattening of congressional careers would be consistent with impressionistic knowledge of changes in American politics during the last forty years. For example, today, newly elected members of Congress are presented with a battery of seminars, workshops, retreats, lectures, and publications all designed to teach them how to organize a congressional office; how to utilize congressional procedures; how to get reelected; and how to get publicity. While the impact of these sessions is difficult to measure, it is often implied that the learning curve for many members of Congress levels off quite early these days. Modern members seem quick to learn much of what they feel they need to know about serving (staying?) in Congress.

Moreover, these same members now are said to be free to act on this knowledge. The modern House's more equitable distribution of resources combined with its expectations that participation and legislative involvement will not be biased against those newly elected to Congress fosters consistency rather than variability across careers. Further the intracareer electoral climate seems to have changed in a way that fits with increased behavioral stability. Electoral safety may now decrease legislative ingenuity and risk taking since there is little motivation to alter established, apparently successful patterns of behavior, especially when seemingly minor slips and changes have been magnified into major campaign issues in some instances in recent years. If verified, this would be a change from older conventional wisdom, which held that electoral security likely encouraged rather than discouraged legislative innovation.

Increased attentiveness to legislative activity, particularly on the part of roll call–tallying interest groups, encourages incrementalism if not total stasis on the part of members. Potential challengers are ready to cry "flip-flop" or "political opportunist" at the drop of a hat—whether the issue is stylistic or substantive. Those identified as latecomers to an issue or to a cause run the risk of losing support from both sides. Members are being watched much more carefully than they have ever been watched, even though constituents are not any more knowledgeable or informed than they used to be. Every contribution received, every junket taken, every vote missed, every roll call scale released, every piece of franked mail sent, every joke told, every staffer hired, every trip home not taken now all have the potential to be major issues in the next campaign, or the next, or the next. The fact that this attention is more latent than actual is of no practical consequence to the representative. Both encourage the same response.

In addition to being observed more closely, members of Congress are doing more observing themselves. They are making increasing use of fairly sophisticated district-based polls in order to learn what sells and what does not sell among their constituents. Representatives now have a more accurate fix on the issue positions of the people in their districts, and they also know that stylistically the people prefer to be given as much personal attention as possible—regardless of the tenure or status of their member.

The behavioral modifications that are thought to follow from this altered environment are partially captured in the words of Malcolm E. Jewell and Samuel C. Patterson concerning the case of former senator Walter George (D-Ga.):

> A story is told about the reelection efforts of Senator Walter George of Georgia in 1956. At age 78, with thirty-four years of seniority in the Senate, he was chairman of the Foreign Relations Committee and one of the most powerful figures in Washington, an adviser to presidents and an architect of the nation's foreign policy. For the first time in many years he was facing a serious fight for

renomination, and he returned to Georgia to campaign. As he toured the small towns of his home state, he found that little remained of his once-powerful political organization. Again and again he would ask about old friends and political allies whom he remembered, and would learn in amazement that they had been dead for several years. After a tour of the state he had neglected for so long, Senator George announced that he would retire.

It would be impossible to find a modern equivalent of that story. Today senators and representatives recognize that they cannot neglect their state or district. This is the political base, the ultimate source of any member's power. Although Congress is in session most of the year, the advent of jet planes had made it possible for most to reach their district in a few hours; consequently, constituents expect their representatives to come home most weekends and whenever Congress is in recess. (1986, 54)

If Jewell and Patterson are correct, the experiences of legislators like Walter George and Emanuel Celler may not be duplicated by any current members of Congress. The clear impression is that the cycles in constituency attention, electoral support, formal positions held, and legislative activity that used to characterize legislative careers have been replaced with careers that are marked by stability.

Yet, balanced against the case that career contours have become flatter are the shapes of several recent congressional careers as well as the sentiments posited by Lawrence Dodd and Burdett Loomis, two leading scholars of congressional careers. Dodd has written about an almost mystical development of legislative "mastery," which is thought to occur during a career (1983, 1986). This mastery of electoral and legislative machinery is said by Dodd to separate junior and senior members most of the time. Loomis, drawing to some extent on his extensive observations of the House class of 1974, continues the focus on legislative mastery and the associated development of political skills (see especially 1988b, 5–10, but also 1984). To these authors, modern congressional careers are not devoid of distinct stages and meaningful change.

Anecdotal support for this point of view is readily available. The evolution of Newt Gingrich (R-Ga.) from a so-called bomb-thrower to minority whip says something about changes in the House but also says something about the changes of a House member. While Gingrich probably will never be sedate, his actions in recent years are obviously different from those of his early House service. Finally, on two separate occasions, Vin Weber (R-Minn.) has been used to illustrate a similar point (Hook 1988, 2264; Cook 1989b, 3466). The "education" of a legislator is apparent when Weber describes himself as having gone from "being ready to make every battle with the Democrats a death struggle" to realizing that "you can't make every battle a scorched-earth battle, because this institution is going to have to confront other issues" (Hook 1988, 2264). Weber has not abandoned his activist, conservative principles but admits to having changed stylistically and substantively with the passage of the years, as evidenced by such comments as, "You develop a respect for the institution [Congress]," and, "Republicans need to spend more time on the 'human' issues such as education, housing, and the environment" (Cook 1989b, 3466).

Purpose and Justification

So just what are we to make of congressional careers? It is impossible to know whether careerism is good or bad without knowing about the nature of careers, and this is where we run into trouble. Both the theoretical and empirical underpinnings of research on congressional careers are wanting. A general sense exists that the political life-cycle view of congressional careers is inadequate, but beyond this not much can be said. No satisfactory theory is available to take its place, and the requisite data have not been marshaled to test theories that may be forthcoming. Congressional careers have not been analyzed as a whole. Previous studies have focused on a single aspect of the congressional career, making it impossible to obtain a feel for careers in their entirety.[3] Further, when evidence is presented on these specific aspects of careers, it is, as often as not, inconsistent across indicators and/or contrary to expectations.

For example, speculation about increasing career stasis is brought up short on occasion by empirical findings. The results presented by Bullock and Loomis are not overly supportive of a pattern that is widely thought to have existed; namely, that recent members have acquired formal positions of authority much more rapidly than did cohorts of previous decades. Asher and Weisberg do not conclude that roll call stability began only in the 1970s. Parker does not detect an increase in the stability of constituency activities across careers (although part of the reason for this may be the limited time period for which data on travel home are available). And little evidence exists on changes in (non–roll call) legislative activity over the period in question.

Moreover, even if thorough tests indicated that some of the "expected" shifts had taken place, it would be necessary to find out why. To do this, we need to pay more attention to the interaction of the various components of congressional careers. Only then will we be able to answer questions about whether electoral concerns are responsible for constituency activity; whether there is a trade-off between legislative activities and constituency activities; whether formal positions on the Hill help or hinder a member electorally; and whether these same positions encourage or discourage constituency activity.

Time itself is unsatisfactory as an independent variable (see the literature on presidential popularity; for example, Mueller 1973; Kernell 1978). Life-cycle effects on general political participation are usually explained by such real-life considerations as the difficulties of the very old in getting to the polls and the fact that most young people lack a firm set of stabilizing "roots" in a community (see Verba and Nie 1972). Career stages of members of Congress, if they are found to have any effects, may be surrogates for other things, perhaps electoral situation, perhaps the possession of formal positions, perhaps something else. It may be that, with the addition of these other variables, career stage would cease displaying an independent effect on activity levels. This would not mean career stage is unimportant; it would mean we have specified *why* career stage is important. The interrelationships of the various aspects of congressional careers must be studied in order to determine why legislative activity changes as it does.

Many of the fundamental questions of modern congressional behavior need to be answered with a career-based research design rather than the standard cross-sectional design. How else can we hope to describe the contours of modern congressional careers, to suggest how these contours may have changed over the last few decades, and to explain why these contours look the way they do? How else can we really hope to understand the influence of elections on constituency service or the influence of constituency service on legislative activity? These issues cannot be addressed satisfactorily with cross-sectional data; they require career-based data and proper analytic techniques. That is what I hope to provide in the pages to come.

Since members place their activities and situations in the perspective of their personal congressional histories, analysts would be well advised to adopt this same perspective in trying to describe and to explain congressional behavior. Members do not arrive from another planet, cast a single roll call vote, and quickly depart the premises, yet this is the implication of most traditional approaches to the study of congressional behavior. To be understood properly, this behavior must be studied from the perspective of the people doing the behaving. This is a major reason why a career-based research design is imperative to the study of congressional behavior.

But the desire for a better understanding of individual congressional behavior is not the sole reason for adopting a career-based research design. The nature of congressional careers is closely related to the nature of the institution itself. It is widely believed that careers can affect the features of the institution. For example, Barbara Hinckley (1976), along with many others, believes that one of the most important events in the modern House of Representatives—the 1975 coup against the seniority rule—was largely a result of the sizable number of House members present who were then at the very early stages of their careers (specifically, the large class entering the House in 1975). More generally, as is evident from the words of those wishing to limit congressional terms, there is widespread speculation that the alleged stodginess of the institution in the 1960s and perhaps the late 1980s can be traced to lengthy careers (see especially Huntington 1965). Further, many observers believe that the lack of allegiance to many institutional norms, including seniority, is at least partially attributable to the greater influx of junior members in the 1970s (see Dodd and Oppenheimer 1981).

Naturally, it is also the case that the nature of the institution affects careers. The advent of the committee system and the seniority rule seemed to encourage longer careers (see Cooper 1970; Abram and Cooper 1968) just as the demise of seniority may have encouraged some members to terminate their House careers (see Hibbing 1982b). Further, Cooper and Brady (1981a) point out how leadership careers are influenced by the context of the institution. In larger scope, Kenneth Shepsle (1987) maintains that House careers are influenced primarily by the specialization and division of labor present in the institution.

Some say careers shape the institution; some say the institution shapes careers. But regardless of the causal order of the career-institution relationship (Polsby may have the best approach here in simply viewing the nature of careers as part and parcel of the evolution of the institution toward professionalization and institutionalization), individual congres-

sional careers simply cannot be separated from the study of the institution. Careers are shaped by institutional context just as they in turn feed
back into that context. (The presumed institutional consequences of
careers are evident in the debate over term limitations.) All this makes the
study of congressional careers trickier—but also more rewarding. Learning about the nature of congressional careers will allow us to learn more
about the nature of the institution in which these careers unfold.

Features of the Study

The specific legislators studied are members of the U.S. House, and the
time period employed is the post–World War II era—the era of lengthy
congressional careers. Some of the data utilized begin with 1946; other
data start with 1955, the date the Democrats began what has been until
now uninterrupted control of the House of Representatives; and still
other data pertain only to more limited time periods. But through it all I
have attempted to use data that are truly longitudinal at the individual
level, not just summations of the records of various classes within a
particular session of Congress. Most of the data are objective indicators,
but to some extent I have relied upon interviews I have conducted over the
last few years with approximately fifty representatives and former representatives. Unattributed quotations are from these personal interviews.

After this introductory chapter, I turn to the six main substantive
chapters. Chapter 2 involves the congressional "electoral career" and
deals with questions such as: How does the average share of the vote
received by representatives change as they move through their careers? Is
there some change across careers in the chances of representatives losing
bids for reelection? And has the shape of the electoral career changed
during the postwar years?

The formal positions held by members is the topic for chapter 3. Here I
look for any pattern that may exist in the movement of members of
Congress into and, occasionally, out of various formal positions in the
House. What is the shape of the typical "position career"? Do members
gain positions of influence quickly, then level off, or do they gradually
acquire better positions throughout their entire careers? Has the shape of
this position career changed in the last thirty years? These are some of the
issues addressed in chapter 3.

Chapter 4 deals with the "roll call career"; more specifically, with the longitudinal patterns of representatives' roll call voting records. Chapter 5 concerns "legislative activity" and also discusses activities on the Hill, but it approaches the topic from a broader perspective that includes bill introduction, amendment offering, effectiveness, specialization, and speaking on the House floor. Chapters 4 and 5 attempt to answer questions such as: Over the course of lengthy careers, is it likely that patterns of roll call behavior change appreciably? Do members miss more votes as they move through their careers? Do they become more specialized in the policy matters they address? Do they become more effective legislators? Do they become less active (recall the comments of Vin Weber)? Do they pick their spots better?

Chapter 6 also deals with the "activity career," but the specific activities addressed are quite different from those in chapters 4 and 5. Here the focus is on the non-Washington activity of representatives. Richard Fenno's *Home Style* (1978) sensitized many scholars to the need for more than roll call studies. What is done out in the districts is a crucial aspect of representation and needs to be addressed. In this chapter I look at the "district activity career" as measured by such things as trips taken back to the district and the number of staffers stationed in district rather than Washington offices.

Chapter 7 investigates the relationships among these various "careers." Is the position career related to the electoral career, as the political life-cycle view theorizes? Does a position of authority in Washington often lead to electoral difficulty back home, or does it enhance electoral performance? Is there a trade-off between a high degree of constituency activity and prestige positions on the Hill? How are roll call behavior and level of constituency service affected by electoral performance? Most importantly, what are the behavioral consequences of increased tenure once other factors, such as electoral safety and positions within the House, are held constant? This final substantive chapter will be followed in chapter 8 by a brief summary of the general patterns evident in this study of modern congressional careers.

2 The Electoral Career

Regardless of whether career-based patterns in congressional actions are thought to be cyclical or stationary, explanations for these expectations can generally be traced to electoral concerns. These concerns may or may not be the core element of congressional service that Mayhew (1974a) makes them out to be, but electoral sensitivities do seem to influence many aspects of modern congressional life. The actual nature of these relationships is the topic of chapter 7, but the presumed connection of the electoral career to congressional behavior makes it prudent at this juncture to deal with some basic questions concerning the shape of electoral careers. Are voters strongly supportive of senior members but less supportive of junior and very senior members, as the political life-cycle view maintains? Or, is the tenure level of members irrelevant to their electoral support? Has the relationship between tenure and electoral support changed?

Research on Modern Congressional Elections

Given the presumed relationship of election results to other aspects of congressional service, it is not surprising that congressional elections rank toward the top on any list of well-researched topics in American politics. In fact, so much has been written about the changing nature of elections in Congress and especially the House that only a brief summary is necessary here. The chances of a House incumbent being defeated in a primary or general election have not changed much in the last few decades. Between 1950 and 1956, 92.3 percent of all incumbent House members seeking reelection were successful. Between 1976 and 1982, 92.5 percent of all incumbent House members seeking reelection were successful. Although in the last couple of elections, reelection rates have risen to around 98 percent for House incumbents, the general pattern over the last forty years has been one of stability rather than change. What has not remained stable is the average victory margin of incumbents in the House. Between 1950 and 1956 the mean share of the two-party vote for House incumbents was 60.8 percent. Between 1976 and 1982, the mean share of the two-party vote was 66.1 percent, thus constituting an increase of over 5 percentage points. This change has led to an enormous amount of speculation about the causes and, to a regretfully lesser extent, the consequences of the decline in the level of competition in House elections (see Erikson 1971; Mayhew 1974b; Tufte 1975; Ferejohn 1977; Fiorina 1977a, 1977b; Born 1979; Alford and Hibbing 1981; Alford and Brady 1989; but also see Garand and Gross 1984; Jacobson 1987b).

In addition to the formidable advantages of incumbency, a second major aspect of modern congressional elections is the extent to which aggregate results respond to local rather than national conditions. Former Speaker Tip O'Neill is famous for stating that "all politics is local politics" (O'Neill 1988). At the other extreme are academic models that do a surprisingly accurate job of predicting congressional elections (in the aggregate) with such nationally based information as change in national income and/or presidential popularity (see Kramer 1971; Tufte 1978; Lewis-Beck and Rice 1984).

The truth lies, as it so often does, somewhere in the middle (see Mann 1981, 44–45). Not all politics is local politics. National swings have been a part of congressional election outcomes for a long time. In 1974 the Republican party was associated with a stagnant economy and with Watergate. The 36 Republican House incumbents who were defeated in the 1974 congressional elections, when all is said and done, had little to do with either of these circumstances, yet they were voted out. Try telling them that all politics is local politics. At the same time, if all politics is national, how can we explain those stunning instances in which individual elections go against the tide? There would be no way to account for why Republican challenger Jack Buechner (R-Mo.) defeated Democratic incumbent Robert Young in 1986 despite the fact that no other sitting Democrat was defeated. There would be no way to explain why a seemingly entrenched and secure incumbent like Lionel Van Deerlin (D-Calif.) was defeated in the 1980 election after winning his previous two elections by 3 to 1 margins.[1]

Even more problematic for the "national forces" position is the absence of direction in recent elections. Partisan seat swings of sixty and seventy seats, characteristic of elections past, have been replaced by "swings" of five to ten seats. Little uniformity in the movement toward one party and away from the other is apparent in 1980s congressional elections across the country (see especially Jacobson 1987a). Outcomes seem to hinge more on localized issues such as whether the incumbent has been linked to some type of scandal (see Bauer and Hibbing 1989). For example, six of the seven incumbent losers in the House elections of 1988 were scandal-ridden. All politics may not be local, but the events of the 1980s suggest that the outcomes of congressional elections are becoming less dependent upon uniform national forces and more dependent upon local events and circumstances.

But neither of these two research streams tells us anything about how electoral support varies with tenure, and, as was pointed out in chapter 1, the nature of this relationship is the crux of the difference between the political life-cycle view and revisionist thought. According to the political life-cycle view, representatives are the most vulnerable early in their congressional careers. Those who make it through this difficult early period become safe and remain that way until Washington responsibilities and the march of time lead to greater vulnerability very late in the career. But more recent literature implies that, perhaps after a fleeting moment of instability, modern congressional electoral careers are consistently safe. This notion holds that throughout much of their careers members rack up solid vote totals but probably remain subjectively insecure. These solid vote totals and pesky electoral worries do not come and go in cycles; they persist year in and year out.

It seems as though it would be relatively easy to test the accuracy of the electoral components of both the political life-cycle and the "monotonic" career views, and indeed there has been some research on the tenure–electoral support connection. One surprising aspect of existing research dealing with the degree to which congressional electoral careers are cyclical is that more is known about senatorial electoral careers than House electoral careers. Forays by Matthews (1960, 241) and Barbara Hinckley (1970, 239–40) were followed by a thorough treatment from Warren Kostroski (1978). Of course, with the six-year senatorial term there are not as many data points (i.e., elections) across careers as there are with typical House electoral careers, but conclusions are still possible over a range of four tenure categories.

Unfortunately, the conclusions reached are not identical. Matthews's data on the 1947 to 1957 period indicate a tendency for second-termers to do better than first-termers and for third-termers to do better than second-termers, but he finds that fourth-termers (and above) have an electoral success rate that dips lower than even that of first-termers. Given these data, it is easy to see the genesis of the political life-cycle view. Hinckley's data on the ensuing decade show less of a cyclical pattern and more of what Kostroski calls a plateau effect. First-termers receive the least electoral support, but after that additional tenure matters not. Finally, Kostroski uses data from a fifty-year period and employs many different strategies that, not surprisingly, generate many different conclusions. The one given the most attention is that, excluding senators from states that are electorally safe (mostly the South), first-termers' average success rate is 68.8; second-termers' is 73.4; third-termers' is 82.4; and fourth-termers' and above is 68.2. This is almost a perfect fit with the political life-cycle pattern described by Matthews.

When attention is turned to the House, results are much less developed but at least as confusing. Some scholars have employed a measure of "sophomore surge" to tap the degree of incumbency advantage present. The logic behind this measure is that the greater the increment between a representative's vote totals in the first and second House elections, the larger the electoral advantage attributable to incumbency since the individual was a nonincumbent in the first election and an incumbent in the second (see Born 1979; Cover 1980; Cover and Mayhew 1981). The explicit purpose of this approach is to measure incumbency advantage and not to investigate the total electoral career. Even so, it indicates that the surge in electoral support between running for election and running for reelection to a House seat has become larger in recent years. Thus, we know a little about the changing patterns of electoral careers for House members at these extremely early stages of the career.

But the issue of what happens later in the House electoral career is far from settled. Previous research has little to say on this matter, and what findings there are seem at least slightly contradictory. Works by Cover (1980) and Kurtz (1972), for instance, present evidence that career stage is irrelevant to electoral safety, but a study by Alford and Hibbing (1981) demonstrates that career stage is highly relevant. As will be discussed shortly, part of the confusion here may be due to the sensitivity of conclusions on this issue to the specific measure of electoral security being employed. For now, suffice it to say that previous research on the topic does not permit confident statements about the precise nature of the typical electoral career.

A few additional studies are at least partially relevant to the concept of a congressional electoral career. Robert Erikson (1976), Melissa Collie (1981), and Gary Jacobson (1987a, 1987b) have taken brief looks at representatives' electoral security over time. Erikson discovers that of all members elected to the House in 1952, 36 percent were to suffer electoral defeat by 1972. Collie takes the imaginative approach of looking at the evolution of marginal seats. For example, she finds that members first elected to marginal open seats are seldom able to turn them into to safe incumbent seats. Despite the increase in incumbency advantage, the odds of turning a marginal seat into a safe one apparently did not change much in the late 1960s and 1970s. Jacobson, on the other hand, detects important changes in recent House elections. Specifically, he argues that recent events have "enhanced the reelection prospects of first-term incumbents only. After the first reelection, House members are actually *more* vulnerable now than they were before the changes of the 1960s" (1987b, 44).

While research of this nature is suggestive and at least demonstrates recognition of the need to learn more about how the electoral situation of members of Congress changes through time, as a collectivity existing research suffers from several drawbacks. Much of the data are out-of-date, little attention has been given to changes in the percent of the vote received over careers (as opposed to alterations in the chances of winning), no one has presented thorough data on how electoral careers themselves have changed over time, and, as odd as it may seem, insufficient attention has been given to the House, precisely where electoral careers could be expected to make themselves most visible.

More important, the aforementioned problem of utilizing cross-sectional data to answer longitudinal questions applies more forcefully than ever to much of what has just been summarized. None of the previous research follows several complete classes of individual representatives over the entire course of their careers. Some of it computes averages for all members who at one time or another were second-termers, fourth-termers, or whatever. Some of it computes what happened to a single class of representatives as their careers folded or unfolded. But none of it puts us in a position to determine conclusively the extent to which life-cycle, period, and/or generational effects are at work. And none of it provides convincing evidence of the accuracy or inaccuracy of the political life-cycle view of congressional careers. For this, we need to follow a number of class and individual electoral careers over a long period of time.

The Longest Electoral Career

Returning to the case of Emanuel Celler allows for a good start to explaining electoral careers. In fact, the electoral career of Manny Celler illustrates several important points concerning elections and Congress. At first glance, Celler's career seems to underscore the need for all representatives to give their constituents the impression that the electoral side of congressional service is being taken seriously. Manny Celler won twenty-five elections to the House of Representatives. At this writing, no one has won more. But Celler was defeated in his bid to be elected a twenty-sixth time, and one of the chief complaints voiced was that his presence was no longer being felt back in the district. Never mind that Manny Celler had been ignoring the district for many of his twenty-four successful reelection bids; the point is that if the situation becomes bad enough and if the challenger points out the correct things, nobody is immune from the dangers of appearing to take the voters of the district for granted—no matter how long he or she has been in Congress and no matter what the size of the last reelection margin (see also Matthews 1960, 242; Jacobson 1987a).

The length of Manny Celler's career is astounding. He was still serving in 1972, yet when he was first elected to the House in 1922, Joseph G. Cannon (R-Ill.), though no longer the autocratic Speaker, was roaming the halls of Congress, representing the people of the Eighteenth District of Illinois. When Celler was first sworn in, the last three presidents under whom he would serve, Kennedy, Johnson, and Nixon, were, respectively, 5, 12, and 7 years old. Manny Celler was actually serving in the House during both Teapot Dome and Watergate (although his 1972 defeat meant he was not in the House to see the repercussions of the Watergate burglary); no other national officeholder had a political career that spanned the two major twentieth-century scandals.

But what of the general *shape* of Manny Celler's electoral career? Were its contours consistent with the expectations of the political life-cycle view? Figure 2.1 presents Emanuel Celler's share of the two-party vote throughout his twenty-five congressional elections.[2]

Here we are able to see an electoral career that is an exemplary replica of the political life-cycle view. A shaky start is followed by improvement in electoral support throughout most of his career and an unmistakable tailing off late in the game. Celler's first victory was hard-fought. In a very good Democratic year (the Republicans lost seventy-five seats in 1922), he

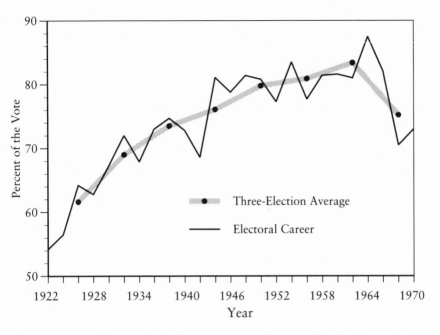

Figure 2.1. Emanuel Celler's Electoral Career

won barely 54 percent of the two-party vote and less than 46 percent of the total votes cast in what was then the Tenth District of New York. In his first race as an incumbent, Celler experienced very little sophomore surge and was only able to increase his share of the vote a couple of percentage points, to 56.5 percent of the two-party vote and 50 percent of the total vote. But in the next election (1926) Manny Celler began to give indications that he was constructing a safe seat. In this race, he received over 64 percent of the two-party vote and almost 60 percent of the total vote. During the decade of the 1930s, he always maintained at least a 2 to 1 margin over Republican challengers. By the end of the 1940s, Manny Celler was generally winning at least 80 percent of the vote, although in bad Democratic years, like 1946, he would "slip" into the high 70-percent range. During the 1950s and early 1960s, landslide electoral victories continued to roll in, reaching a climax in 1964 when, with the help of the no-longer-12-years-old Lyndon Johnson, Manny Celler received 87.5 percent of all votes cast in the district.

After 1964, however, things started to change. Celler's showing in

1966 was down but still perfectly respectable. Then in 1968 problems were clearly evident. After receiving his first serious primary challenge in a long time, Celler was held to barely 70 percent of the general election vote—to most a very strong showing, but in the context of Celler's electoral career, an indication that tougher battles were coming. Things remained about the same in 1970, and then in 1972 Elizabeth Holtzman, claiming that the incumbent was, among other things, ignoring key elements of the party such as women, beat a confused Manny Celler in the Democratic primary by 600 votes.

Manny Celler's fifty years in the House had come to an end just months before he would have passed Carl Vinson as the person with the (then) longest period of service ever in the body and just a year before the position he vacated, chairman of the House Judiciary Committee, was to receive an unbelievable amount of national and international attention as a result of the hearings on the articles of impeachment for the president of the United States. But for those 600 votes, the television cameras would have been trained on an increasingly fragile, 85-year-old Emanuel Celler rather than the suitably cautious and thoughtfully competent Peter Rodino, and who knows what effect this substitution may have had on history.

Figure 2.1 also contains a "smoothed-out" version of Celler's electoral career, obtained by calculating the three-election averages for his vote totals from 1924 to 1970. This smoothing out indicates an electoral career that, until 1968, was marching toward ever greater levels of safety. The biggest improvements came early in the electoral career, but for the most part Celler continued to improve his vote totals at only slightly reduced increments into his twentieth term. In fact, there never was a flattening out for Manny Celler. When it became apparent that he had stayed too long, the plunge in vote-getting power was swift. But is the general curvilinear shape anticipated by the political life-cycle view and illustrated by Manny Celler's electoral career typical of most modern electoral careers?

The Typical Modern Electoral Career

To make this determination, data on all congressional elections from 1946 to 1984 were recorded. As a preliminary step, I present in figure 2.2 the average electoral career as measured by the share of the two-party vote for all those serving at some time during this forty-year period.

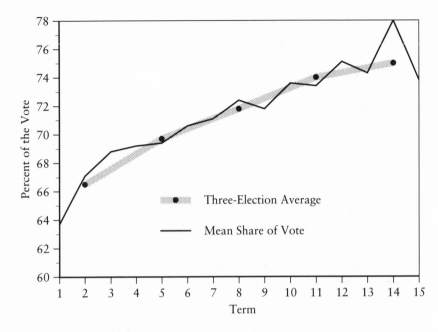

Figure 2.2. Mean Share of the Vote, by Tenure, 1946–1984

The pattern portrayed in figure 2.2 raises some questions about the existence of a late-career dip in electoral support—an important feature of the political life-cycle view. The largest jump comes between the first and second reelection bids. The average junior surge in the postwar era is about 3.5 percent (of the two-party vote), from a little less than 64 percent to a little more than 67 percent. The increase in mean share of the two-party vote between second and third reelection bids is less than 2 percent, and subsequent increments tend to be even smaller. Surprisingly, however, with a couple of minor exceptions, these increments continue to be positive throughout the typical congressional career. Not until the fifteenth term is there a meaningful drop from the mean vote received at the previous tenure level (from a 78-percent average for all members seeking their fourteenth reelection to 73 percent in bids for the fifteenth reelection). It is doubtful that this downturn constitutes the significant late-career drop in electoral clout anticipated by the life-cycle view of congressional careers, especially since after the fifteenth reelection bid the slow growth in mean electoral support reappears. Small N's beyond the fifteenth reelection bid, however, make firm conclusions difficult.[3] Figure 2.2 also presents the average electoral support for three-term chunks of the typical career. Again we see smaller improvements late in the career but little indication that these small increments eventually become negative increments. There is little solid evidence here that at some point additional tenure becomes an electoral liability.

One of the problems with research in this area is that both the share of the incumbents' vote (presented in figure 2.2) and the percentage of incumbents who are victorious have been used to measure electoral success. One measure takes into account the average share of the vote received (regardless of the number who won or lost). The other measure describes the percentage of incumbents running for reelection who are in fact reelected (regardless of their margin of victory or defeat). Both are legitimate variables measuring legitimate aspects of electoral support. But the comparison of results derived from these two quite different operationalizations often creates confusion.

Some of this confusion can be cleared up with a more comprehensive data base and a more comprehensive treatment of the matter. In figure 2.2, data on mean share of the vote are presented. In figure 2.3, the success rates for incumbents at various tenure levels are presented. The first noteworthy but wholly unsurprising aspect of the figure is the very high success rates of all House incumbents. Eighty-four percent of incumbents seeking their first reelections were victorious from 1946 through 1984—and this figure is well below the percentage of representatives at other tenure levels who were successful in securing reelection. After the first reelection, success rates are always over 92 percent and usually around 95 percent. As was the case with mean percentage of the vote, data on percentage victorious indicate that additional tenure brings additional electoral support. This is particularly evident when viewing the smoothed-out data in figure 2.3 from the first through the ninth reelection bids. Here we see a fairly steady, though modest, increase in the percentage of incumbents defeating their challengers. After the tenth term, the declining number of cases causes the term-by-term averages to fluctuate more severely, so conclusions must be qualified, but there may be a hint of greater electoral uncertainty in the eleventh and thirteenth terms. Still, somehow it does not seem right to refer to reelection rates of 93 and 95 percent as reflecting "greater electoral uncertainty." Moreover, the smoothed-out, three-election average suggests no downturn late in the typical career, only a flattening of the increase.

Overall, after the first term, there may be a slightly smaller relationship between tenure and percentage victorious than there is between tenure

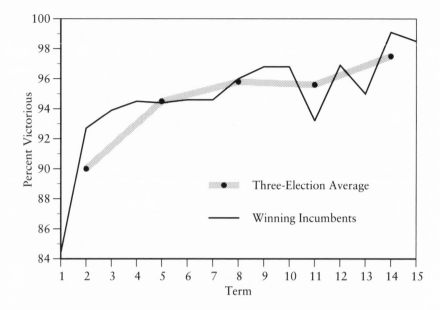

Figure 2.3. Percentage of Incumbents Who Win Reelection, by Tenure, 1946–1984

and share of the vote. The references by Hinckley and Kostroski to plateau effects in Senate electoral careers are not totally out of place in describing variations in the ability of House incumbents at different tenure stages to secure reelection. Finally, despite some slight intimations to the contrary, there continues to be little evidence of the late-career downturn in electoral support that is a key part of the political life-cycle view of the electoral career.

Primaries

One of the messages of Manny Celler's electoral career is that incumbents cannot ignore primaries. Students of congressional elections should not either. Although Celler's support in general elections was declining in the twilight of his career, he was in fact defeated in the Democratic primary of 1972. General elections are only part of the electoral story. Still, instances of incumbent representatives being defeated in a primary are even rarer than incumbent defeats in general elections. From 1960 to 1984, for example, there were 315 incumbent losses in general House elections and only 94 incumbents who lost in House primaries. From 1946 to 1984 there were only 157 incumbent losses in primaries. Nonetheless, while the numbers are small, the potential for primary difficulties is obviously present.

Who is most likely to encounter defeat from within the party? Not surprisingly, southern representatives get picked off in primaries more frequently than the national average. Focusing again on the 1960 to 1984 period and excluding instances in which redistricting seemed to be a major reason for the primary loss (mostly in 1972 and 1982), we are left with 81 primary defeats. Exactly 24.9 percent of the congressional contests during this time were held in southern districts, yet 34.6 percent of the 81 primary losses were in the South. Representing a southern district does increase the chances of a primary loss, although perhaps not by as much as many observers may have expected.

Relatedly, being a Democrat increases the chances of suffering a primary defeat. Of all incumbents during this time period, 61.7 percent were Democrats; yet 76.5 percent of all primary losers were Democrats. Part of this tendency is due to the higher percentage of Democrats in the South, which, as we have just seen, increases the odds of encountering a stiff challenge in the primary. Still, even if the analysis is restricted to the non-South, Democrats are somewhat more likely than Republicans to lose in a primary.

How do the odds of losing in a primary change through the course of a career? In contrast to the tendency of incumbents to decrease their chances of losing general elections as they grow older, the chances of losing a primary contest actually go up with increasing tenure (see figure 2.4). During the first, second, and third reelection bids, the odds are less than 1 in 100 that an incumbent will lose in a primary. During the fourth, fifth, and sixth reelection bids, these odds increase, but only to slightly over 1 percent. These increases continue at the same fairly gradual pace until by the thirteenth, fourteenth, and fifteenth reelection bids the chances of losing in a primary are 4 out of 100 and slightly more than 5 out of 100 in subsequent reelection bids. Thus, while primary defeats are not common occurrences, they are not unheard of, especially later in a career.

Of course, part of the slightly greater tendency of old-timers to lose in primaries can be explained by the fact that southern representatives are more likely to be around at the very high levels of tenure. The one-party dominant nature of southern politics during most of this time period

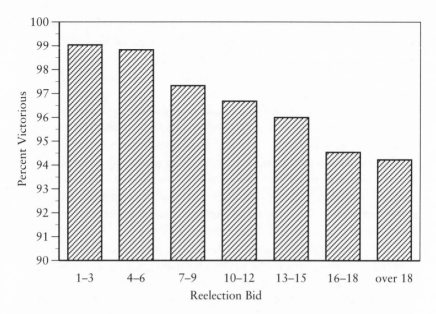

Figure 2.4. Incumbents' Chances of Surviving Primary Election Stage, Three-Election Average, 1960–1984

means that if there were to be any competition at all for House seats in the South, it needed to come from within the Democratic party. This is part, but not all, of the explanation for the direct relationship between tenure and primary defeats.

But regardless of the explanation, it is surprising to note that after about twelve terms in the House the chances of being defeated are at least as high in primary elections as they are in general elections (compare the data mentioned here with those contained in figure 2.3). The career of Manny Celler is somewhat typical in this regard. So too is the career of Joseph W. Martin, Jr. (R-Mass.), Speaker of the House in the 1940s and 1950s. Martin, like Celler, was defeated in a primary (1966) by a new-generation politician, in this case Margaret Heckler.

Changing Contours of the Modern Electoral Career

As far as the typical postwar electoral career is concerned, the political life-cycle view misses the mark. Data on the percentage of incumbents successfully running for reelection and on the average share of the vote received by incumbents indicate an improvement in electoral performance over the course of the typical career and do not lead to the conclusion that late-career electoral difficulties are commonplace. At the same time, figures 2.2 and 2.3 make it plain that there is a strong positive relationship between tenure and electoral support. It just happens to be more linear than curvilinear, albeit with smaller increments more common later in careers. On the whole, the late-career decline that is such an important element of the political life-cycle view of congressional careers actually seems to affect very few individuals—and even then not in the manner posited. It may be that life cycle–based expectations have been overly influenced by a fairly small number of well-publicized, very senior members who ran into electoral difficulties.

But the key question now becomes how this electoral career has changed from the 1940s to the 1980s. Has the typical career evolved from a cyclical pattern in the 1950s and 1960s to a more static one in the 1970s and 1980s? Is Jacobson correct in believing that first- and second-term incumbents in recent decades are doing better electorally than their counterparts in the 1950s and early 1960s? Are senior members more or less vulnerable than they were previously? How are these patterns affected by the attrition of members as each class ages? How are they affected by the breakup of the one-party South? How have the contours of electoral careers changed over the course of the last forty years?

Comparing Four Decades

Before presenting data on specific classes of incumbents, it may be useful to break the pertinent time period into four equal parts. Though not purely a longitudinal approach (since anyone who was a twelfth-termer, for example, within that specific ten-year period will be included), it is a step toward longitudinal analysis, and it has the advantage of allowing us to view changes without being misled by the idiosyncrasies of a particular class. I have computed and constructed the typical electoral career for representatives of the four different decades in the data set. These careers are pictured in figure 2.5.

The data are presented in small, separate, line graphs to facilitate comparison. The lines are reasonably stable and can be extended out to fifteen terms because five classes are averaged together in each figure.[4] On

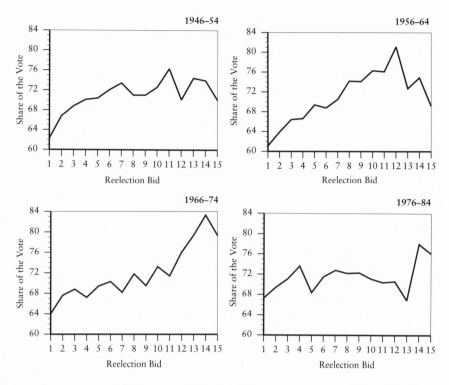

Figure 2.5. Decade-by-Decade Analysis of the Relationship between Vote Share and Tenure, 1946–1984

the basis of these procedures, the unavoidable conclusion is that a marked change in the contours of House electoral careers has occurred. The pattern in the first two decades of the postwar period (1946–54 and 1956–64) is obviously curvilinear. In both periods, after starting in the low 60-percent range in the first reelection, the average share of the vote for all incumbents seeking reelection moves toward 70 percent. After about seven terms, the line for the 1946–54 decade flattens out, blips up briefly in the eleventh reelection, and is moving downward when the endpoint for the figure (fifteenth reelection bid) is reached. In the 1956–64 period, rather than flattening out, the average share of the vote continues to build with additional tenure until after the twelfth reelection bid when, having reached the lofty height of an 81-percent average share of the vote, it drops fairly sharply in the last eight years portrayed in the figure.

The two most recent periods yield entirely different patterns. In the 1966–74 decade there is never any downturn. Instead, average share of the vote goes up with tenure, slowly at first and then rapidly after the eleventh reelection attempt. The thirteenth, fourteenth, and fifteenth reelections are clearly the electoral high points for representatives in the mid-1960s to mid-1970s. The most recent decade is different yet. The other three decades at least shared the feature of growing vote totals for the first six or seven terms, before diverging after that. From the mid-1970s to the mid-1980s, however, incumbent vote share rises for a couple of terms but then actually begins a slow decline. This slow decline continues all the way out to the fourteenth reelection when there is a sudden increase, but the distinctiveness of this era is readily apparent. During the last ten years of the time period, additional tenure has not meant additional electoral security, at least as measured by average share of the vote. Incumbents running for their thirteenth reelection do no better than incumbents running for their first.

Additional evidence of the change in the nature of the House electoral career can be obtained by fitting lines to the four sets of data points in figure 2.5. For the time being, let us assume a linear relationship exists between length of service in the House and electoral security, as measured by share of the two-party vote. The straight lines that most nearly approximate the data for each of the decades are presented in figure 2.6.

The "lines of best fit" show an increasing effect of tenure on vote share. In the 1946 to 1954 period, every two years brings an average increase of .51 percent in share of the vote. It would take twenty years and ten elections at that rate to increase vote share by 5 percent. In the 1956 to 1964 decade every two years brings, on average, an increase of .93 percent. And in the 1966 to 1974 decade each additional election brings an expected increment of 1.06 percent. Thus, a fifteenth-termer during this particular decade would be predicted to do 16 percent better than a first-term representative, other things being equal.

It would seem career stage was having an ever greater impact on electoral performance. An additional term in the late 1960s meant more of an increase in vote share than did an additional term in the late 1940s. Moreover, tenure was becoming an increasingly accurate predictor of vote share. The first three lines of table 2.1 show that the adjusted R^2 for the line of best fit rises from .40 in the 1946–54 period to .54 in the next decade and then to .80 in the 1966–74 decade.

But the increasing relevance of career stage to vote share comes to a

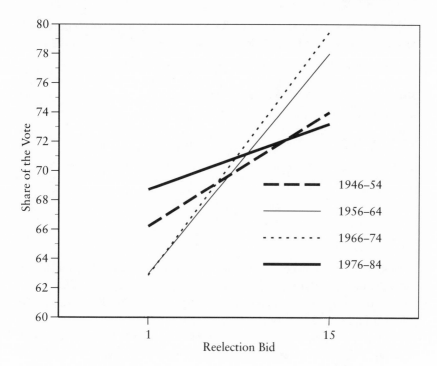

Figure 2.6. Lines of Best Fit for the Vote Share–Tenure Relationship, by Decade, 1946–1984

quick stop in the last decade of the time period (1976–84). The slope of the line of best fit falls to just .31, indicating that it takes three terms in the late 1970s and early 1980s to increase vote share as much as one term had in the previous decade. Further, the ability of career stage to predict vote share is much reduced (the adjusted R^2 is only .14). The key point is that in recent years tenure level has been largely irrelevant to the electoral performance of House incumbents.

Checking for Curvilinearity

But in light of figure 2.5, it is apparent that fitting straight lines to the relationship between tenure and vote share is a misspecification. In some instances the relationship appears curvilinear, just as Matthews's description posited. One way to check for curvilinearity is to compare the R^2

Table 2.1. Summary Statistics of the Relationship between Tenure and Share of the Vote Received, 1946–1984

Decade	Linear (Adj.) R^2	(Adj.) R^2 with Logged Ind. Var.	Curvilinear R^2 Minus Linear R^2
1946–1954	.40	.65	+.25
1956–1964	.54	.68	+.14
1966–1974	.80	.62	−.18
1976–1984	.14	.14	.00

Source: Computed by the author.

obtained in a standard regression with the R^2 obtained when (in this case, with diminishing returns expected) the independent variable is logged. If the R^2 of the loglinear relationship is higher than the R^2 of the linear relationship, curvilinearity is present.

The second column of table 2.1 reports the R^2 for the loglinear relationship, and the third column reports the relative strengths of the linear and curvilinear specifications. From 1946 to 1954 the relationship between tenure in the House and electoral performance was clearly curvilinear. Explanatory power increases .25 from .40 to .65 when the logged tenure variable is substituted for the regular tenure variable. From 1956 to 1964, there were also some elements of curvilinearity as indicated by the slightly more modest .14 improvement in the R^2 when the independent variable is logged. But in the last twenty years there is no evidence of curvilinearity. This is apparent in figure 2.5 and especially in table 2.1 where we see, for the 1966–74 period, a linear R^2 that is markedly higher than the R^2 associated with the nonlinear specification. Then, in the most recent decade, there is no difference in the fit of the linear and curvilinear models (see column 3 of table 2.1)—both are quite weak.

This is evidence of an important shift in the contours of the House electoral career. Prior to the mid-1960s, the curvilinear expectations of the political life-cycle view were realized. Early postwar congressional careers were characterized by growing shares of the two-party vote while late careers were likely to display no growth and perhaps even decline, as extra-long tenure in the House became a liability on occasion. The data suggest that in the 1950s and early 1960s, several representatives stayed too long.

It would be tempting to say that since the mid-1960s electoral careers have been basically flat, thus completing a neat transition from cyclical to static career patterns. It would also be wrong—or at least incomplete. By the late 1970s and early 1980s, this is essentially what had happened. During this time there is, for the most part, no relationship between length of tenure and electoral performance. The slope of the relationship is very flat, and the explanatory powers, whether with a linear or curvilinear specification, are trivial.

But the period from 1966 to 1974 is different than the time before and after it. Unlike the ensuing decade, there is a strong relationship between tenure and vote share; but unlike the preceding decades this relationship is less curvilinear than linear, thanks in part to the strong performance of thirteenth, fourteenth, and fifteenth-termers during this decade (see figure 2.5). Although the confusing effects of a step-level increase in incumbency advantage may somehow contribute to the linear relationship between tenure and vote share in the late 1960s and early 1970s, the findings presented here do not lend support to the notion that the mid-1960s increase in incumbency advantage is primarily due to the improved electoral performance of first-term members—rather, this improvement seems to have come a bit later.

Incumbents Successfully Running for Reelection

Before conclusions on these points are taken too far, it would be wise to investigate the relationship of career stage to the second commonly used indicator of electoral safety—the percentage of incumbents who are successful in their attempts at securing reelection. In figure 2.7, following the format of figure 2.5, data are plotted for this relationship by decade.

In the first decade of the period we see a massive jump between the first and second reelection bids in the percentage of incumbents who won. Three of four first-term incumbents won in the late 1940s and early 1950s, but well over 90 percent of the second-termers did. Slow and uneven improvement in the odds of victory is evident until the ceiling of 100 percent is reached in the ninth term. The only reasonably sharp drop (to 93.3 percent) occurs several terms later with the fifteenth-termers.

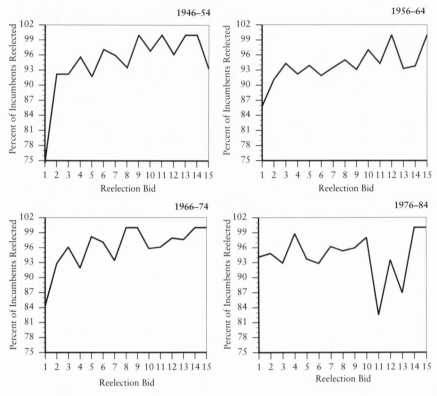

Figure 2.7. Decade-by-Decade Analysis of the Relationship between Percentage Reelected and Tenure, 1946–1984

The second decade shows a more modest early career rise (thanks to a better performance in the first reelection bid), then a slow climb to 100 percent victorious (no twelfth-termers lost in this decade), followed by some possible weakening very late in the career. The third decade is not that much different from the second, but the fourth and final decade (1976–84) is, once again, very different. No early career increase is apparent for those experiencing more recent careers. In fact, no variation exists across the stages of the career except for the relatively low success rates of eleventh- and thirteenth-termers. Respectively, 82.5 and 87 percent may seem little cause for embarrassment, but in the context of a steady stream of mid–90-percent success figures, these two numbers do stand out.

Figure 2.8 and table 2.2 highlight the distinctiveness of recent career

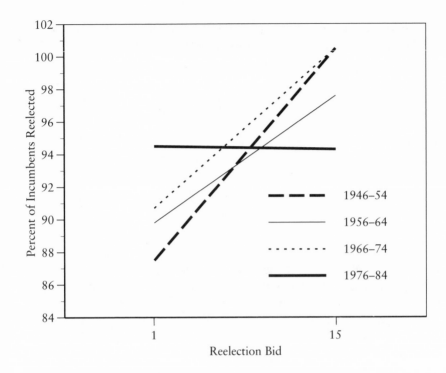

Figure 2.8. Lines of Best Fit for the Percentage Reelected–Tenure Relationship, by Decade, 1946–1984

patterns. In figure 2.8 the ordinary least squares regression lines are plotted for the four decades. The slopes for the first three are all positive and fairly similar in magnitude. Moreover, as can be seen in the first three rows of table 2.2, about one-third to one-half of the variance in the percentage victorious can be accounted for by variation in career stage in each of the three decades. Further, a curvilinear specification is preferable to a linear one in all three cases. It is not surprising that the relationship would be curvilinear given the fact that a natural ceiling is coming into play (success rates, after all, cannot exceed 100 percent).

This is certainly not the case, however, in recent years. In the 1976 to 1984 period there is not a positive slope to the relationship between tenure and the percentage of incumbents winning reelection. Indeed, there has been no slope at all. As figure 2.8 reveals, the pattern in the last decade stands out like a sore thumb from the pattern found in the preceding thirty years, with the very slight (but statistically insignificant) nega-

Table 2.2. Summary Statistics of the Relationship between Tenure and Percentage of Incumbents Reelected, 1946–1984

Decade	Linear (Adj.) R^2	(Adj.) R^2 with Logged Ind. Var.	Curvilinear R^2 Minus Linear R^2
1946–1954	.34	.61	+.27
1956–1964	.45	.55	+.10
1966–1974	.44	.64	+.20
1976–1984	.00	.00	.00

Source: Computed by the author.

tive slope serving to highlight its uniqueness. Increasing years of service explain absolutely none of the variance in the percentage of incumbents who were electorally successful. In recent years, there simply is no relationship—linear, curvilinear, or otherwise—between tenure and percentage successful.

Southern Politics and Electoral Careers

But the central concern of this work is with true longitudinal patterns, and these patterns can be confused when the data are aggregated, even across fairly short periods of time such as decades. This potential aggregation problem could be particularly vexing given what is known about congressional elections in most of the South during the early portions of the time period. For years, the one-party South meant long careers and lopsided general election contests for many incumbent representatives from the region. Aggregating data may result in mean vote shares for senior incumbents being inflated because of this situation. In fact, one reasonable explanation for the substantial changes in the contours of electoral careers is that decades ago southerners boosted the mean for senior members. As the region's Republican party gained in strength and as the South became correspondingly more competitive at the congressional level, categories reflecting the electoral performance of senior members came down, and the slope for electoral performance regressed on tenure became correspondingly flatter.

Table 2.3. Summary Statistics of the Relationship between Tenure and Share of the Vote Received, Non-South Only, 1946–1984

Decade	Linear R^2	Linear Slope	Curvilinear R^2	Curvilinear Slope
1946–54	.57	.50	.65	7.1
1956–64	.19	.23	.36	4.4
1966–74	.72	.58	.79	8.0
1976–84	.15	.27	.14	3.5

Source: Computed by the author.

This is a sensible alternative explanation for the changes uncovered, so it deserves a systematic test. This test involves removing the eleven states of the Old South and replicating the analysis. The results are presented in table 2.3. As was the case when the South was included, the most recent decade is the one in which additional tenure matters the least to the predicted share of the two-party vote. For 1976–84, the amount of variance explained by increasing tenure, whether the formulation is linear or curvilinear, is the most meager, and the slope is the most gradual (although the curvilinearity of the 1956–64 decade pulls the linear slope for that period slightly below the linear slope for the last decade).

To be brief, when the analysis is confined to the non-South, basic conclusions are not altered at all. If regression lines are fit to data from the non-South just as they were to data for the entire country in figure 2.6, we see patterns from decade to decade that are nearly identical. The only possible exception to this conclusion is that from 1956 to 1964 the exclusion of the South does reduce the effect of additional tenure to some extent, but this is not sufficient basis for rejecting the overall conclusion that in the late 1970s and early 1980s the effects of tenure on electoral performance have practically vanished.

Beyond the slight changes in the 1956–64 period, the only important difference produced by excluding the South is that the intercepts (not shown) are always quite a bit lower than the intercepts reported for the entire country. The slopes remain surprisingly constant when the South is excluded. What this means is that while southern elections on the whole are much less competitive than elections in other parts of the country, the degree to which increasing tenure decreases competition is fairly constant across regions. Thus, earlier conclusions that tenure has less of an influence on electoral performance than it did decades ago appear valid—or at least are not produced by the confounding effects of the breakup of the one-party South.

Comparing Selected Classes

Still, to obtain the clearest picture of longitudinal effects, information on individual classes is the most valuable. Data are available for all House classes from 1946 to 1984, but presenting the trend line for each of the twenty classes would result in a truly unwieldy figure. Thus, figure 2.9 presents information on four equally spaced, representative classes; namely, those of 1944, 1954, 1964, and 1974. Two lines are presented for each class: the solid line is the actual mean share of the vote, and the dotted line is the mean share of the vote when party effects are controlled. This correction takes into account the differing numbers of Republicans and Democrats at each election and the varying success of the parties in these same elections. For example, in 1948, Democratic congressional candidates on average did 7.9 percent better than they did in 1946; therefore, the corrected share of the vote for 1948 was obtained by subtracting 7.9 percent from each Democrat's actual share of the vote and adding 7.9 percent to each Republican's. If the number of Republicans in each class were identical to the number of Democrats, the correction would, of course, alter nothing. But with some classes being disproportionately populated by members of one party or the other, it is possible that partisan ebbs and flows could obstruct clear interpretations of the effects of additional tenure on electoral performance.[5]

We see from figure 2.9 that each class is distinct in its electoral pattern.[6] The class of 1944 is on an electoral roller coaster, increasing its share of the vote in the first, second, and third reelection bids, decreasing in the fourth, fifth, and sixth, and recording its best performances in the seventh and eighth reelection attempts. (Individual class data are presented only out to eight terms because of the small number of representatives in any given class who remain in the House after sixteen years.) The class of 1954 is also on a roller coaster, but a much calmer one. There are ups and downs, but the range is more constrained than was the case for the class of 1944.

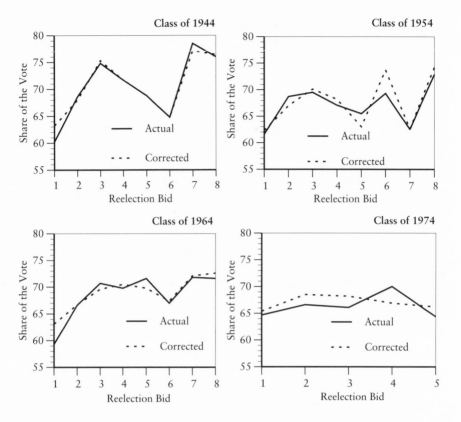

Figure 2.9. Class-by-Class Analysis of the Relationship between Vote Share and Tenure, Classes of 1944, 1954, 1964, and 1974

This movement toward greater stability across tenure levels continues in the two most recent classes. Outside of a slight dip in the sixth reelection bid, the class of 1964 remains remarkably consistent from the third to the eighth reelection attempt. The class of 1974 is even more static, though we are only able to observe this class over five data points. From the first reelection bid through the fifth, the share of the vote deviates only in the most modest fashion. Members of the class of 1974 are not able to make lasting, significant improvements on the 64.7 percent of the vote they averaged in their first reelection bid. In their fifth reelection bid (in 1984) they received only 64.4 percent of the vote. The other three classes pictured in figure 2.9 improved from their first to their fifth reelections by 8.6 percent, 3.9 percent, and 12.3 percent, respectively.

A big part of the reason for the lack of electoral improvement in the class of 1974 is the fact that it starts at such a high level with the first reelection bid. Whereas the earlier classes average around 60 percent of the vote in their first reelection attempts, the class of 1974 received nearly 65 percent of the vote, thereby making it much more difficult for large increments to appear in subsequent elections. As mentioned earlier, this finding coincides with suggestions in previous literature that such a shift had occurred (see especially Born 1979; Jacobson 1983).

Even so, the inability of the class of 1974 to build substantially on its early performance is noteworthy. In three terms the class of 1964 went from 60 to 70 percent of the vote; by way of contrast, in three terms the class of 1974 went from 65 to 66 percent of the vote. Not only are first-termers doing better electorally than they used to, but also there is some indication that more senior members are doing a little worse. Non-southern members with ten terms or more averaged less of the two-party vote from 1976 to 1984 than they did from 1966 to 1974 (69.5 percent as opposed to 70.6). The result is a flatter electoral career.

On the basis of these four classes it would indeed seem to be the case that the contours of the electoral career have changed. When individual classes other than those displayed in figure 2.9 are analyzed the message is basically the same. There is less volatility across careers than in the past. Tenure, in fact, at least as of the late 1970s, appears to be generally useless as an indicator of electoral security.

Mortality Effects

Although simple aggregation problems are largely alleviated by a focus on individual classes, mortality (or attrition) effects may be skewing the picture presented. In figure 2.9, for example, only members of the class of 1974 who were still around in 1976 were obviously included in the calculations leading to the second reelection bid for that class. A smaller number remained in the 1978 elections, and so on. Thus, as members of this class retire, voluntarily or involuntarily, the number of cases available to calculate the mean share of the vote is reduced (see notes 3, 4, and 6). More important, there is reason to expect that those who remain are not representative of the original class (after all, they survived and the others did not)—a situation that could bias results one way or another.

These potential mortality effects have been insufficiently appreciated by students of congressional careers. To determine whether or not mortality effects are distorting the basic findings of this chapter, I analyzed the electoral performance of what might be called each class's electoral "Olympians"; that is, those members of the class who ran for reelection at least seven times. The number seven was selected somewhat arbitrarily in an effort to achieve both a suitably lengthy career and a reasonable number of cases. Figure 2.10 reports the results of this comparison for three typical classes.

The figure presents some startling results. When those members serving only a few terms (six or less) are excluded from the analysis, we continue to find that recent electoral careers are very flat (see the line for the class of 1970). What is surprising is that earlier electoral careers appear mostly flat as well. The Olympians of the class of 1960 gain an average of about 3 percent of the vote over the course of fourteen years in Congress, and the Olympians of the class of 1950 lose about 3 percent over the same length of time, but on the whole stability seems to rule. In fact, the lines for the classes never cross; later classes merely shift upward.

I checked this tendency toward flat mortality-corrected electoral careers by looking at other classes and by employing other minimum career lengths (in figure 2.10, there were only 14 Olympians in the class of 1950; 16 in the class of 1960; and 14 in the class of 1970). By using six reelection bids as a minimum, the number of cases is more than doubled, but conclusions remain the same. When mortality effects are controlled, typical classes of representatives do not improve significantly upon their mean performance in the first reelection bid. This is particularly true with recent careers but seems largely true of earlier careers as well.

Why are electoral careers less cyclical when mortality controls are introduced? A comparison of the electoral performance of Olympians with the electoral performance of all members of the class then running for reelection makes the answer easier to understand. Early on, the discrepancy between the share of the vote for the entire class and for the Olympians is usually sizable, no doubt reflecting the fact that those who are most likely to be around for awhile are those who hail from generally safe districts. The two lines slowly converge as the terms wear on. Indeed, this situation only makes sense since the composition of the groups is becoming more and more similar as the mortality of the overall class brings it closer to the Olympians with each passing election. In the seventh reelection bid, the means for the two groups are identical since, by definition, the two groups are compositionally identical. As the terms

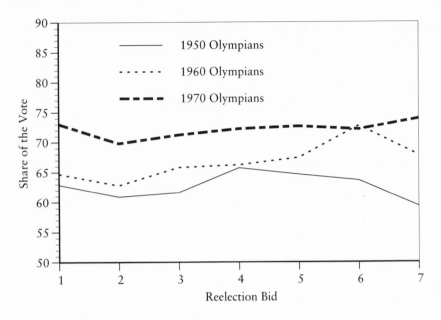

Figure 2.10. Class-by-Class Analysis of the Relationship between Vote Share and Tenure, Controlling for Mortality Effects, Classes of 1950, 1960, and 1970

pass, the typical pattern is for the class as a whole to inch its way up to the Olympians.

These findings should encourage students of careers to be cautious. What precisely is meant by the phrase "typical" career? If it is the average features of a career lasting more than a few terms, the patterns in figure 2.10 are the most accurate. Means computed on the basis of everyone then in the House are distorted because they include data on those members who stayed only one to six terms. The gradual attrition of these interlopers, given their *relatively* poor early electoral performance, makes the electoral career look more variable than it otherwise would.

What does the adjustment for mortality effects mean for conclusions about the diminishing role of tenure in explaining electoral support? Nothing if the focus is on the current situation. Recent electoral careers have little variance across tenure regardless of whether all members or only Olympians are included. What the restriction to Olympians suggests is that mortality effects may have made earlier careers appear somewhat more cyclical than they in fact were.

Table 2.4. Predicting Electoral Support in the Eighth Reelection Bid with Support in the First, Classes of 1950, 1960, and 1970

Class	R	R^2	Slope	Constant
1950	.25	.06	.34	40.0
1960	.21	.04	.25	53.0
1970	.56	.32	.73	31.0

Source: Computed by the author.

Individual Careers

In spite of all these corrections and adjustments, we still may not have properly addressed the real degree to which individual careers embody electoral fluctuation. For example, even though the mean share of the vote for individual classes appears to vary across terms less than it used to, it is theoretically possible that the individual careers used to compute these class means are bouncing all over the lot. One of the best ways to determine whether or not individual careers are more stable is to attempt to predict later electoral support from earlier support. If early support is more predictive for recent careers than it is for earlier careers, this is strong evidence that electoral careers have become more consistent.

To provide information on this matter, I regressed vote share in the eighth term on vote share in the first term for the 1950, 1960, and 1970 classes. The basic expectation is that early vote share will be a better predictor of late vote share for the class of 1970 than it is for the earlier classes. The results, presented in table 2.4, generally support these expectations.

As is readily apparent, while early share of the vote can hardly be considered determinative for any class, it does a better job of predicting late-career electoral support for more recent careers than for earlier careers. The amount of variance explained by early support is much greater for the class of 1970 than for either the class of 1960 or 1950 (R^2 = .32 as opposed to only .04 and .06, respectively). Further, each percent increase in early support for the class of 1970 is predicted to increase late vote support by .73 of a percent while for the earlier two classes the impact is only around one-third and one-fourth of a percent.[7] Electoral

careers have stabilized in the sense that performance in the first reelection
bid is a better predictor of performance in a later reelection bid.

Conclusion

In the 1950s, incumbents seeking their first reelection to the House were
successful about 80 percent of the time and averaged approximately 60–
65 percent of the vote. After a few more terms, they were successful
nearly 95 percent of the time and received around 70 percent of the vote.
Such variance across tenure levels is not common anymore. In the late
1970s and early 1980s, incumbents seeking their first reelection to the
House were successful approximately 93 percent of the time and averaged
68 percent of the two-party vote. But after a few terms modern representatives seem to be in virtually the same spots as when they were new,
with reelection rates around 93 percent and average share of the vote in
the high 60-percent range.

To be sure, there are important suggestions in the data that electoral
careers in the 1950s may not have been quite as cyclical as they first
appear. Back then, the one-party South provided a boost to the mean
figures for senior members, and, most importantly, mortality effects de-
pressed the mean figures for junior members. However, the importance of
these facts should not be overstated. As table 2.3 indicates, the biasing
effects of southern elections for our purposes are surprisingly small. Mortality effects, while serious, are reasonably constant across decades and
therefore have affected recent elections as well as elections occurring in
the 1950s. Further, one of the more important findings in this chapter is
that, individual career by individual career, early electoral performance is
now a better predictor of late-career electoral performance than was the
case decades ago. Finally, although earlier decades provide a useful baseline, to some extent the more important conclusions pertain to the relationship of tenure and electoral success in the 1980s.

Additional tenure in recent Congresses seems to be neither electoral
credit nor debit. Challengers and some reformers may claim that extended tenure means it is time for an infusion of new blood; incumbents
may argue that their House experience is a decided asset to the district;
but voters seem not to care and are apparently reaching their voting
decisions on the basis of other information (or else equal proportions of
voters view additional years of service as liability and asset).

What is it about the modern House that makes tenure irrelevant to variations in mean electoral performance? This question will be addressed at somewhat greater length in chapters 7 and 8, but a few words of speculation are in order here. Traditionally, legislative involvement was contingent upon tenure and was thought to have some influence on voter choice. Thus, one possible explanation for the irrelevance of tenure to electoral support is that legislative involvement is no longer contingent upon tenure, perhaps as a result of the alleged decline of apprenticeship, the proliferation of committee and party leadership positions, and related moves toward democratization in the body. A second, more general explanation is that modern voters may be increasingly influenced by matters that are not purely legislative. Constituency service comes to mind. If Fiorina (1977a, 1989) is correct about voters now frequently deciding on the basis of constituency service–oriented activities, there is little reason to expect old-timers to do better electorally than their junior colleagues, assuming junior members now use the full range of resources at their disposal (the frank, staffers, paid trips home, etc.).

Slightly more extreme are those explanations maintaining that additional tenure is not only irrelevant but often dangerous. Al Ullman's comment about powerful representatives now being more vulnerable than newly elected representatives is an example, although it is not made clear why this dislike for the well-positioned recently blossomed. Perhaps senior members' connections and legislative clout make it more likely they will be tainted by the appearance of some type of misconduct—or perhaps simply the appearance of being a political hack. Whatever the explanation, those members of the House who look forward to greater electoral safety with the passage of the years are likely to be disappointed.

What does all of this mean for the political life-cycle view of congressional careers? At least as far as the electoral career is concerned, the political life cycle has never been particularly prevalent in the postwar House, although it was a slightly more accurate description years ago than it is now. This view appears to capture the modest beginnings and gradual improvements of the electoral career of the 1950s, but closer analysis reveals a portion of even that movement to be artifactual.

Moreover, the life-cycle view seems mistaken in holding that there will be a noticeable decline in electoral performance as soon as the representative accumulates substantial Washington responsibilities. There is some indication that very senior members (like Emanuel Celler) may see their vote-getting abilities atrophy, but this happens, if at all, only after twenty-five to thirty years in the House. It is not something that need concern representatives serving more typical stints. Given the advanced stage at which the decline hits, and given that most victims of this decline have been thoroughly immersed in Washington responsibilities for years and years prior to being hit, maintaining that the voters are taking their revenge on representatives who have "gone Washington" is problematic. As far as recent electoral careers are concerned, the evidence conclusively supports the view that they are largely flat. House electoral careers in the 1980s are marked more by constancy than by movement. Tenth-termers cannot expect to be treated much differently by the electorate than first-termers. Of course, since first-termers, by and large, are treated quite well, this may not be all that hard for senior members to handle.

Nonetheless, there is a new electoral environment. As stated in the *Congressional Quarterly Weekly Report*, "It was once conventional wisdom that the most vulnerable incumbents were the newest ones. But this is not the case anymore" (Cook 1989a, 1064). Republican adviser Eddie Mahe agrees, noting that a freshman now is usually "tough" to defeat because "he's been busting his butt since day one" (quoted in Cook 1989a, 1065). Instead, Mahe says the best strategy is to look for those members who may have become fat and lazy (he defines this as, among other things, spending little time back in the district and maintaining a small number of district offices). For their part, incumbents now receive explicit instructions on how to avoid being blindsided. Says Beryl Anthony of the Democratic Congressional Campaign Committee, "We don't wait for [nonincumbent] Republicans to wake them up. We wake them up" (Cook 1989a, 1065).

3 The Formal Position Career

The U.S. House of Representatives, consistent with one of the defining characteristics of legislative bodies (see Loewenberg 1971, 4), was designed to be collegial. In the abstract, all members were to have equal say on policy matters. In reality, a multitude of formal positions in the House give more influence to some members than to others and cause the influence of a particular member to vary from issue area to issue area. These formal positions are so important that representatives often go to great lengths to acquire and keep them.

Committee Positions

Serving on a Committee

During the 100th Congress (1987–88), Dan Glickman (D-Kans.) was a member of the Democratic Steering and Policy Committee in the House, the committee that recommends which Democrats will serve on the various standing committees. In reference to two Democrats eager to obtain seats on the prestigious Ways and Means Committee, Glickman once said, "I couldn't turn around the corner without Sander Levin or Jim Moody following me" (Hook 1986, 3073). Their strategy must have been properly formulated because just after the session convened Levin and Moody were assigned to fill the only two openings on this vital, tax-writing committee.

Some members have even adjusted their voting records in order to make themselves more palatable to the individuals deciding who would and would not obtain formal committee positions. One particularly blatant case involved Phil Landrum (D-Ga.), who, like Levin and Moody, wanted desperately to acquire a seat on the Ways and Means Committee (see Shepsle 1978, 147–48). Landrum knew that to acquire this plum he would have to become more supportive of the party, which is exactly what he did, at least according to the story told in the House's recorded roll call votes. In the 87th Congress (1961–62), Landrum's party-support score, a scale running from 0 (indicating total opposition to the party leadership) to 100 (representing perfect consistency with the party line) jumped 30 points from what it had been in the 86th Congress.[1] Despite Speaker John McCormack's (D-Mass.) support, Landrum failed to get the coveted Ways and Means assignment. Thus, he was forced to maintain his strong support of the Democratic leadership. At the beginning of the 89th Congress, Landrum was finally given a Ways and Means slot. With no reason to continue going out of his way to please the party bigwigs, Landrum promptly reverted to his erstwhile antiparty voting record. In fact, over the years it worsened to the point where Landrum opposed the Democratic leadership more often than he supported it.

The amount of machinating involved in committee assignments is virtually impossible to overestimate. The resulting conflicts are frequently intense. In 1985, for example, while organizing for the 99th Congress, then majority leader James Wright (D-Tex.), who had been assigned by Speaker Tip O'Neill (D-Mass.) to negotiate with Republican leader Robert Michel (R-Ill.) on the ratio of Democrats to Republicans on standing committees, agreed to give the minority party additional representation on most committees. Republicans were given approximately thirty more committee seats than they had held the year before, even though the overall percentage of Republicans in the House (the traditional baseline for calculating party ratios on the committees) changed minimally with a net gain of only fourteen seats for the Republicans as a result of the 1984 elections.

All seemed to be going well until the individual committees began to set up ratios and make assignments for their respective subcommittees. Republicans on two key committees—Judiciary and Energy and Commerce—objected bitterly to the subcommittee ratios announced by the Democratic majority on the full committees. The dispute was particularly ugly in the Energy and Commerce Committee, where Republicans boycotted all committee sessions and made daily speeches on the floor condemning the ratios on several key subcommittees, including Telecommunications, Health, Investigations, and Energy. Finally, on 20 March 1985, the Democrats on the committee acceded to most of what the striking Republicans were after, and the committee delinquently set about its important business.

But disputes over committee assignments are frequently as bitter within parties as they are between parties. As the Republicans organized for the 100th Congress (1987–88), an old split resurfaced between those states with large Republican delegations and those with smaller numbers of Republican representatives. In 1987, small-state Republicans, for the first time in decades, were able to win many of the desirable committee assignments for their own candidates. One of the beneficiaries was Jim Kolbe (R-Ariz.), a hardworking, respected, moderate who lost his bid for a seat on the Appropriations Committee in 1985 because he was from a state with a small delegation and won in 1987 for the same reason. The conflict in 1987 was especially messy because it pitted the number two man among House Republicans, minority whip Trent Lott (R-Miss.) who pushed for most small-state candidates, against the number one man, minority leader Michel who tried valiantly to salvage more positions for members of large state delegations like Illinois. It was, as one of the leaders of the small-state uprising, Tom Tauke (R-Iowa), put it, "as naked a power play as you can have around here" (Hook 1987, 961).

Chairing a Committee

Controversies over who should chair committees are generally even more acrimonious, although there is the occasional atypical representative who lives in fear of chairing a committee. (One such member from upstate New York retired when it became apparent that if he did not, he would be promoted to the chairmanship of an important committee.) In 1910, the power play over committee assignments became just a little too naked, and Speaker Joseph G. Cannon (R-Ill.) was stripped of many of his powers in this area. In place of selection by the Speaker, the seniority rule became the major force in the determination of committee leaders. The seniority rule holds that the majority party member with the longest continuous service on a committee will be given the opportunity to chair that committee (see Hinckley 1971 for a general discussion of the seniority rule).

The automatic quality of the seniority rule is, at the same time, its great advantage and its great disadvantage. The advantage of having a universalistic rule for the selection of committee leaders is that it removes the motivation for conniving on the part of the courtiers. No matter how cleverly done, these tactics will not assist the would-be usurper. As stated by former senator William Proxmire (D-Wis.), "If there were not seniority, there would be all kinds of politicking and maneuvering to see who's going to be chairman of this committee or that committee, and there would be backbiting and all sorts of problems. . . . Seniority is a way of avoiding all kinds of difficulties" (quoted in Tobin 1986, 31–32).

On the other hand, the automatic features of the seniority rule occasionally permit a clearly undeserving member to be the committee chair. The joke about the seniority system really being the senility system has occasionally been right on target. One former representative described to me the sad sight of a nearly 80-year-old Melvin Price (D-Ill.) trying to lead the Armed Services Committee when he was neither physically nor mentally capable of doing so and called the scene "a total human tragedy." On the Senate side, Appropriations Committee chairman Kenneth McKellar (D-Tenn.) became so senile that he would, according to long-time congressional correspondent Samuel Shaffer, start questioning a witness at a committee hearing, fall asleep, wake up, and, with appropriate indignation, charge that the witness had not answered his question (Tobin 1986, 37–38).

And on occasion the seniority rule—even in its prime—was less automatic than many believe.[2] When Carl Vinson was about to retire from Congress and his chairmanship of the Armed Services Committee, what he wanted most was for L. Mendel Rivers (D-S.C.) to be his successor. The problem was that two members besides Vinson had more seniority than Rivers. Vinson swung into action and had one of these representatives (Paul Kilday, D-Tex.) appointed to the Military Court of Justice and convinced Speaker McCormack to move the other (Overton Brooks, D-La.) to McCormack's Science and Space Committee chair. Low and behold, the new chairman of the House Armed Services Committee in 1965 was L. Mendel Rivers.

So there are acknowledged problems with the operation of the seniority system. These problems, combined with the reform-minded atmosphere of the late 1960s and early 1970s, led to fundamental changes in the application of the seniority rule. While the senior majority-party member of a committee will still generally be its chair, this situation is not as universal as it was twenty years ago. The widely described "coups" of 1975, in which three senior committee heads (F. Edward Hebert of Louisiana, Rivers's successor as chairman of the Armed Services Committee; Wright Patman of Texas, chairman of the Banking and Currency Committee; and W. R. Poage of Texas, longtime chairman of the Agriculture Committee) were deposed by the Democratic Caucus and replaced by less senior members, were not the only events indicating times had changed. The removal of several senior subcommittee chairs, the 1985 ouster of Hebert's successor, Price, from the Armed Services Committee chair and his replacement by Les Aspin (D-Wis.) who was *seventh* in line according to the seniority rule, and the near removal of Aspin two years later also demonstrate that seniority is not what it used to be.

Though seniority is followed most of the time, senior committee members now realize their behavior is not beyond reproach. A junior member who had just voluntarily retired when I visited with him in the early 1980s made a statement to me that aptly summarizes the changes: "Before the reforms, we younger members were expected to laugh at the jokes of the chairman; after the reforms it is amazing how funny *our* jokes became." An important shift in power had occurred on the Hill.

Party Positions

But committee positions are not the only key formal posts in the modern House of Representatives. Parties are the other basic organizing element of Congress, and party leadership slots produce every bit as much competition as committee positions. Robert Peabody (1976) has brought together accounts of many modern party leadership contests, including the 1965 battle between Gerald Ford (R-Mich.) and Charles Halleck (R-Ind.) for the position of minority leader, the five-way contest for majority leader in 1971 among Representatives Boggs, Udall, Sisk, Hays, and O'Hara, and Tip O'Neill's victory over Sam Gibbons (D-Fla.) and several other in-the-end unannounced candidates for the position of majority leader in 1973 after Boggs's death in a plane crash. Tony Coehlo's (D-Calif.) victory in the contest for the position of majority whip in 1987, in which he beat back the challenges of two formal rivals (Charles Rangel, D-N.Y., and Bill Hefner, D-N.C.), was yet another hard-fought party leadership battle, as were Newt Gingrich's (R-Ga.) 1989 defeat of Edward Madigan (R-Ill.) for the position of Republican whip and William Gray's (D-Pa.) 1989 victory in the race to succeed Coehlo as Democratic whip.

Moreover, as Burdett Loomis (1984, 185–86; see also Sinclair 1983) reminds us, the number of party positions increased markedly in the last twenty years. Democrats, for example, now have the Speaker, party leader, whip, deputy whips, caucus chair, caucus secretary, Campaign Committee chair, Steering and Policy Committee members, and a variety of other party positions. And the "lesser" party positions are not just cosmetic. Coehlo's work as head of the Democratic Congressional Campaign Committee was instrumental in his 1987 victory in the contest for majority whip, and the position of whip itself has apparently become part of the "leadership escalator" (Ehrenhalt 1987, 3–4; Canon 1989), as is reflected by the decision to make it an elective rather than appointive position. The proliferation of party leadership opportunities, like the growth in the number of committee and subcommittee positions, must be incorporated into any thorough treatment of career patterns.

The Importance of Formal Positions

These formal positions, whether they are party positions or committee positions, go a long way toward defining the career of a representative. One headline in the *Congressional Quarterly Almanac, 1985* (16-G) announced simply, "Influence Measured by Assignments." Position is often required to make things possible. For example, John Moss (D-Calif.) was always an activist legislator, but the breadth, intensity, and effectiveness of his interests took on new meaning after he ousted Harley Staggers (D-W.V.) from the chairmanship of the Investigations Subcommittee of what was then called the Interstate and Foreign Commerce Committee. Often it is difficult to be taken seriously in the House without the proper position from which to operate. Formal position is not the only thing that defines a representative's role in Congress, but it has a lot to do with it.

This argument should not be taken too far. There are instances in which a member has been able to shape the position rather than the other way around. Wayne Hays (D-Ohio) took a post no one wanted (chairman of the House Administration Committee) and managed to make himself one of the most feared people in Washington. On the Senate side, Robert Byrd (D-W.V.) built the power base that would eventually make him the majority leader of the U.S. Senate when he had the lowly position of secretary of the Democratic Conference. In this capacity he proceeded to do the jobs nobody else in the Senate was willing to do. Byrd rolled up a huge stack of IOUs and called them in when he defeated Edward Kennedy for the Democratic whip position in 1971 (see Shaffer 1980, 171–84).

In fact, one House staffer told me that *all* power in Washington is personal power and has nothing to do with positions held. To illustrate his point, this legislative assistant used the case of the late Claude Pepper (D-Fla.), popular supporter of the elderly and their causes. According to this source, "Pepper went from a middling position as chairman of the Aging Committee to a top-of-the-line position as chairman of the Rules Committee, yet his power did not change much if at all." The staffer was clearly surprised that Pepper's influence had not been altered appreciably despite a change in position. His point of view is not without merit— certainly influence on the Hill does not derive solely from position—but his surprise makes an equally important point. There *are* commonly held expectations about which positions have more clout than others. To ignore this basic fact and to assume that all power derives from the person would be to seriously misrepresent the nature of the House as an institution and would lead to a wholly incomplete understanding of congressional careers in the modern House. (The staffer's surprise over this particular case may also reflect a lack of appreciation for the changed role of the Rules Committee by the time Pepper had become chair.)

The purpose of the remainder of this chapter is to present information on such issues as how positions in the House are distributed and how career stage affects a representative's chances of obtaining quality formal positions. What guidance is supplied by previous research? As mentioned in chapter 1, probably the most serious examinations of change in the typical formal position career are contained in Loomis (1984) and Bullock and Loomis (1985). Here we find succinct accounts of the expectation that in earlier decades progression to quality formal positions was painstakingly slow but that in more recent Congresses advancement has come much more rapidly. The empirical test they present is sensible but limited by some very understandable factors. First, Bullock and Loomis rely on data from four or five scattered Congresses. While this is a great improvement over most work in the area, it does leave room for more complete treatments. Second, because of the many different career options available in the House, separate (and frequently conflicting) results are presented for "power committee" positions, committee leadership positions, subcommittee leadership positions, and party leadership positions. This is by no means unreasonable, but it does make more difficult the task of sorting out and summarizing the precise changes that have occurred.

These difficulties are apparent in their findings. A look at the tables in the two relevant articles seems to support the interpretation that the expected shift in formal position career patterns does not occur for some positions and for some classes but does occur for other positions and for other classes. In fact, as noted in chapter 1, the extent to which the evidence runs contrary to expectations is somewhat disconcerting. Often, members of the more recent classes appear to be slower to advance to certain positions than do members of earlier classes. Since this finding flies in the face of conventional wisdom and since formal positions are such vital elements of congressional careers, a more comprehensive test is needed of the hypothesis that representatives now acquire formal positions more quickly than they used to.

The Perception of Formal
Positions in the House

To make this task more manageable, the assistance of numerous close observers of Congress was invoked. In March of 1986, I prevailed upon forty top-level congressional staffers, forty political scientists who specialize in legislative politics, and forty journalists with congressional press passes to complete a brief questionnaire. Requests to these three small random samples generated an average response rate of about 65 percent (see Stubben and Hibbing 1987 for additional details of the survey and sampling procedures). The respondents were asked to assign estimates of the amount of prestige associated with fifteen formal positions in the House during the last few decades. As can be seen from table 3.1, some of these were party positions and some were committee positions. The possible range was defined by the position of Speaker on one end with an automatic rating of 100 and, at the other end, by the position of a simple member of a "less desirable" (defined shortly) committee, automatically rated 1.

The mean ratings of the selected positions are presented in table 3.1. To avoid having an unreasonable number of positions listed on the questionnaire, the standing committees were grouped into three categories, along the lines suggested by Fenno (1973) and employed by Smith and Deering (1984) and others. The so-called prestige committee category includes Appropriations, Rules, and Ways and Means. The large category of policy or constituency committees includes Agriculture, Armed Services, Banking, Budget, Education and Labor, Energy and Commerce, Foreign Affairs, Government Operations, Interior, Judiciary, Merchant Marine,

Table 3.1. Rating of Selected House Positions in the Modern Era

Position	Rating
Party leadership	
Speaker	100
Majority leader	80
Majority whip	59
Caucus chair	39
Deputy whip	34
Member of the Steering and Policy Committee	30
Committee leadership	
Chairman of a prestige committee	72
Chairman of a policy/constituency committee	59
Chairman of a less-desirable committee	34
Subcommittee leadership	
Chairman of an appropriations subcommittee	56
Chairman of a subcommittee of a policy/constituency committee	40
Chairman of a subcommittee of a less-desirable committee	17
Committee membership	
Member of prestige committee	34
Member of a policy/constituency committee	17
Member of a less-desirable committee	1

Source: Author-conducted survey of staffers, journalists, and congressional scholars.

Public Works, Science and Technology, Small Business, and Veterans Affairs. Finally, the less desirable committee category is composed of the District of Columbia, Administration, Post Office and Civil Service, and Standards of Official Conduct (now Ethics) committees.[3]

With the Speaker initialized at 100, the mean score for the majority leader was 80; majority whip and the other party positions fall off fairly dramatically after that. The position of chair of one of the prestige committees was, on average, perceived to hold only a little less prestige (72) than majority leaders. A typical chair of a policy or constituency committee was thought by the respondents to be about as prestigious as the position of majority whip (59.5 to 59). And the position of chair of a less desirable committee was ranked down with the positions of deputy whip, caucus chair, and Steering and Policy Committee member. As to subcommittee chairs, Appropriations subcommittee chairs were viewed as having practically as much influence as the leaders of the full policy and constituency committees (56.5 to 59.5). On average, respondents felt that more prestige accrued to being chair of a subcommittee of a policy or constituency committee than to being chair of a full committee in the less desirable committee category.[4] Being on a committee but not chairing it or any of its subcommittees was generally ranked quite low: even membership on a prestige committee received only an average rating of 34—the same as the chair of a less desirable committee.

By and large, these ratings are in accord with traditional descriptions of the hierarchy of positions in the House. While the ratings in table 3.1 are simplifications, they are reasonable simplifications. These ratings permit additional analyses of how the distribution of positions in the House has changed in the last thirty years and also of how the distribution of positions typically changes over the course of modern congressional careers. In the remainder of this chapter, I focus on Democratic members of the House from 1955 to 1986 (the 84th through 99th Congresses). This time period was selected because during these three decades there have been no changes in the majority party, the Democrats having held control of the House since the 1954 elections. Thus, careers can be analyzed without the confusing circumstances of a committee chair becoming ranking minority member solely because of a partisan shift in the overall chamber. The restriction to Democrats is undertaken because only members of the majority party fill many of the positions utilized in the questionnaire.

The Increasing Number of Formal Positions in the House

Careers are intimately related to the nature of the institution in which they take place. Changes in congressional careers affect Congress as an institution, and changes in Congress as an institution affect congressional careers. As far as positions are concerned, the institution changed markedly during the time period employed here, with the major change being that there are now many more positions available than there were thirty years ago. This point is evident from a glance at table 3.2.

This table was created by applying the position ratings in table 3.1 to each Democrat in each Congress. To illustrate, in the 84th Congress,

Table 3.2. Mean Position Score and Degree of Skewness in Formal Position Distribution among House Democrats, 1955–1986

Congress	Mean position score	Skewness (S.E.)	N
84 (1955–56)	35.5	.85 (.16)	231
85 (1957–58)	35.2	.77 (.16)	234
86 (1959–60)	34.5	.94 (.14)	283
87 (1961–62)	36.7	1.05 (.15)	262
88 (1963–64)	37.9	1.00 (.15)	255
89 (1965–66)	37.2	1.05 (.14)	290
90 (1967–68)	41.7	.84 (.15)	247
91 (1969–70)	42.6	.70 (.15)	243
92 (1971–72)	42.6	.60 (.15)	255
93 (1973–74)	48.0	.56 (.16)	242
94 (1975–76)	46.8	.82 (.14)	286
95 (1977–78)	47.1	.77 (.14)	284
96 (1979–80)	47.8	.73 (.15)	274
97 (1981–82)	50.6	.63 (.16)	239
98 (1983–84)	48.9	.80 (.15)	262
99 (1985–86)	50.3	.78 (.16)	250

Source: Computed by the author.

James Haley (D-Fla.) was chairman of the Indian Affairs Subcommittee of the Interior Committee. Since Interior is a constituency committee, Haley received 40 points for holding this position (see table 3.1). Haley also was a member of the Veterans Affairs Committee, for which he received an additional 17 points (see table 3.1). Thus, Haley's total for the 84th Congress is 57 points.[5] Similar calculations were undertaken for each of Haley's Democratic colleagues in the 84th Congress, and the average score for all Democrats was then computed. This is the figure reported in the first column of table 3.2 for the 84th Congress. Figures for the remaining Congresses were computed in the same manner.

The growth in the mean scores is quite clear. From about 35 points in 1955—the equivalent of membership on two policy or constituency committees—the average position ratings for a Democrat grew to over 50 points in 1985—not far from the equivalent of chairing an Appropriations subcommittee or a full policy and constituency committee. Does this mean the typical House Democrat in 1985 was more prestigious than the typical House Democrat thirty years earlier? Of course not. Does this mean there were a larger number of positions in 1985 than in 1955? Of course.

While the number of full committees grew by only two during this time period, subcommittees proliferated at a brisk pace, increasing from 83 in the 84th Congress to 140 in the 96th, before dropping off just a little in the last few Congresses. With so many more chances to chair a subcommittee, it is not surprising that the average Democrat in 1985 held better positions than the average Democrat in 1955. But this increase in the number of committees and, especially, subcommittees is only one of the reasons for the increase in the average prestige rating for Democrats. In addition, existing committees were allowed to grow in size (particularly Ways and Means), new party positions were created, and the committee ratio of Democrats to Republicans was made more favorable to Democrats on several key committees. All these factors contributed to the growing number of positions available to House Democrats (see also Smith and Deering 1984, 51).

The Distribution of Formal Positions

While the increase in mean position ratings for Democrats can be accounted for in a fairly straightforward fashion, a more important matter involves the *distribution* of positions in these Congresses. Was there simply a uniform quantum leap upward during this time period for all Democrats in terms of the positions they held, or has there been a redistribution of these positions?

To begin to answer these questions, I present in figure 3.1 (and table 3.2) the skewness statistic for the distribution of the positions held by Democrats in each of the sixteen Congresses. This statistic, also called third moment, is 0 if the distribution constitutes a normal, perfectly

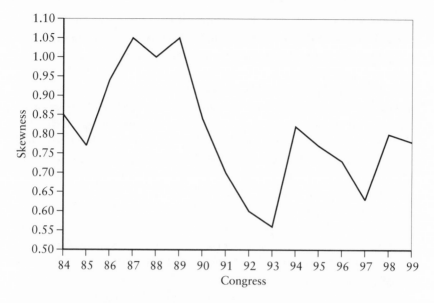

Figure 3.1. Variations in the Distribution of Formal Positions among House Democrats, 1955–1986

symmetric, bell shape. Positive skewness statistics, as we have here, indicate there are more cases to the left of the mean (representatives with less prestigious positions) than to the right of the mean. Thus, it is axiomatic that the values to the right of the mean must be more extreme. Not surprisingly, all sixteen Congresses display positive skewness statistics, thereby indicating prestigious positions tend to be dominated by a fairly small number of representatives while the great majority of representatives have only a modest array of positions to their credit. This kind of pattern would probably apply to most organizations.

But the intriguing element of the skewness statistics is the way they vary in size across the time period. After a modest beginning in the first two Congresses (1955 through 1958), we observe a fairly sharp increase in the degree of skewness from 1959 through 1966. This then is the high point of the age of committee chairs—a time when a fairly small number of individuals dominated their committees, assigned themselves or a small cluster of their friends to key subcommittees, and on more than one occasion frustrated the party leadership. This is the era when, more than any other time in postwar history, a few individuals controlled the formal positions of the House of Representatives. This eight-year period was the time when the distribution of positions in the House was the most un-even. And it would have been still more uneven if the procedures I employed gave credit for multiple subcommittee positions on a single committee.

After the 89th Congress, the size of the skewness statistic drops noticeably. From a high of 1.05 in 1965–66, the skewness statistic falls quickly and steadily for the next eight years, bottoming out in the 93d Congress (1973–74) at .56, practically half of what it had been just a few years before.[6] This late-1960s and early-1970s decline in the skewness statistic was partially a product of the reform-oriented activities advocated by the Democratic Study Group (see Dodd and Oppenheimer 1981, 41), particularly the 1971 decision to limit individual members to one subcommittee chair. In addition, the proliferation of positions in and of itself pushed more members higher on the scale, thus reducing the crowding problem at the lower end and, correspondingly, reducing the skewness statistic.

Some cursory treatments of Congress imply that the process of democratization began with the election of the Watergate class of 1975. After all, when the members of this class entered the House, they promptly deposed three senior committee chairmen, they transferred the committee assignment task from the Democratic members of the Ways and Means Committee to the Steering and Policy Committee, they expanded the Ways and Means Committee by almost 50 percent, and they barred major committee chairmen from serving on other committees (see Shepsle 1978, 256).

But the data reveal that the distribution of formal positions in the House was actually more skewed in the 94th Congress than it was in the previous three. Upon reflection, this is not surprising since many of the relevant reforms were in the works long before 1975. Still, this explanation does not account for the *increase* in skewness in the 94th Congress. What happened in 1975 was not a reversal of the consequences of congressional reform but the result of an influx of new Democrats without an accompanying reduction in the number of senior Democrats. The fallout from Watergate and a weak economy combined to produce an extraordinary boost in Democratic House membership in 1975 (from 242 to 291). Even with the reforms, members were not handed quality formal positions immediately, so the influx of new members, along with the continuing presence of older, position-holding members, causes a momentary blip in the skewness statistic. Thus, somewhat paradoxically, when the members of the large Democratic class of 1975 were sworn in, the distribution of positions became more skewed.

From 1975 to 1982, the distribution of positions across the Democratic membership of the House declined again. In truth, the consequences of the 1975 reforms are probably more evident in this steady decline than in the temporary increase occurring in 1975. In addition to the effects of these important reforms, the voluntary retirement rate among senior position-laden Democrats was unusually high in the late 1970s (see Hibbing 1982b). The departure of these well-placed elderly representatives no doubt also contributed to the late-1970s decentralization. Since 1983, the skewness statistic has come back up a little, but it is clearly operating on quite a different level than that which existed in the early 1960s.

The data and procedures used here depict the decentralization and democratization of the House of Representatives that has been the topic of so much conversation in recent years. They allow us to present empirical evidence on a matter that to this time has been treated largely with anecdotes, some occasional data on subcommittee chairs, or information on a class or two of representatives. These procedures suggest that the time period in which a small number of committee chairmen dominated all the formal positions in the House was actually fairly brief, lasting only from about the 86th to the 89th Congress, although I hasten to point out that these references are to formal positions only, not to overall power in the body. Formal positions in the House were distributed about as evenly in 1957 as they were twenty years later in 1977. Moreover, the data indicate that the trend toward a more equitable distribution of formal positions among House Democrats was under way long before the Watergate elections of 1974. In short, the usual claims of a wider distribution of formal positions in the last ten years than in the previous twenty are generally on target but are inaccurate with regard to some important specific aspects.[7]

Formal Positions over the Course of a Career

With this institutional information as background, it is time to address the issue of how individual formal position careers are shaped. Certainly there are practically as many paths through the formal positions of the House as there have been members. Some careers are amazingly stable as far as positions-held are concerned. Consider the case of James Delaney

(D-N.Y.), who entered the House in 1949 and immediately joined the Rules Committee. He spent the next twenty-eight years there, casting several monumental votes along the way (see, for example, Mayhew 1974a, 151),[8] and became the chair of the committee only in his last term, the sole instance in which his formal position score was different from the rest of his career. Similarly, Edward Patten (D-N.J.), after first being elected to the House in 1962, spent a single term on the Science and Technology Committee before jumping to Appropriations where he remained—without getting a subcommittee chair—for the next sixteen years. It is not a coincidence that these two examples of stability in formal position careers involve individuals on prestigious committees in the early portion of the time period. Position stability was generally greater in the fifties and sixties, and prestige committees usually inspire members to stay around awhile.

On the other end of the spectrum are the numerous examples of representatives who have jumped frequently from position to position. One of the most extreme was Olin Teague (D-Tex.), who began his House career in 1946 on the Veterans Affairs Committee. By 1955 he had worked his way up to chairman, but he had also taken a spot on the District of Columbia Committee—in fact he had a subcommittee chair on the latter. In addition, Teague was a charter member of the Science and Aeronautics Committee, and he subsequently chaired the Manned Space Flight Subcommittee. In 1971, the personally popular Teague capitalized on his racquetball connections and good-old-boy style to swipe the chairmanship of the Democratic Caucus from a startled Dan Rostenkowski (D-Ill.), who forgot to cover his backside while eyeing the position of majority leader. Two years later, Teague traded his Veterans Affairs chair (while retaining the number two ranking) for the top position on Science and Aeronautics, and two years after that, "Tiger" Teague, as he was commonly called, rotated out of the caucus chair as is required by caucus rules. Before retiring in 1978, he also added several terms of service on the Ethics Committee to his continuing positions on Science and Aeronautics and Veterans Affairs. Teague's House career could hardly be characterized as standpat.

Teague's Texas colleague, Omar Burleson, was a rarity in that he gave up a full committee chairmanship in 1971 in order to transfer to the bottom of the seniority ladder on another committee. Such an action makes more sense when it is noted that he moved to the Ways and Means Committee from the chairmanship of the pre–Wayne Hays Administration Committee (although Burleson also was forced to give up the chairmanship of a powerful Foreign Affairs subcommittee). Still, the norm is for this kind of switch to be made before the member becomes chair of a committee. In Burleson's case, he was strongly encouraged to move by the powerful Texas delegation and by the oil industry, both of which wanted a forceful and sympathetic voice in Ways and Means' discussions of oil depletion allowances and the like.

While recognizing the unique quality of most individual careers, it is nonetheless important to determine the nature of the *typical* formal position career in the modern House. To provide some sense of this typical career, figure 3.2 graphically depicts the mean formal position career of four classes of representatives: the classes of 1957, 1963, 1969, and 1975. I have inspected the data for all sixteen classes in the time period. However, since presenting the curve for each class would be a little much for one graph, I selected four equally spaced classes that do not distort the message that comes through upon observation of all sixteen classes.

Immediately evident is the shift upward as we move toward the more recent past. The class of 1957 in its first term averages 15.9 points, less on average than a single membership on a policy or constituency committee. Contrast this with the class of 1975, which in its first term compiled an average formal position rating of over 30, nearly the equivalent of a chairmanship of a policy or constituency committee subcommittee. These results are not unexpected given previous findings involving the increase in the number of formal positions available. The more important aspect of this figure concerns the shape of the formal position career once the change in the intercept is taken into consideration. This is where we encounter one of the most crucial tests of the assumption that the traditional, slow-to-acquire-positions career has given way to a modern career path in which formal positions are bestowed upon House Democrats at a much earlier stage.

The major difference in the career contours is that the more recent classes of 1969 and 1975 tend to rise briskly the first four terms while the earlier classes of 1957 and 1963 experience sluggish growth from their second through their fourth terms. The class of 1957 only improves, on average, 5 points over the course of these four years, and the class of 1963 improves only about 6. Contrast this with the class of 1969, which goes up almost 12 points, and the class of 1975, which sees an average improvement of 13 points. By far, the largest difference between classes at comparable career stages occurs at the fourth term where the class of

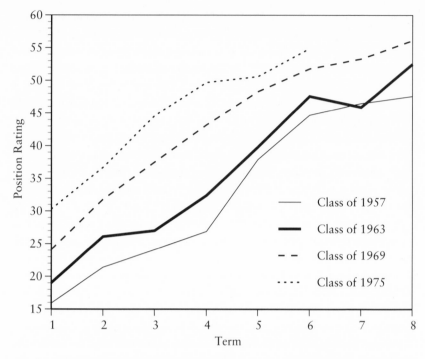

Figure 3.2. Mean Position Rating for House Democratic Classes of 1957, 1963, 1969, and 1975

1957 is at 26.9 and the class of 1975 is at 49.7. As expected, after the fourth term, the earlier classes begin to make up lost ground.

With the traditional slow-to-build career path, members did not begin to make significant improvements in their formal positions until after eight years or so in the House. But with more recent House careers, members are more likely to make improvements right away and then to flatten out after four or five terms. In this way, the findings presented in figure 3.2 offer modest support for conventional expectations concerning a shift from slow to fast rates of position acquisition.

But the large differences in the number of positions available make it difficult to compare. The fourth term of the class of 1957 took place in the 88th Congress (1963–64) when the average score for all Democrats was 37.9. The fourth term of the class of 1975 took place in the 97th Congress (1981–82) when the average score for all Democrats was 50.6. To facilitate comparisons of the different classes, I have computed a z-score for each representative. The z-score is a standardized score that reflects the degree to which a particular value is above or below the mean. Thus, a z-score of 0 means that the value in question is exactly equal to the mean for all values in that Congress. A z-score of +1 indicates a value that is one standard deviation above the mean, and a z-score of −1 indicates a value that is one standard deviation below the mean. With a z-score, the focus becomes the mean share of formal positions held by a given class *relative to all formal positions available in the pertinent Congress*. Figure 3.3 contains the standardized position scores for the same four classes of Democratic representatives utilized in figure 3.2.

The standardization has had the effect of reducing the disparity in the scores for representatives in their first terms. Unlike figure 3.2, position scores for first terms are now nearly identical across the four classes. The standardization of these scores, however, does nothing to alleviate the different shapes of the position careers across the classes—if anything, it exacerbates these differences. The four classes all increase by about the same amount from their first to their second terms, but after this, the similarity ends. From the second to the third term, the class of 1957 improves ever so slightly, the class of 1963 actually sees its positions-held situation decline relative to other Democrats in the 90th Congress, and the class of 1969 improves only modestly. The class of 1975, however, improves markedly, from .48 standard deviations below the mean to very nearly the mean (−.09) for all Democrats. As we move from the third to the fourth term, the class of 1969 makes up a lot of ground on the class of 1975, but the two earlier classes lag far behind, even though the scores have been standardized. At the fourth term of their respective careers, the mean position scores for the classes of 1957 and 1963 are −.53 and −.50, respectively, while the classes of 1969 and 1975 have already surpassed the average score for all Democrats in the corresponding Congress at .02 and .12, respectively. However, by the seventh term, the earlier classes have nearly caught up. Thus, significant movements come early for recent classes; later for earlier classes. In this important respect, the shift from classic career to revisionist career is readily apparent.

Further analysis makes it possible to be more specific about when the change in the shape of the formal position career occurred. While I will not present the position career for each of the sixteen classes, inspection of the pattern indicates that, outside of the class of 1959, which appears to be something of an aberration, most early classes display a relatively sluggish increase in their third and fourth terms.[9] The major change in

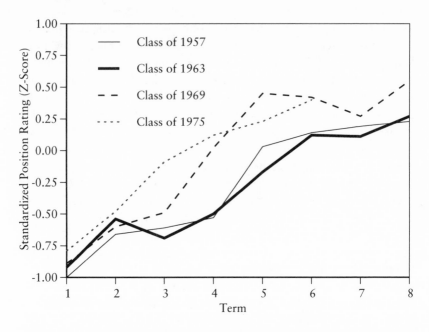

Figure 3.3. Standardized Mean Position Rating for House Democratic Classes of 1957, 1963, 1969, and 1975

the shape of the position career in the House clearly comes between the classes of 1967 and 1971, with the class of 1969 serving as a perfect transition. The earlier classes not presented (1959, 1961, 1965, and 1967) have patterns that look very much like the classes of 1957 and 1963 (see figure 3.4), and the later classes not presented (1971 and 1973) have patterns that look quite a bit like the class of 1975 (see figure 3.4).[10] If one specific period had to be selected during which the position career ceased being traditional and assumed its modern contours, the period from 1967 to 1971 would have to be it. If 1969 is used as the breakpoint, the different contours of the old and new careers are quite evident. This is the message of figure 3.4.

The findings in this figure, like those in the previous figure, have been standardized on the basis of how many and what kind of formal positions were available in any individual Congress. The first and second terms of the old and new career patterns are very nearly identical, but in the third term, the distinctive features of the post-1969 congressional position career are apparent. Third-termers in more recent Congresses have a much greater share of the action (to the extent that holding formal com-

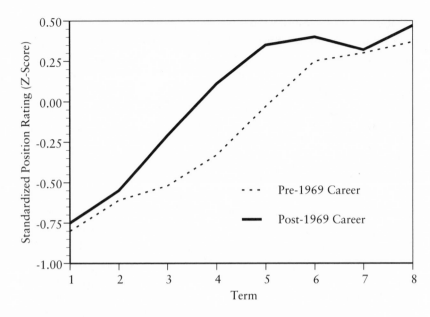

Figure 3.4. Standardized Mean Position Rating for Pre- and Post-1969 House Democratic Classes

mittee and party positions indicates having a piece of the action) than third-termers in pre-1969 Congresses. The quicker acquisition of quality formal positions continues in the fourth and fifth terms. On average, fourth-termers in post-1969 Congresses rank above the mean position score for the relevant Congress (z-score of +.11). Fourth-termers in earlier Congresses, however, rank .33 standard deviations below the mean for whatever Congress marked their fourth term (z-score of −.33). Even by the fifth term, the typical old-style career does not yet reach the mean position rating for all Democrats in that Congress (z-score of −.03). New-style careers continue their climb, reaching a z-score of +.35.

But between the fifth and six terms the old career narrows the gap substantially. By the seventh and eighth terms there is in essence no difference between the old- and new-style careers. And beyond the eighth term generalizations are difficult because of the small number of individuals in any given class remaining after sixteen years in the House. The differences between the old and the new style of position career thus are largely confined to the third, fourth, and fifth terms. As suggested by conventional wisdom, the new style of position career is one in which members acquire positions more quickly. In the modern House, members improve their formal position situation markedly between the fourth and tenth years of service. Many move into subcommittee chairmanships, and most do even better than this. In the House of the late 1950s and 1960s, the major strides with regard to formal positions came only after at least eight years of service. Not until then did members begin to acquire key committee, subcommittee, and party positions.

Mortality Effects and the Position Career

Again there is a need to be sensitive to the possibility that the contours of careers are distorted due to the varying composition of a class at different career stages. With regard to formal position careers, it is theoretically possible that even if the members of a class retain identical positions across entire careers, the curve of the class might go up steeply. Such an occurrence would take place if the members with less prestigious positions were more likely to serve shorter time periods in the House. As the class is made up increasingly of well-positioned members, the mean score for the class would go up even though the positions of the members of the class remain the same from Congress to Congress.

To provide some sense of what the results would look like sans the potential bias of mortality effects, I constructed the formal position curves for only the Olympians (those serving more than seven terms) of the four classes highlighted in this chapter. So whereas the results in figure 3.4 include all members of a class who were participating in the Congresses in question, this approach includes only those members who served at least eight terms. As such, the number of cases generating the mean z-scores is stable within classes ($N = 5$ for the class of 1957; $N = 17$ for the class of 1963; $N = 10$ for the class of 1969; and $N = 28$ for the class of 1975). The variance among the four classes is, of course, due to the differing sizes of the classes at entry as well as the differing rates of attrition each class experienced, but within classes, from first term to eighth, the N remains the same.

There is no need to present the results graphically since the story told by the mortality-corrected data is not fundamentally different from that of figure 3.3. Again the formal positions held by third-, fourth-, and fifth-termers are much less notable for the earlier classes than for the later ones. Before the third term and after the fifth, however, formal positions held are not that much different in the old and the new careers. Thus, we can be reasonably confident that the shift in the contours of the congressional career is not a product of mortality effects. Even with these effects controlled, the relatively rapid advancement of more recent classes is evident.

Conclusion

Have formal position careers in the House changed shape? Is conventional wisdom accurate when it holds that progression to quality formal positions used to be much slower than it is today? The scale of position prestige employed here, based as it is on the perceptions of key congressional observers and participants, is open to challenge but perhaps no more serious challenge than the more traditional research approach, which implicitly assumes that, to take one example, all subcommittee chairmanships are of identical value to all members of the House. Moreover, placing all positions on a single metric puts us in a better position to provide general rather than position-specific answers to the questions posed above.

A clear difference exists between the old (pre-1969) and new (post-1969) House career. Probably the best visual image of this change is found in figure 3.4. The gap between the two lines is indicative of the degree to which careers have changed *after the proliferation of positions that occurred across this time period is taken into consideration,* something previous research has failed to do. To put it somewhat differently, the contours of the formal position career have changed. Representatives in the early stages of their careers are likely to have a greater relative share of the formal positions available than was the case with the pre-1969 congressional career. The reforms of the late 1960s and early 1970s did more than increase the number of formal positions in the pool; they led to a measured amount of redistribution in these positions.

While formal positions are obviously acquired more quickly in the 1970s and 1980s than they were in the 1950s and 1960s, several qualifications to this general conclusion are warranted. First, the gap between the old and the new may be smaller than some congressional scholars would have anticipated. The standardized scores for the old and the new classes at comparable career stages never differ by more than .5 standard deviations.

Second, differences are generally restricted to a certain stage of careers. Before the third and after the fifth or sixth term, the old and new careers are quite similar. Of course, the differences would appear much greater and longer lasting if the focus of attention were on the percentage of members with, say, subcommittee chairmanships or if it were on unstandardized overall formal position scores (see figure 3.2). But an emphasis on such raw numbers really says nothing more than that there are a greater number of formal positions in the House than there used to be— an unarguable but hackneyed point. To obtain an accurate feel for the relative extent of position-holding by various classes and for how this position-holding varies across careers, we must turn to the results generated by standardized figures. These tell us that, relative to their colleagues in the pertinent Congresses, modern classes in their third, fourth, and fifth terms possess somewhat better shares of the positions available than their counterparts in the 1950s and 1960s Congresses. Otherwise, position share has not changed from old- to new-style career.

Third, the shift did not come as a result of the Watergate class's entry into the House in 1975. From the perspective of the distribution of formal positions, decisions such as the one to limit each member to one subcommittee chairmanship had a much greater impact than the dethroning of three committee chairmen. Rather, the evolution in the direction of a new career contour as well as the movement toward overall democratization of the distribution of formal positions (see figure 3.1) were both under way long before 1975. This conclusion is slightly contrary to the implications found in the work of Loomis (1988a) and Schneider (1989).

Although at first glance it may not seem to be true, these findings on the changing contours of the formal position career are not inconsistent with the notion that the congressional career has shifted from cyclical toward static contours. While the modern position career, unlike some other career components we will analyze, is not flat, this would be an unreasonable expectation. The formal positions held by newcomers will never match the quality and quantity of the formal positions held by more senior members. Still, it is now the case that, after the first four terms or so, less movement up the formal position scale occurs in recent careers than in the more traditional careers of the 1950s. To illustrate, figure 3.4 indicates that from the fourth term to the eighth the typical new formal position career rises from .08 to .47 standard deviations above the mean, an increase of .39. The typical old formal position career, during a comparable period of time, went from −.37 to +.40 standard deviations away from the mean, an increase fully twice as large as modern members typically experience.

Progress now comes quickly before members settle in for the long haul. After the initial few years of service we see that the position career, like the electoral career, is less influenced by life-cycle effects than it was in the old-style House career. Having established this, it is time to turn our attention away from elections and positions and toward the actual behavior of representatives as they move through their House careers.

4 The Roll Call Career

"When I came to Congress in 1960," a former representative told me, "Carl Vinson [D-Ga., and longtime chair of the Armed Services Committee] had a rule that committee members were permitted one question in all the committee deliberations that took place their first term; that's it—one question in an entire term; they were permitted two questions in their second term; three in their third; and so on. With this kind of attitude, you can see why it took members some time before they were legislatively active."

"Of course my involvement in legislation changed over my career," another ex-representative told me; "I became much more productive. To give you an example, when I was young I offered an amendment to a bill we were considering in the Interior Committee. Well, all this amendment did was make [committee chair and dominant force Wayne] Aspinall [D-Colo.] mad as hell. This, in turn, doomed the bill. I would never have done that years later; I would have known better."

And yet a third former representative, a retiree from a border-state district, had this to say about ideological change in congressional careers: "Most members remain pretty stable in their [ideological] positions. I can think of a few who didn't. Edith Green [D-Oreg.] became more conservative; Paul Rogers [D-Fla.] became more liberal; John Buchanon [R-Ala.] also became more liberal, particularly on racial issues. But most stay fairly constant. If there is an overall tendency, it is probably to moderate. This comes because you must develop a sense of what can be done. If you don't, you will go crazy. As the years pass, you lose the sense of good versus evil. My biggest lesson in Congress was discovering that my enemies did not have horns."

These three quotes all address the topic of how the legislative activity of

House members may change over the course of a career. In the next two chapters, I present tests of various hypotheses concerning the evolution of the legislative aspect of congressional careers. Some of these hypotheses are embedded in the statements above; others are derived from the literature and so-called conventional wisdom. But none of them has yet received what could be described as a systematic test. Like many other aspects of the congressional career, legislative activities have been subjected to a substantial amount of cross-sectional analysis and a piddling amount of truly longitudinal research.

In addition to this cross-sectional bias, extant research on legislative activity tilts much too heavily toward investigations of roll call votes. Perhaps because of the ready availability of data, explaining why some representatives vote yea and some vote nay on an issue or set of issues is a favorite pastime of legislative scholars. While roll calls are of undeniable importance, as demonstrated by the three comments introducing this chapter, they constitute only a small portion of a representative's overall legislative activity. In this and the next chapter, I hope to correct these two serious deficiencies in our understanding of legislative activity in the House by providing research that is longitudinal and by broadening the focus so that legislative activity is viewed as something more than just casting roll call votes. In this chapter, the focus is on traditional roll call behavior. In chapter 5, the topic becomes the general legislative activity of members of Congress: how many bills they introduce, how many amendments they offer, how many speeches they give, and how specialized and successful their legislative agenda happens to be.

Roll Call Voting Research

Although it is only one facet of a member's legislative activity, roll call voting patterns still seem the logical place to begin this investigation of the legislative aspects of the congressional career. For one thing, there is research on which we can draw. Even though the emphasis to date has been on cross-sectional variation in roll call activity, this does not mean that this stream of research is totally irrelevant to the task at hand. Many of the roll call studies are instructive (see MacRae 1958; Mayhew 1966; Shannon 1968; Cherryholmes and Shapiro 1969; Turner 1970; Clausen 1973; Fiorina 1974; Matthews and Stimson 1975; Kingdon 1981; Poole and Daniels 1985, to name just a few), and many of them are, at one point or another, related to the issue of change in voting behavior over the course of a career (see Collie 1984 for a summary of this literature).

The most basic point of intersection involves the stability of roll call decisions. One of the best-known cross-sectional findings is that there is a stable left-right continuum to voting (see especially Schneider 1979; Poole and Daniels 1985; Poole and Rosenthal 1985). Members of Congress, it is held, can be reasonably placed on a single ideological continuum. In other words, this research suggests there is a substantial amount of constraint across issues. Liberals on foreign policy tend to be liberals on domestic policy.

This finding is not totally consistent with those of Clausen (1973) and, to some extent, Sinclair (1976), who find it beneficial to look at congressional voting issue area by issue area. Others feel claims of unidimensionality may be inflated due to an improper appreciation for the kinds of baseline predictions that could be achieved simply by chance, given that (setting aside not voting) the representative has only two options: yea or nay (on this topic, see the exchange between Hammond and Fraser 1983a and 1983b and Weisberg 1983).

Happily, there is no need for us to enter this war zone. Our concern is with the stability of voting behavior over time rather than across issues at a single point in time. If the major focus of attention with the cross-sectional research is the *constraint* of roll call voting across issue positions, the focus of longitudinal research must be the *consistency* of roll call voting across the years (see Converse 1964 for the standard discussion of constraint and consistency).

Although conceptually they are two quite distinct issues, it is often assumed that there will be some relationship between constraint and consistency; that stability across issues will go along with stability across time. Indeed, it would be difficult to explain how there could be substantial across-issue constraint if on specific issues there were not some degree of consistency across time (that is, it would be difficult to explain constraint if representatives, like Converse's respondents, were devoid of reasonably stable attitudes on specific issues). Perhaps partially for these reasons, it seems to be assumed that roll call voting at the individual level is fairly consistent across time.

The voting histories that representatives carry with them on most issues are assumed to be quite influential. Why? There are several possibilities, many of which are mentioned by Kingdon in *Congressmen's Voting Decisions* (1981, 274–78). First, reliance on voting history saves time. There is little reason to renew information search and research if these efforts were undertaken in preparation for a vote on the same issue a few months or years previously. Second, it is a safe strategy, assuming there was no huge public outcry as a result of the vote the last time. Third, explaining inconsistencies in voting patterns is arguably more difficult than explaining voting patterns that the constituency views as mostly wrong. Fourth, the forces that led to a particular vote the last time are probably not that much different from those existing this time around. Finally, there are the larger, social-psychological explanations having to do with stored mass, inertia, and becoming set in one's ways. For these reasons and others, a sensible initial expectation is that roll call voting behavior at time t will be a good predictor of voting behavior at time t + 1.

Are these expectations supported by empirical evidence? This is difficult to say as the evidence is thin. Somewhat surprisingly, Kingdon, after presenting a persuasive case for the importance of voting histories and after extensive interviewing of representatives about their decision-making processes, concludes that "voting history . . . does not seem to be sufficiently important in my data to give us the kind of confidence we would need in order to accept an incremental process as our dominant explanation for congressmen's voting decisions" (1981, 277). Kingdon's statement appears to contradict Asher and Weisberg who, after the most complete examination of roll call behavior at the individual level over time, conclude that "the tremendous continuity in congressional voting should be explicitly recognized. . . . Any static theory that ignores this impressive stability is failing to incorporate a central characteristic of legislative decision making" (1978, 423).

Indirect evidence in support of the Asher and Weisberg position is available from attempts to determine the source of change in Congress (see Brady and Lynn 1973; Fiorina 1977b, 54–55; Fenno 1978, chap. 6; Brady and Stewart 1982, 333). These studies generally conclude that change is much more likely to come from turnover in the membership of the body (that is, generational replacement) than from individual members adopting new positions (conversion). The country's major legislative initiatives have been enacted after unusually high levels of membership turnover such as the country experienced in 1932 and 1964 (see Brady 1988). Shifts and modifications in individual beliefs have difficulty competing with the kinds of change that can be produced by replacing old members with new members.

Even as we start from an assumption that representatives will display stability in their roll call patterns over time, there remains the question of just how much stability. Certainly, roll call instability across time in a given district will almost always be greater if there is membership change in the district than if a single individual continues to hold the seat. Certainly, voting history will usually be a strong factor in many roll call decisions (see also Clem 1977). But this is not the same as saying that consistency will be absolute.

Just how consistent is roll call behavior? When there is change across careers, does it follow a pattern? Is the member quoted above correct in speculating that there will be a tendency to moderate as the years go by? If there is a tendency to observe greater moderation with the passing years, is it the result of mortality effects? Erikson and Wright (1985) have demonstrated that, other things being equal, the most successful candidates electorally are conservative Democrats or liberal Republicans. In earlier research (Hibbing 1982b), I found evidence that representatives with extreme ideological positions are more likely to retire voluntarily than are moderates. If extremists are more likely to leave Congress voluntarily and involuntarily, then a moderating tendency may appear simply as a result of extremists dropping out.

Regardless of the most frequently taken path, it behooves us to pay careful attention to those individuals who embark on something of an ideological odyssey during their House careers. As mentioned by the retired representative quoted earlier, some members display a surprising amount of flexibility in their roll call behavior. Edith Green (D-Oreg.) began her career in the 1950s with party-support scores (corrected for nonattendance) in the 80- to 90-percent range. By career's end in the early 1970s, her support for the Democratic party was barely 50 percent. Is it possible to explain why some members are less consistent than others in their roll call behavior?

Finally, careful attention should be paid to whether or not the tendency to alter voting patterns is the same in recent as in earlier House careers. In chapter 2, we found some indication that electoral support is now more constant over a career than it used to be. Have there been similar changes with regard to the contours of roll call activity? Or perhaps the anticipated overall stability has remained an unvarying component of careers in the House since the 1940s. So even if most members seem to be consistent across time in their roll call voting patterns, many important questions remain to be answered. These questions have to do with the specific level of stability, the direction of any movement that may appear, the type of representative who does not follow the typical pattern of temporal stability, and change across the decades in the contours of the roll call voting career.

Problems with Analyzing Roll Call Voting Longitudinally

Getting a fix on the stability of roll call voting across the phases of a House career is easier said than done. The major problem is that the context of the roll call vote is never constant. Although similar issues come up year after year, seldom can it be said that two roll call votes are identical. Perhaps the wording has changed, amendments have been added, the public mood has shifted, and/or the center of gravity within the House has moved. The problem is compounded in direct proportion to the lengthening of a career. On top of this, if single-issue votes at different career stages constitute the variable of interest, the problem of selecting appropriate votes arises.

Asher and Weisberg (1978) tackle these problems in several different ways. They present four case studies, each with slightly different research designs. The most revealing in terms of career-based change in roll call activity involves votes on raising the debt ceiling, an obvious choice given the regularity with which votes on this issue are taken. Asher and Weisberg analyze the 225 representatives who served continuously from 1964 to 1971 and find that 45 percent of them were perfectly consistent in their support for or opposition to increasing the debt ceiling. Another 21 percent always supported the increase when their party controlled the White House and always opposed the increase when their party did not control the White House. This means the remaining 34 percent could not be described as being consistent in any sense of the term. Although Asher and Weisberg take this finding to be support for the belief that roll call voting is "evolutionary" or stable, it strikes me as a surprisingly high level of inconsistency.

When they turn their attention to foreign aid, Asher and Weisberg do not analyze individual-level voting change except at just two points of a career. These two points were designed to bracket a change in administration. Consistency across these two data points was displayed 85 percent of the time. While 85 percent is fairly high, bear in mind that 50-percent consistency would occur by chance and that this is consistency across only two temporally proximate data points. With additional time and additional votes, there would naturally be additional inconsistency. Overall, we might conclude that there is more consistency than inconsistency but that the level of consistency is hardly overpowering.

Their third case study involves a comparison of 1956 and 1960 votes on school construction legislation. Here, the level of consistency is quite high: 239 (90 percent) of the 265 representatives who voted on both bills were consistent. An additional 36 eligible representatives missed one or both votes, which is indicative of yet another difficult procedural matter arising when individual votes are employed. Finally, with regard to Asher and Weisberg's fourth case study (civil rights), no data are presented relevant to the consistency of individual representatives on similar issues across time.

Thus, while the work of Asher and Weisberg is likely the best on the topic, it hardly adds up to the conclusion that perfect across-time consistency is present throughout an entire career. Most of their data correlate voting at only two points of a career; the findings on occasion indicate a surprising amount of inconsistency in roll call behavior; and the problem of abstentions is bothersome. Finally, Kingdon points out that some of the more important, cutting-edge issues may have no precursor in the representative's voting history (1981, 277). Thus, by stressing recurring votes such as those on the debt ceiling and foreign aid, Asher and Weisberg may be presenting only part of the story. The larger point, perhaps, is that nowhere do we see findings pertaining to consistency across entire careers, and these could be fundamentally different from those based on, say, two votes within the space of a few years.

There is a solution to many of these problems, but the solution creates more problems. The solution to which I refer involves the use of scales of overall roll call activity rather than particular votes—votes that may or may not be comparable from year to year and decade to decade. This practice reduces the attendance problem, taps a broad base of voting activity, eliminates the need to quibble about representative and unrepresentative votes, and is available over the course of many years, particularly if the well-known *Congressional Quarterly* indices of party support, presidential support, conservative coalition support, and overall participation levels are employed.

The major drawback of using these scales is the fact that, despite common usage, they are not strictly comparable from year to year (see also Pritchard 1986). For example, measures such as the presidential-support scale are heavily dependent upon many matters, including the proclivity of a president to take a position on certain types of issues. A presidential-support or a party-support score of 80 percent in one year is not necessarily identical in meaning to a score of 80 percent in the next year. To reduce this problem, at various points I again convert the raw scale scores (after attendance correction) into z-scores. This means that if average levels of party support for all representatives shift down 10 points from 1981 to 1982 but an individual representative's relationship to that mean remains unaltered from 1981 to 1982, the standardized score will be the same. Such an adjustment is far from perfect. For example, it standardizes scores by individual Congresses; thus, to the extent ideologically biased membership change takes place from one Congress to the next, it is possible for the standardized scores to change even if in some abstract sense a member's roll call behavior may have been the same from one Congress to the next. Still, all things considered, a standardization of roll call scales is probably the best way to gain some compass on the nature of roll call consistency across modern, usually lengthy House careers.

Roll Call Voting

Participation

The proper place to begin is with consideration of simple participation in roll call votes. As members move through their House careers, do they participate more or less in recorded votes? The obvious expectation is that participation will decline with age. Such a finding would be consistent with the fact that participation diminishes from middle age to old age among the general population (the period of life corresponding to most congressional careers). It should be mentioned, however, that such conclusions are moderately contentious and subject to a variety of interpretations (see, for example, Verba and Nie 1972; Beck and Jennings 1979; Jennings 1979; Jennings and Markus 1988).

A cursory inspection of changes in roll call participation over careers may be slightly misleading. As an example, the class of 1967 had an average roll call participation rate of 91.1 percent in its first Congress, the 90th. By the 97th Congress, the remaining members of the class of 1967 participated in 89.3 percent of all roll calls, only a slight drop from that which they produced in their first Congress. It turns out, however, that a

91.1-percent participation level was .68 standard deviations above the mean for the 90th Congress while 89.3-percent participation in the 97th Congress was right at the mean for all members. This is another way of saying that overall participation rates in the 97th Congress were higher than in the 90th Congress (a mean of 89 compared to a mean of 84). Since the 97th, participation rates have continued their climb (all the way to 95 percent in the first session of the 101st Congress). So in the context of what are considered high and low levels of participation *at the time*, roll call participation on the part of classes such as 1967 probably changed a good deal during their House stay.

One way to determine just how much change occurred is to standardize scores within each Congress. Figure 4.1 indicates that the overall trend in the postwar years has been toward slightly lower *relative* participation rates as tenure increases. The solid line in the figure represents the mean z-scores for all eligible members (those with extended illness and those ineligible for all votes in a particular Congress are not included). On average from 1947 to 1982, first-termers participated .18 standard deviations above the mean for their respective Congresses, but by the seventh and eighth terms members were participating at well below mean levels.

The dotted line in figure 4.1 provides the participation levels for the subset of members who served more than seven terms within the time period (N = 238), in this way eliminating the effects of attrition as discussed in chapter 2. With these mortality effects controlled, the drop in participation across a career is even more pronounced, due to the fact that initial participation levels of those who stay at least eight terms in the House are much higher than those who stay a shorter period of time. Perhaps the discrepancy in early levels of participation is an indication of who is more interested in a House career, or perhaps it is indicative of who needs to spend more time in the home district because of electoral difficulties, or both.

At any rate, while the high participation rate of careerists is interesting, the major finding in figure 4.1 for our purposes is the decline in relative participation across the typical House career. Fitting a counter variable to the two lines reveals that the downward slope of participation rates is statistically significant (at the .01 level) and averages −.03 standard deviations per term for all eligible members and −.06 for those members who stay at least eight terms. If we can say nothing else about roll call change over the course of a career, we can say that members tend to participate in fewer roll calls (relative to their colleagues) as their careers progress.

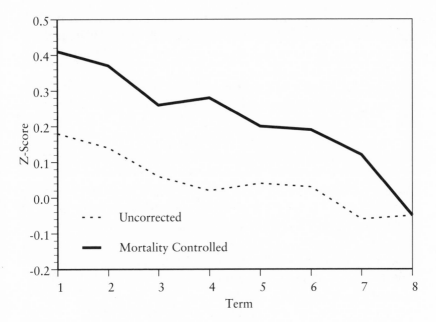

Figure 4.1. Standardized Roll Call Participation by Tenure, with and without Mortality Effects, 1947–1982

More interesting than whether or not members vote is the nature of voting patterns exhibited when they do participate. To investigate changes in voting patterns over careers, I will focus on the extent to which a member's votes support the party with which that member identifies and the degree to which a member's votes tilt to the liberal or the conservative end of the ideological spectrum. Information on presidential-support scores, another commonly used voting scale, will not be presented due to the difficulties created by changes in the party and/or the individual occupying the presidency.

Party Support

How is party support likely to be altered as the House career unfolds? If members of Congress are similar to members of the American public, it might be hypothesized that party voting would increase with age. Although the research in this area has been characterized by much controversy (see, for example, the exchange between Shively 1979a and 1979b and Abramson 1979), by the tendency to draw longitudinal conclusions on the basis of cross-sectional data (see, for example, Campbell,

Converse, Miller, and Stokes 1960, 210), and by haggling over the pros and cons of cohort analysis (see, for example, Glenn 1976; Jennings 1979; Markus 1983), the consensus is that partisanship strengthens with age. The least problematic data set would seem to be the one analyzed by Jennings and Markus (1984). Surveying the same individuals over a seventeen-year period, they concluded that "party identification remains fairly supple into the late twenties in the usual course of events but hardens considerably soon thereafter" (1016).

But there is no reason to assume automatically that what happens to partisan attachments in the mass public will be replicated in the roll call voting behavior of representatives. For one thing, if Jennings and Markus are correct, most of the "firming up" of partisanship will have occurred by the time members enter Congress. Moreover, factors such as electoral concerns mean that the political world of the representative will be quite different than that of an ordinary citizen. A fortified electoral base and an extended career permit many members of Congress enough security and freedom to ignore party wishes when they so prefer.

Congressional Quarterly has long recorded what it refers to as party-unity votes. These are votes on which a majority of voting Democrats oppose a majority of voting Republicans. Party-support scores indicate the extent to which each member supports his/her party on these party-unity votes, from 0 to 100 percent. *Congressional Quarterly*'s raw scores were then corrected for nonattendance using the equation

$$[\text{party support}/(\text{party support} + \text{party opposition})] \times 100.$$

As with simple participation, overall levels of party support have varied in the last forty years. Unlike the gradual increase in mean participation levels over the years, mean unstandardized party support has followed a curvilinear pattern with high figures recorded in the late 1950s and 1980s (see Rohde 1989 on the recent increase in party-support voting) and lower figures in the 1970s. Given these contextual variations and given the fact that the scales are not strictly comparable from Congress to Congress, it seems most sensible to focus on relative or standardized rather than absolute or unstandardized party support (although it turns out this decision does not affect conclusions one way or the other). Accordingly, the solid line of figure 4.2 presents standardized party support by tenure for all eligible representatives, and the dotted line contains similar figures for only those members who served at least eight terms.

It is clear from the figure that party support does diminish with increas-

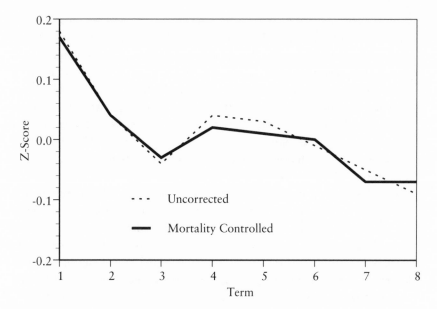

Figure 4.2. Standardized Party-Support Scores by Tenure, with and without Mortality Effects, 1947–1982

ing tenure in the House of Representatives. First-termers, on average, support their party .2 standard deviations more than the mean level of support for all representatives in the pertinent Congress, but, as was the case with participation, by the seventh and eighth terms, they are well below mean levels of party support. Unlike the results for participation, the correction for mortality effects does not alter the results much at all, so no special attention needs to be given to careerists as opposed to all members. On average, each additional term in the House brings a decrease of $-.03$ standard deviations in party support for Olympians only and also for all members. This trend is easily significant at the .01 level. Apparently, we can be somewhat confident that the need (or willingness) to support the party diminishes with tenure.

Ideological Voting

The literature provides little guidance in formulating expectations for career-based change in the ideological tint of representatives' roll call records. Studies of citizens in general suggest a tendency toward greater conservatism with the years (Campbell, Converse, Miller, and Stokes 1960, 210–11; see also McClosky 1958). This conclusion is consistent with the belief that, with time, people become more set in their ways. Again, adequate tests (that is, tests employing longitudinal rather than cross-sectional data) have yet to be conducted, and even if they had been they may not speak at all to the situation faced by a representative making a roll call decision. Do representatives become more conservative the longer they stay in Congress, or is the retired representative quoted at the beginning of this chapter correct in his belief that members display a moderating tendency as the years go by?

Absolute scales of ideological voting are the least comparable scales from year to year, so the focus will again be standardized scores. As is apparent from figure 4.3, the most common tendency is for representatives to become slightly more conservative relative to their House colleagues. It would appear the Edith Greens of the House outnumber the John Buchanons. Figure 4.3 indicates an overall movement toward more conservative roll call records after the scale (in this case, the widely used attendance-corrected conservative coalition support scale) has been standardized according to the scores of all members in the relevant Congresses.[1] After starting generally below the mean of roll call conservatism in the first couple of terms, members, on average, finish the first sixteen years of their House careers above the mean. Each term brings an average increase in support for the conservative coalition of about .02 standard deviations, although since we are speaking in relative terms, this movement could reflect an influx of liberal new members as much as actual movement on the part of the old (more on this shortly).

Special mention needs to be made of the correction for mortality effects presented in figure 4.3. While this correction is identical to that contained in figures 4.1 and 4.2, it takes on additional importance in figure 4.3. This additional importance accrues as a result of what is commonly known about congressional politics during this era. For virtually all of this time period, southern members were significantly more likely to serve longer careers in the House than were nonsouthern members and were also more likely to support the positions associated with the conservative coalition (in fact, this latter point is practically definitional). This being the case, it is possible that any claimed movement toward conservatism would simply be the result of the disproportionately low rate of mortality for southern members. The attrition of the more liberal northern members allows the southern members to exert increasing influence on the mean conservative coalition support figures, and this rather than any career-cycle effects could be responsible for the gradual increase in conservatism evident in the solid line of figure 4.3.

Despite the logic of this argument, the dotted line in figure 4.3 demonstrates that the movement toward conservatism is not just an artifact of southern politics. Here we find that even when the focus of attention is on just those members who served more than seven terms (in other words, even when results are not confused by some representatives dropping out along the way), there appears to be an increase in support for conservative positions from the first one or two terms to the seventh and eighth terms.

The data also contain some indication that representatives moderate their roll call voting records with the passing of the years. The standard deviation around the mean level of conservative coalition support is higher for first-termers (almost 36) than for eighth-termers (about 30).[2] An even bigger drop occurs when mortality effects are controlled. There is a slight tendency for representatives to lose their ideological fervor as they serve additional years. The twin findings of increasing conservatism and increasing moderation may seem contradictory. What they demonstrate is that liberals move to the middle more than conservatives do.

Before concluding this section, a comment is in order on the magnitude of the roll call changes uncovered. On the one hand, roll call change across the typical career should not be overstated. Figures 4.1, 4.2, and 4.3 display modest changes, usually running from z-scores of $-.2$ to $+.2$. The results presented here do not suggest a very large "throw." Some readers may interpret these findings as support for the Asher and Weisberg claims of longitudinal stability in roll call behavior. Such a conclusion would be partly right and partly wrong.

It seems to me there *are* important changes in roll call behavior over the course of the typical career. However, a sense of proportion must be maintained. Liberals are not frequently becoming conservatives; party diehards are not frequently becoming party bashers; and perfect attenders are not frequently becoming incorrigible truants; but there is some movement, on average. While a shift from a z-score of $+.2$ to $-.2$ may not sound like much, assuming a normal distribution, such a shift constitutes a relative movement across approximately 16 percent of the membership, or 70 representatives (normal distribution tables indicate that 8 percent of the cases can be expected to be between the mean and a z-score of .2). While each of us is likely to carry different ideas of what is consistent and what is inconsistent, this degree of movement, simply on the basis of career-cycle effects, seems fairly substantial.

In sum, if one were given the assignment of describing normal career

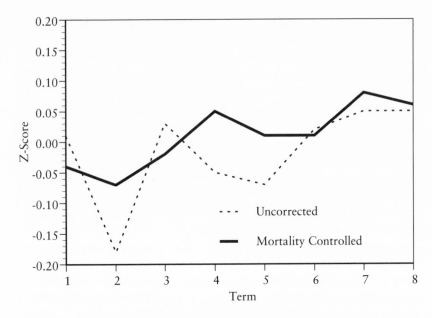

Figure 4.3. Standardized Conservative Coalition Support Scores by Tenure, with and without Mortality Effects, 1957–1982

progressions in roll call behavior, the proper account would include references to a decrease in participation, a decrease in support for the party, and a slight ideological movement to the right, particularly for liberals. This account would recognize that these changes are, for the most part, at the margin but would draw attention to the fact that broad-based scales of roll call behavior over sixteen years indicate a greater amount of change than studies of narrowly specified issue votes over only three- to six-year periods.

Changing Contours of the Roll Call Career

To this point, the evidence presented has been aggregated across the approximately thirty-five years for which roll call scales have been made available. As such, many of the criticisms raised in chapter 1 regarding the state of career-based research could be applied to the first portions of this chapter. Moreover, highly aggregated data make it impossible to determine how careers have changed over time. Have postwar careers always been marked by declines in participation, in party support, and in liberalness, or is this something new? Or are recent roll call careers more static than early postwar careers? To answer these questions, we need longitudinal data by class or even by individual.

Compared to most other variables employed in this study, the theoretical justification for expecting roll call career contours to become flatter is not as compelling. Still, such a movement would not be inexplicable. Perhaps more consistent electoral support across careers could be expected to translate into participation scores that are also more consistent. Perhaps the potential in modern congressional politics for any blemish or inconsistency on the record of participation and ideological location to swell into a major campaign issue encourages stasis. Perhaps the declining role of parties in congressional elections makes it less likely party-support scores will be higher among newer members who tend to be relatively needy, marginal, and inexperienced. After all, today there is little variation across careers in electoral success, and, even if there were, the parties are no longer indispensable to those who are trying to build the foundations of a long career in the House. Thus, it might reasonably be expected that, if anything, roll call careers in recent years are flatter than they were in the 1950s.

Participation

The overall decline in participation across careers is still evident when the class is the unit of analysis (not shown). Nine of the eleven classes have negative slopes, and nine of the eleven classes have participation rates in the eighth terms that are below participation rates in the first terms. But there is no pattern at all to the slopes. Participation declines across careers are not any more or any less distinct in the early portions of the time period than in the later.

Party Support

The story is similar as far as party support is concerned. There is no identifiable change in career contours over the time period. As can be seen in figure 4.4, where the standardized results for four typical, evenly spaced classes are presented for purposes of illustration, the slope is generally downward, but there is no particular tendency for the slope to be steeper earlier or later in the period. It is the case, however, that during the first two or three terms of the early careers, party support dropped

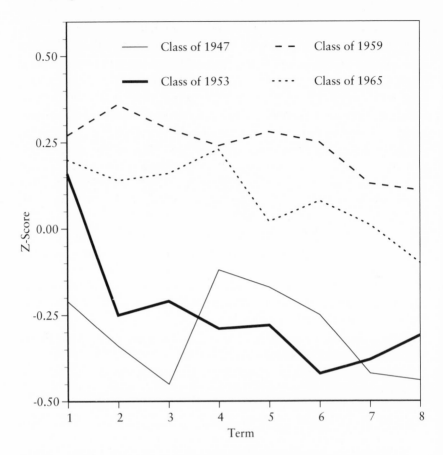

Figure 4.4. Class-by-Class Analysis of the Relationship between Party Support and Tenure, Controlled for Mortality, Classes of 1947, 1953, 1959, and 1965

noticeably. For the more recent two classes, there was no corresponding early-career decline.

To provide a more systematic test, I fitted a regression line to each class's mortality-corrected party-support pattern (the independent variable was simply years served). I then regressed the resulting class slopes on a counter variable to see if there was a pattern of decreasingly negative slopes over time. The resulting coefficient was not significant and was actually mildly negative (b = −.003). This confirms that there has been no tendency for career-based changes in party support to become less extreme later in the time period. The class-by-class analysis does reveal important differences, even as most of the classes analyzed (nine of eleven) do display some downward movement in mean party support. Some classes (see the classes of 1947 and 1953 in figure 4.4) are almost always below the mean of party support, and others (see the classes of 1959 and 1965 in figure 4.4) are almost always above the mean, but there appears to be no firm pattern of contour change associated with the movement from earlier to later House roll call careers.

Ideological Voting

Has the modest overall tendency for classes to grow more conservative with additional tenure become more pronounced or less pronounced in recent years? Because measures of ideological voting were not systematically collected and recorded as early as participation and party-support scores, we are not able to view as lengthy a time span in this section, but it is possible to analyze careers from 1957 to 1982.

As a result, figure 4.5 presents the patterns in conservative coalition support for only three rather than four classes: 1959, 1963, and 1967. Immediately evident is the difference in the general ideological outlook between the heavily Democratic class of 1959, the mixed class of 1963, and the heavily Republican class of 1967, which came in on the heels of the strong Republican showing in the midterm election of 1966. Not surprisingly, the inclinations of the three classes are liberal, less liberal, and conservative, respectively.

But the key question is how these classes are affected by increased tenure. The first two (more liberal) classes became more conservative, consistent with the overall findings presented in the previous section. The (more conservative) class of 1967, however, did not become more conservative with additional tenure; neither did it become more liberal. To some extent, these three classes illustrate a common tendency in the data set. Liberal classes move toward the center with passing years in the House— the slope for the liberal classes (those with initially negative z-scores) is positive and statistically significant. Conservative classes (1957, 1961, 1965, and 1967) do not mirror liberal classes by moving to the left and do not parallel liberal classes by moving to the right. Instead, conservative classes invariably produce slopes across time that are insignificant both substantively and statistically; in other words, conservative classes do not

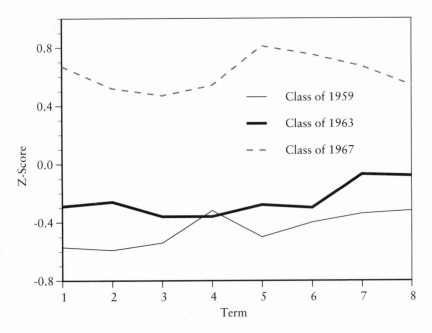

Figure 4.5. Class-by-Class Analysis of the Relationship between Conservative Coalition Support and Tenure, Controlled for Mortality, Classes of 1959, 1963, and 1967

move noticeably one way or another. With liberals becoming more conservative and with conservatives treading water, it is easy to visualize how the results presented earlier could indicate increasing conservatism and increasing moderation at the same time.

Over-time changes in the contours of roll call careers appear to be limited. Although the most recent career in figure 4.5 is flatter than the two earlier careers, this is largely due to the tendency for conservative classes to move less than liberal classes. When all classes are included, there is little evidence that career-based shifts in ideological position have become either more blatant or more muted. Instead, the movement toward conservatism on the part of liberal classes and the largely consistent ideological orientation of conservative classes seem to be fairly constant throughout this time period. The slope of the slopes for conservative coalition support is close to 0 and far from statistical significance, thereby indicating little systematic contour change.

Table 4.1. Predicting Roll Call Scales in the Seventh Term with Roll Call Scales in the First Term, by Class

Class	N	Party Unity R^2 (Slope)	Ideology (CCS) R^2 (Slope)
1947	26	.06 (.20)	
1949	28	.29 (.55)	
1951	25	.59 (.75)	
1953	31	.46 (.86)	
1955	19	.12 (.37)	
1957	9	.66 (.67)	.79 (.79)
1959	30	.39 (.73)	.77 (.78)
1961	19	.45 (1.06)	.85 (.79)
1963	32	.82 (.96)	.95 (.79)
1965	30	.60 (.88)	.93 (.89)
1967	15	.75 (.87)	.92 (.88)
1969	19	.63 (.85)	.92 (.89)

Source: Computed by the author.

Is Early-Career Voting Determinative?

Aggregation even to the class level may hide stability or, more likely, instability across individual careers. The preferred test of roll call career stability is to determine whether or not for recent careers early behavior is more predictive of late-career roll call behavior than it is for earlier careers. To make this determination, each class member's roll call scores in his/her first Congress were used to predict that same member's roll call score in the seventh term of service. The predictive capabilities of each class were recorded and are presented (along with the slope) in table 4.1.

As noted earlier, ideological scores have not been recorded for as long as party-unity scores, but both roll call scales provide fairly clear evidence of increasing predictability of individual roll call careers. Taking party unity first, the scores of the twenty-six careerist members (those serving seven terms or more) of the class of 1947 (80th Congress) in their first term gave very little indication of what their scores would be in their seventh term (R^2 = .06). The predictive capabilities of first-term scores improved for the next few classes, particularly for the class of 1951, but consistently high predictive qualities, as well as consistently high slopes, do not appear until the most recent four or five classes in the study. Averaging these recent classes together, approximately 70 percent of the variance in seventh-term party unity is explained by individual variations in first-term party unity.

According to table 4.1, early-career conservative coalition support scores have always been a reasonably accurate predictor of later-career conservative coalition support scores; however, stability does seem to be growing in the sense that first-term scores are more accurate predictors of seventh-term scores than used to be the case. For the classes of 1957 and 1959, first-term ideological scores explain less than 80 percent of the variance in seventh-term scores. For the classes of 1963, 1965, 1967, and 1969, over 90 percent of the variation is accounted for by early roll call activity. The regression slopes register corresponding gains.

When analyzed at the individual and not the class level, stability across careers in roll call behavior has become more evident. Knowing how a member voted during the first term of service now permits more accurate predictions of future voting behavior than used to be the case. In light of this evidence, it is difficult not to conclude that roll call careers have become more static, stable, and predictable and less variable, cyclical, and idiosyncratic.

A Look at the Roll Call Careers of Individual Members

For the next few pages, the focus shifts to specific representatives, not typical representatives, typical classes, or typical Congresses. While this approach is not the most helpful for purposes of making generalizations about the nature of congressional careers, it does serve as a reminder of the tremendous diversity that can be masked by a total emphasis on summary data. In short, to get a feel for the special cases and special characters of Congress, we need to reserve space for the study of individual careers.

The House class of 1947 contained some truly noteworthy members, including John F. Kennedy (D-Mass.), Richard M. Nixon (R-Calif.), Carl Albert (D-Okla.), Jacob Javits (R-N.Y.), Olin Teague (D-Tex.), and Otto Passman (D-La.). It also contained some individuals who had atypical roll call careers. Members who change their roll call positions dramatically across a career are always eye-catching. Watkins Abbitt (D-Va.) recorded an attendance-corrected party-support score of 75 percent his first term in the House, but by his tenth term his party-support score was down to 16 percent, a drop of 1.82 standard deviations. John Bell Williams (D-Miss.) went Abbitt one better by beginning with a party-support score of 79 and ending up ten terms later with a party-support score of 8, thus producing a plummet of more than 2.5 standard deviations during his career in the House. (Williams was stripped of his seniority by the Democratic party after openly supporting Barry Goldwater in 1964—a situation that both indicates how disaffected Williams was with the party and explains why his 1965–66 roll call figures were even more extreme.) There was also the occasional odd bird who increased party support over the years. Harold Donahue (D-Mass.), for example, recorded a 1.24 standard deviation shift upward in party support, from 81 in the 80th Congress to 97 in the 89th.

A perusal of roll call histories indicates that Walter Baring (D-Nev.) may have evolved away from his party as much as any postwar representative. Baring began his career with a 93-percent party-support score but twenty years later produced scores that had fallen to the vicinity of 10 percent. The legendary master of parliamentary dilatory tactics, H. R. Gross (R-Iowa), was not always the rock-ribbed Republican he was at the end. Gross began his career with party-support scores in the mid-60s before gradually building to the mid- to upper 90s. Albert Herlong (D-Fla.) remained fairly stable in party support but apparently lost interest in roll calls altogether. His participation dropped from 88 percent as a first-term representative to 45 percent as a tenth-termer, a drop of 4.26 standard deviations.

If we look to slightly more recent Congresses, changes in conservative coalition support as well as changes in party support can be addressed. Again, we find plenty of roll call oddities and odysseys. Silvio Conte (R-Mass.), George Shipley (D-Ill.), Richard Ichord (D-Mo.), and Paul Findley (R-Ill.) all shifted ideological positions more than the norm. But the largest ideological shift of all may have been that of John Anderson (R-Ill.), who began his career in the 87th Congress with reasonably strong party-support scores and a 100-percent conservative coalition support

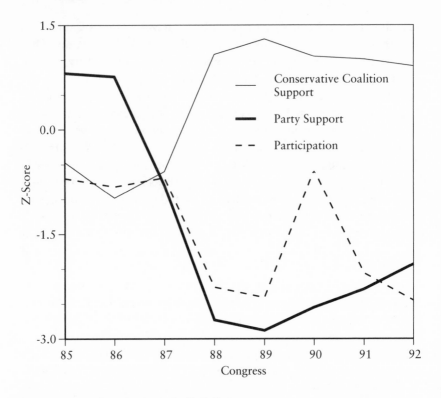

Figure 4.6. Walter Baring's Roll Call Career

score. By the 96th Congress (1979–80, when he was making a bid for the presidency), Anderson's conservative bent was a thing of the past, and he supported the conservative coalition only about 7 percent of the time, even after we correct for his understandably low attendance during the 96th. If we exclude the 96th Congress from Anderson's record, he still finished his House career with conservative coalition support scores in the low 50s, a far cry from how he entered Congress.

To be sure, most members remain reasonably steadfast even during lengthy careers. Peter Rodino (D-N.J.), Richard Bolling (D-Mo.), and Gerald Ford (R-Mich.), for example, all maintained virtually constant party-support ratings both in absolute and relative terms. But it is important to note that no two roll calls are identical, and in some instances change over a career is truly dramatic. This last point is illustrated in the

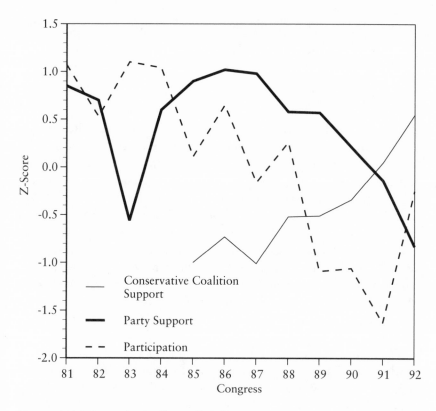

Figure 4.7. Wayne Aspinall's Roll Call Career

roll call careers of Walter Baring and Wayne Aspinall (see figures 4.6 and 4.7). Here we obtain a glimpse of Baring's spectacular two-term transformation from a strong liberal Democrat in the 86th Congress to an equally strong conservative opponent of Democratic policies, and we see Aspinall's later but more gradual estrangement from Democrats, liberals (particularly environmentalists), and roll call voting in general.

So there is substantial variation in the roll call careers of individual members even though aggregated data can, on occasion, lure us into concluding that nearly all members are extraordinarily consistent in their intracareer roll call activity. Representatives have been known to lose interest in roll calls, to discover an interest in roll calls, to turn against their party, to warm to their party, to become more conservative, and to become more liberal. Examples of all these activities can be found through an inspection of individual roll call careers. Summary statistics are just that.

Summarizing Roll Call Careers

But on the whole, postwar roll call careers in the House of Representatives follow a pattern. This pattern consists of a general tendency for members to become more conservative, less supportive of their party, and less likely to participate in roll call votes. These tendencies were evident when data were aggregated across the entire period from 1947 to 1982 as well as when individual classes and individual careers were analyzed. And although I have presented standardized results, these precise tendencies for all three roll call scales are evident in the raw or unstandardized data as well (not shown)—they are just a bit messier since they reflect institutional as well as individual changes. The apparent movement toward slightly more conservative roll call voting across careers is not solely a function of an influx of liberal new members distorting standardized figures.

The decline in participation over the course of a career is not a particularly earth-shattering finding, but the decrease in party support and increase in conservative coalition support are of somewhat more significance. The increase in conservatism was accompanied by a homogenization of most classes as they aged together. However, the tendency for liberals to moderate toward the mean was clearly more prevalent than instances of conservatives moderating toward the mean from the other side.

Important changes in roll call behavior frequently occur over the course of a career both in absolute and in relative terms. This is not to say previous voting history is irrelevant to roll call decisions. It clearly is, as is evidenced by the fact that the movements detected here, except among a few intriguing individuals, were usually quite modest. It is not the norm for liberals to become conservatives and vice versa or for party stalwarts to become party gadflies. But perhaps more than previous research has let on, the norm is for substantial evolution to take place over ten or twenty years in the House. A fair amount of shifting occurs on the margin, and over a lengthy period of time (such as is involved in many modern careers), repeated marginal change adds up to more than marginal change.

It is difficult to know when change is significant and when it is so minor that representatives' voting histories dominate all other potential explanatory variables. My opinion is that the scope of change portrayed here as attributable to career stage is important and larger than the literature would lead us to expect. At the same time, it appears as though variation in roll call careers has diminished over time. This increasing stability was not evident when class means were analyzed, but it was evident when the first-term scores of individual class members were used to predict their scores fourteen years later. Early roll call activity is now more predictive of later roll call activity than was the case two to three decades ago.

Modern representatives may be slightly less willing than their predecessors to budge from their own past roll call behavior. If they do budge, they simply move with the herd, usually maintaining their relative niche within the House on those occasions when the body moves slightly left (as in 1965–66) or right (as in 1981–82). Early-career ideological and party-support patterns are now more constraining on late-career behavior. (Less can be said about simple participation since the truth of the matter is that in the modern House virtually everyone votes on every roll call, so there is little variation for which to account.) No doubt this change is at least partly due to the increased surveillance afforded roll call votes not by voters directly but by interest groups, journalists, and potential challengers.

These findings, in conjunction with those reported in chapters 2 and 3, are consistent with the notion that recent congressional careers are less cyclical and more constant than the congressional careers of days gone by. The behavior of modern members is more likely to parrot their own previous behavior. But to this point such conclusions cannot be extended beyond the roll call component of legislative careers, and, as argued at the beginning of this chapter, roll call activity is but a small slice of overall legislative activity. In the next chapter, attention is directed at non–roll call aspects of the legislative career.

5 The Legislative Activity Career

"Longevity promotes competence. You have to actually advocate incompetent legislators to get the turnover some want." This is how political scientist Nelson Polsby explained his lack of concern over the small number of new representatives entering recent Congresses (quoted in Rovner 1988, 3362). Political columnist George Will essentially agrees. In a recent essay opposing proposals imposing congressional term limitations, Will wrote that "compulsory rotation of offices would bring in 'fresh faces,' but another name for them is 'rookies,' people with a lot to learn in a town where there is a lot to know. Forcing out veteran legislators would increase the power of the permanent government—congressional staff, executive bureaucracies" (Will 1990). But there are those who disagree or at least feel the advantages of term limitations outweigh the disadvantages detected by Polsby and by Will. Representative William Frenzel (R-Minn.) has introduced into each of the last ten Congresses a bill limiting the number of terms a person can serve in Congress. Numerous interest groups strongly support the idea, the citizens of three states recently limited the terms of their state legislators, and polls consistently show better than 2 to 1 support for mandatory congressional term limits.

Setting aside for the moment the merits of each point of view, these comments at least begin to nudge debate on this important issue in the proper direction. They indicate that the issue is not simply membership turnover levels, as is so frequently implied, but legislative competence and contribution. Polsby feels that senior legislators are more competent, and Will feels that inexperienced legislators are ineffective rookies. Both may be correct, but as far as I can tell, the presumed positive relationship between legislative contribution and length of legislative service is untested. No doubt Polsby and Will can point to many competent veterans and inept rookies in Congress, but competent rookies and (especially) inept veterans are also in evidence on the Hill. The question is whether or not the anticipated relationship withstands systematic analysis. The purpose of this chapter is to provide a partial answer to this question.

While the concepts of legislative competence and contribution are too broad and subjective to operationalize in the manner they deserve, we can make a modest start. Unfortunately, as noted in the previous chapter, existing research has been preoccupied with roll call studies to the detriment of other aspects of the "legislative career." Much of the research seems to deny the basic fact that there is more to the legislative process than the final vote (see Van Doren 1990 for an excellent discussion of this matter). There is introducing legislation, committee work, speaking on the floor, offering amendments on the floor, the degree to which members specialize or generalize in their legislative interests, and the degree to which members are successful in getting legislation advanced.

Still, there have been a few efforts to measure certain aspects of non–roll call legislative activity. For example, the issue of whether or not an "apprenticeship" norm exists, or used to exist, requires information on the extent to which legislative activity increases after the first term or two, although even here the most frequently cited studies—Asher's (1973, 1975)—rely almost exclusively on legislators' perceptions rather than their behaviors.[1] Michael Mezey, on the other hand, does present behavioral data, albeit only for three years, and concludes that "while freshman participation has increased at a faster rate than non-freshman participation, a substantial gap persists between freshman participation levels and the participation levels of non-freshmen" (1981, 16; see also Mezey and Gaudry 1979). Unfortunately, Mezey is not able to track members across careers since the data are treated as three separate cross sections.

Edward V. Schneier, using the number of floor amendments offered and passed as his measures of legislative activity, finds that "in 1960–61, House members with fewer than four years of service collectively offered a total of two amendments; neither passed." He continues, "In 1980–81, freshmen and sophomore representatives offered almost a fifth of the amendments on which there were roll call votes" (1988, 122). Once again, while suggestive, data on two widely separated Congresses are of limited use in coming to grips with variance in participation over the course of a career (see also Canon 1990, 147–54).

The desire to draw conclusions about the health of another hallowed congressional norm, specialization, has also forced scholars to measure non–roll call legislative activity. Steven Smith (1986) details the growing influence of non–committee members on House floor proceedings, particularly the offering of amendments (see also Bach and Smith 1988; Schneier 1988, 122–23; on the Senate, see Sinclair 1986). Others have analyzed the extent to which legislators are able to secure advancement of their bills (see Matthews 1960; Frantzich 1979; Moore and Thomas 1989; Hibbing and Thomas 1990). This naturally requires devoting attention to non–roll call legislative activity. And, finally, there are those who have used legislative activity to categorize legislators according to various criteria, such as the show horse/work horse distinction (see Payne 1980; Langbein and Sigelman 1989; on the classification of Connecticut state legislators, see Barber 1965).

Thus, the fixation on roll call analysis has not been total; research on other aspects of the legislative process exists. The problem is that the data are usually aggregated for the purpose of providing some sense of how the institution itself has changed. Truly individual-level data are generally presented as two or three separate cross sections. While this approach is instructive in its own way, it fails to provide an adequate sense of the nature of legislative careers or of whether the contours of these careers have changed. Even the widely discussed expectation that apprenticeship has declined (in addition to Asher 1973 and 1975 and Mezey 1981, see Dodd and Oppenheimer 1977, 49; Jewell and Patterson 1986, 106; Ripley 1988, 113–14; Ornstein, Peabody, and Rohde 1989, 19–20) has never been given a true behavioral test.

Data now available allow many of these deficiencies in our understanding of legislative activity careers to be rectified. In beginning this process, I employ five different variables. Each deserves brief explanation. Several of these measures can be traced to Donald Matthews's classic analysis of the U.S. Senate. In a brief appendix (1960, 274–79), Matthews suggests several measures that strike me as being extremely useful in the study of legislative behavior. But with the exception of a research note by David Olson and Cynthia Nonidez (1972, 269–77) in which they apply Matthews's measures to the House of Representatives for a single Congress (1965–66), most of the promising operationalizations suggested by Matthews seem to have received scant attention. It is time for a renaissance of interest in these specific measures and, more generally, in the need to develop better measures of legislative activity than the overused, prepackaged scales of roll call voting behavior. Measuring true legislative involvement and contribution is an admittedly daunting task but not so daunting that all attempts are to be avoided.

Five Measures of Legislative Activity

The first of the five basic measures of legislative activity I employ is an indicator of floor speaking. The annual index of the *Congressional Record* lists, for each representative, remarks on various topics. It is also possible to determine whether the remarks were actually made or just inserted and whether they pertained directly to a piece of legislation or to something more ceremonial in nature (commending a constituent on the occasion of her one-hundredth birthday or a school basketball team on its state championship). Thus, we can identify and count speeches made on purely legislative matters (for present purposes, the number of noncontiguous page entries for remarks pursuant to the consideration of a piece of legislation). As Matthews notes (1960, 275), such a measure has obvious limitations. For example, it ignores the quality and impact of a speech, concepts that are intractably subjective. Nevertheless, this measure should provide a rough idea of who is participating in debate on the floor of the House and of how this level of participation changes throughout the course of a career.

The second measure is the number of amendments a member offers during floor debate. This information is also collected in the annual index of the *Congressional Record*. This particular variable is not employed by Matthews, but it is used by Olson and Nonidez, and it would seem to be a valuable indicator of an important component of legislative activity. How often does each individual member offer an amendment to proposed legislation on the floor of the House of Representatives? How does this pattern of offering amendments change for a representative through the years? Are there life-cycle effects apart from changes in the aggregate offering of amendments by the entire membership (on aggregate changes, see Smith 1986)?

The third measure, like the fourth and fifth, is most easily available from the *Congressional Index* not the index of the *Congressional Record*. It involves sponsoring bills themselves rather than sponsoring amendments to bills. Information on bill sponsorship is recorded in the *Congressional Record*, but unfortunately this listing includes all bills, even those for which the member was merely a cosponsor. In the modern House, cosponsoring legislation is often done quite casually, and most cosponsors are not feverishly at work trying to guide the particular piece of legislation through the legislative maze. The cosponsorship of some bills has numbered in the hundreds, and on occasion members have been known to vote against legislation they cosponsored. To avoid counting those bills for which the member was not a serious bill sponsor, I used the *Congressional Index*, which, unlike the *Congressional Record*, makes it possible to identify those bills for which the member was the sole or lead sponsor. While this procedure may be a little too restrictive, it is better to err on this side than the other. Only *bills* are counted; resolutions have been excluded. These procedures should afford an indication of the activity level of each member with regard to the sponsorship of real legislation.

The fourth measure is designed to tap breadth of legislative interests. It is computed by dividing the total number of a representative's bills into the number of those bills that were referred to the most frequently involved committee. To take an example, suppose Congressman Smith sponsored ten pieces of legislation during the 99th Congress. Further suppose that four of these were referred to the Interior Committee, five to Agriculture, and one to Merchant Marine. The representative's specialization score would be 50 percent since five-tenths of the legislation introduced had to do with issues that fell under the jurisdiction of just one committee. If each bill had been referred to a different committee, then Smith's specialization score would have been 10 percent.[2]

The final measure is legislative efficiency and has two components. The first is simply the percentage of a member's bills passing the House during that particular Congress. If four of Smith's ten bills passed, this first element of legislative efficiency is recorded as 40 percent. The second component is the percentage of a member's bills that are reported out of committee, regardless of whether or not they pass once on the floor. These two measures of efficiency are weighted equally and combined into a single measure (in this way bills that pass the House will be double counted since they will have also passed at the committee stage). As before, private bills, cosponsored bills, and resolutions are ignored (many of the resolutions that are not ceremonial are proposed constitutional amendments that usually face very poor odds). This measure of efficiency may be the most questionable of the lot, as it obviously constitutes only one small aspect of what the term *efficiency* connotes to some readers.

Still, it should provide some sense of how one part of being an efficient legislator fluctuates over the course of a congressional career. (Only those Congresses in which a member sponsored at least four bills are included in the analysis of specialization and efficiency.)

These five measures provide a needed supplement to information on roll call activity. They direct attention away from the simple act of voting to other equally important stages of the legislative process, such as bill introduction, debate, and emendation. They also provide some sense of a representative's range of legislative interests and the ability of that representative to operate successfully within the confines of the legislative arena. The five variables just described still do not give committee-stage activities sufficient attention, but at least they constitute a substantial improvement over those studies that imply the legislative process begins and ends with a single roll call vote.

Floor Speaking, Amendment Offering, and Bill Sponsoring

I turn first to the three measures that deal with the sheer volume of legislative activity: speaking on the House floor, offering amendments on the House floor, and sponsoring (not cosponsoring) legislation. These measures may have little practical policy influence (particularly floor speaking, of which Matthews writes, "Perhaps no point of view is more universally popular among [senators] than that most of this talk [speeches on the floor] is meaningless" [1960, 243]), but at the least they are all indicators of a willingness to participate in the legislative forum.

Aggregate changes in congressional activity levels have been documented by others, at least as far as the introduction of bills and amendments is concerned. The various editions of *Vital Statistics on Congress* (see Ornstein, Mann, and Malbin 1990) provide summary data on the number of bills introduced by Congress. These figures document a sharp rise from 13,169 bills and joint resolutions introduced into the 84th Congress (1955–56) to 22,060 bills and joint resolutions introduced into the 90th (1967–68). Since 1969, however, there has been an even sharper decrease, such that by the 99th Congress (1985–86) only 6,499 introductions were made. As concerns floor amendments, Steven Smith (1986) offers the most thorough data, with information on selected, usually alternating, Congresses between 1955 and 1986. The number of amendments rose sharply, peaking in the 95th Congress, before falling off thereafter at a reasonably brisk pace.

Information on speeches given is not widely disseminated. My data reveal there has been less variation in this measure of legislative involvement than for bill and amendment sponsorship. Still, there has been some fluctuation. For many Congresses the mean number of speeches (given the coding procedures described earlier) by members ran around 40. Beginning in the 93d Congress, speech making increased until it reached a mean of 78 in the 95th Congress, and while it has decreased a little since then, it remains higher than was the case in the 1960s. In light of the significant procedural changes in the House over the years pertaining to all three measures, I will rely primarily on data that have been standardized by Congress (see chapters 3 and 4). The issue thus becomes *relative* activity rather than raw activity.[3]

The main concern here is with the degree to which activity levels vary across House careers. Beyond the notion that participation should increase after service as an "apprentice" during the first few years in the House, the literature provides little in the way of theoretical expectations about the relationship between tenure and the volume of legislative activity. Who participates more, the midlevel or the very senior representative? The literature is mute, but on the bright side, the lack of guidance in past research affords us greater speculative range.

It may be that the relationship between tenure and volume of activity is curvilinear with very junior members being discouraged from participating and very senior members, those well into their protectionist phases, lacking the motivation to participate. Alternatively, it may be that very senior members, immersed as they usually are in committee and perhaps party responsibilities, are more likely than midlevel and, especially, junior representatives to sponsor bills and amendments and to take to the floor in their defense. This latter, "linear" scenario seems the most likely.

In figure 5.1 it is possible to view alterations in relative legislative activity across careers. For purposes of obtaining this figure, the z-scores of all first-term members who started their careers from the 84th through the 93d Congress were averaged. Corresponding procedures produced the results for other career stages. Individual classes and members will be analyzed shortly. By controlling for period changes, a better indication of life-cycle effects is possible. Obviously, the figure suggests that increased tenure does indeed bring increased legislative activity. A relatively rapid rise in activity levels (especially speeches and amendments) occurs be-

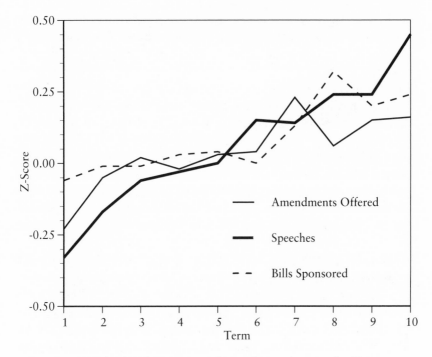

Figure 5.1. Standardized Measures of Legislative Activity, by Tenure, 1953–1985

tween the first and second terms, then there is a leveling off very near the mean for the respective Congresses during the second through about the sixth terms, followed by sharper increases in legislative activity after the sixth term. Thus, the relationship appears slightly S-shaped. But this deviation from linearity is so minor that it does not come through in a systematic test. When a quadratic term is added to the linear term, the increment to R^2 is not significant, and, more appropriate to the two-bend pattern described above, a cubic term does not significantly improve upon a linear specification either.[4] This is not all that surprising since a simple linear term explains 96 percent of the variance in a composite measure of legislative activity (average z-scores for speeches, amendments, and bills).

Even after using appropriate controls for period effects, it is still apparent that legislative activities and tenure are positively related. Further, on the basis of these findings, little justification exists for dichotomizing members of the House into freshmen and nonfreshmen. Substantial variation exists among nonfreshmen. The more senior the member, the more legislatively active, on average, that member is likely to be. With experience comes greater relative legislative involvement. Change is particularly dramatic from the first to the second term and after the fifth or sixth term. With this overall pattern in mind, the question becomes whether or not there has been an alteration in the relationship between tenure and these three measures of legislative activity. In chapters 2, 3, and 4 it appeared as though life-cycle effects were less noticeable in recent than in earlier Congresses. Will this pattern appear for volume of legislative activities as well?

Apprenticeship

This question takes on special significance in light of previous research and speculation on the decline of apprenticeship. For decades, apprenticeship was said to be one of the major established norms of Congress (see Matthews 1960, 92–94). More recently, members and scholars alike have questioned the existence of an apprenticeship norm (see especially Ornstein, Peabody, and Rohde 1989; Rohde 1988). Often we hear that the apprenticeship norm is dead. Ornstein, Peabody, and Rohde quote a junior Democratic senator who states that "all the communications suggest 'get involved, offer amendments, make speeches. . . . We're all equals so you should act accordingly'" (1989, 20). Contrast this description of the modern Congress with the description of the early-1960s House offered to me by the recently retired representative quoted in chapter 4. He related that in some committees first-term representatives were allowed only one remark during the entire term, only two in the second term, and so on.

The concept of a norm seems to inspire strong feelings and disagreements (see Schneier 1988; Rohde 1988; for an earlier overview, see Williams 1968). One issue is whether a norm can be detected by either asking the people involved whether a norm exists, observing whether members behave as though a norm exists, or determining whether certain behaviors are related to rewards, sanctions, or even reputation within the institution. While I feel norms are best understood with the latter approach (see Hibbing and Thomas 1990), for now it would behoove us to set aside any connection to norms and to focus simply on the activity levels of newer members relative to more senior members. If differences exist between new and old members, they are, after all, not necessarily due to the existence of a norm that discourages the participation of younger members. These differences may simply reflect different priorities among members. Schneier quotes a legislative assistant who says his representative "really can't get involved in much legislation. Right now our first priority is reelection" (1988, 119).[5] So the question becomes, norms aside, how have the relative legislative activity levels of first-term representatives changed over the years?

Perhaps the best way to answer this question is to compare the standardized activity levels (in this case, a composite of bill sponsorship, floor amendment introduction, and speech making) of first-termers to eighth-termers, as is done in figure 5.2. Some readers may be surprised to discover a decline in relative first-term activity levels from earlier classes to later ones. In contrast, eighth-termers have become more active during the same period first-termers have become less active. The *apprenticeship norm* may or may not be dead but *apprenticeship* is stronger than it has been in decades.[6]

An early reader of this manuscript commented that it was not surprising freshmen participation declined since in the postreform House there are fewer opportunities for "freestanding" bills and floor amendments. This remark encourages me to emphasize again that the issue is *relative*, not absolute, participation levels. My point is not that freshmen participate less than they used to. The reader is correct in noting that procedural reforms and an institutional emphasis on omnibus bills have reduced many forms of legislative activity for practically all members. The point is that, even when these contextual changes are neutralized, as they are in figure 5.2, new members now participate less relative to nonfreshmen than was the case twenty years ago. (This conclusion applies when first-termers are compared to eighth-termers, as in figure 5.2, or to any other tenure-based group.)

While figure 5.2 helps to make an important point, it violates a theme of this work by setting up a dichotomy between first-term members and others. The preferred approach is to view careers as continuous rather than consisting of only two parts. As such, classes should be observed across their congressional careers. In figure 5.3, this is the approach taken. The standardized legislative activity index is presented for four selected classes.[7] The figure generally confirms what was evident in figure 5.1: legislative activity usually starts low, jumps quickly, levels off for several terms, and rises sharply again late in careers, perhaps after twelve

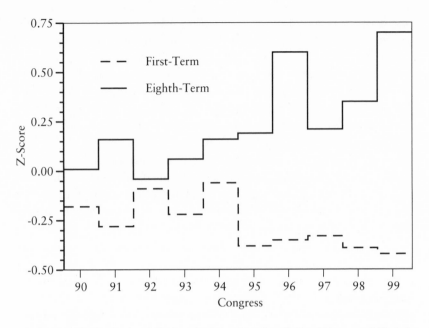

Figure 5.2. Relative Legislative Activity Levels of First-Term and Eighth-Term Representatives, 1967–1986

to fourteen years in the House. We do learn that the class of 1971 was unusually activist, with its members rising above the mean for legislative activity already by their second term (the 93d Congress) and continuing at higher relative levels than the members of the other three classes presented in the figure. This, however, does not seem to represent a tendency for more recent classes to be more activist. The classes of 1969 and 1973, for example, were not nearly as legislatively active as the class of 1971.

In fact, for the most part, analysis of individual classes suggests no contour shift as we move from earlier to more recent classes. If anything, the classes entering in the 1950s were slightly flatter (less of an increase in the legislative activity index across careers) than later classes. Increasing tenure in the House does bring increasing legislative activity, but the specific shape of this relationship has remained reasonably constant and, by and large, is accurately reflected by the aggregated career pattern presented in figure 5.1. If there has been any shift at all, the discrepancy between new- and old-member activity levels has grown.[8]

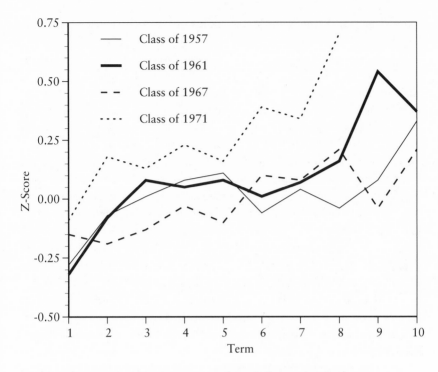

Figure 5.3. Class-by-Class Analysis of the Relationship between Legislative Activity and Tenure, Classes of 1957, 1961, 1967, and 1971

Legislative Specialization and Efficiency

Legislative involvement is not adequately captured merely by counting the number of speeches, bills, and amendments for which a representative is responsible. Frequently, representatives have become key legislative players not by spending all their time in the well or at the hopper but by picking their spots, by understanding the process, by developing expertise in a limited policy area, and by knowing what is possible and what is not. In the Senate, Richard Russell (D-Ga.) was an example of a powerful legislative force who was not a legislative activist. On the House side, the merits of legislative specialization were for years personified by Wilbur Mills (D-Ark.), longtime chair of the Ways and Means Committee. Though to a large extent such concepts as legislative focus, efficiency, and impact defy quantification, crude indicators of focus and efficiency are available.

As mentioned previously, I have followed Matthews's lead by using the set jurisdiction of the standing committees to help measure legislative specialization. The more jurisdictional concentration is evident in the bills a representative sponsors, the more that representative is thought to be legislatively specialized. My measure of legislative efficiency is similar to what others have claimed to be a measure of legislative effectiveness. I have chosen *efficiency* because the phrase more accurately reflects the variable and because legislative *effectiveness* (see Matthews 1960; Frantzich 1979) is a term with clear normative overtones and certainly implies much more than the simple variable I have constructed could deliver. This particular formulation entails the percentage of a member's bills that make it out of committee as well as the percentage of bills that pass the House altogether. Of course, given general patterns of partisanship, the efficiency scores of minority-party members typically will be considerably lower than those of majority-party members (see Moore and Thomas 1989). However, if the partisan control of the body remains the same across the time period (which it does), conclusions about career-based change should still be valid.

The expectation is that the specialization and efficiency of legislators will increase with the passage of the years, as members grow to understand the nature of the legislative process and the value of specialization within that process. Certainly, Polsby and Will anticipate this kind of movement. If they are correct, is this variation across careers greater for earlier than for later classes of representatives (due to the proliferation of formal positions and of opportunities for involvement)?

Figure 5.4 presents findings on career-based changes in legislative specialization and effectiveness when the sixteen Congresses included in this portion of the study are aggregated. The level of specialization over the course of the typical 1953–85-era career has clearly increased with tenure. The same can be said for efficiency. Once general institutional changes are taken into account (by using standardized scores), life-cycle effects on legislative specialization and efficiency are apparent. On average, as they become more senior, representatives become more specialized and efficient relative to the other members of the House.

The relationship between tenure and specialization is slightly curvilinear (ditto for efficiency), with sharper increases later in careers. A simple linear specification accounts for 86 percent of the variance in

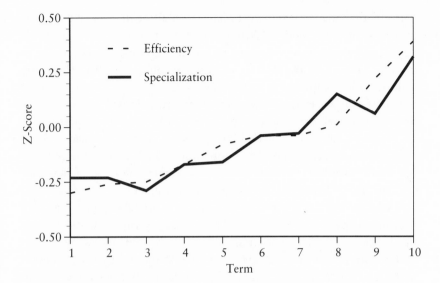

Figure 5.4. Standardized Legislative Efficiency and Specialization, by Tenure, 1953–1985

specialization. When a quadratic term is added, 92 percent of the variance is accounted for and this increment to R^2 of 6 percent is statistically significant (.05). In fact, when the quadratic term is entered alone it accounts for 92 percent of the variance—the same as is explained by the linear and quadratic terms together. Apparently, the effects of tenure on specialization are somewhat subject to the law of increasing returns, with smaller increments early and larger increments late.

It is instructive to compare the career contours of legislative activity (figure 5.1) with the career contours of legislative specialization and efficiency (figure 5.4). While both figures reveal upward trends with additional tenure, the increase in activity comes much sooner in a typical career than does the increase in specialization and efficiency. Note that in figure 5.1, activity levels reach the mean (z-score = 0) practically by the second term. Specialization and efficiency, on the other hand, do not reach these levels until the sixth or seventh term of House service. This could suggest that from the second to the sixth or seventh term many members are participating in the legislative process at reasonably high rates but have not yet acquired the focus and understanding of the process that make for a successful rather than merely active legislator. Alternatively, the later increases in specialization and efficiency may be connected to the acquisition of better committee positions, perhaps a subcommittee chair, while increases in simple legislative activity could be produced even by those lacking a legitimate committee base. These possibilities will be explored more thoroughly in chapter 7, when the interaction of positions held and legislative involvement will be scrutinized. What remains for us in this chapter is to look at how legislative specialization and efficiency have varied for individual classes and members.

Legislative specialization, like apprenticeship, is a once-revered congressional norm that, according to conventional wisdom, has fallen upon difficult times. The age of the issue-hopping dilettante is alleged to have replaced the age of the lifelong student of a particular policy area. The measure of specialization employed in this chapter raises questions about the accuracy of this speculation. It actually documents an *increase* in specialization, from around 40 percent in the 84th Congress to around 50 percent in the 97th, 98th, and 99th Congresses. But has there been an alteration in the tendency of members to become more legislatively focused as their careers wear on?

Figure 5.4 shows that members tend to become more focused if conclusions are based on a composite of all classes in the time period. Figure 5.5 presents the results for the same four selected classes used in figure 5.3. The classes are only taken out to eight terms because of the small number of representatives in any individual class who survive this long in the House (remember also that all representatives sponsoring fewer than four bills in a term are excluded from analyses of specialization and efficiency).

The class of 1971 was not only legislatively active but also legislatively specialized. Again, however, this fact may not necessarily indicate that the movement toward specialization is now coming earlier. The classes of 1969 and 1973 both have low specialization scores into their sixth terms. On the other hand, the class of 1975 became legislatively specialized fairly early, surpassing the mean of the relevant Congress (the 96th) already by its third term. By its sixth term (in the 99th), its mean z-score for specialization was .38, easily the highest of any class at a comparable stage. So there is at least a hint that representatives are becoming legislatively specialized a little earlier in their careers, but until more classes have had the chance to work through extended careers it will remain just a hint. We can be more definite about the fact that there is no suggestion of a flattening in this aspect of congressional careers.[9] If anything, there is more variance between early and late career.

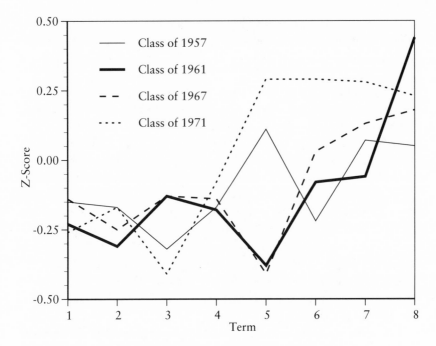

Figure 5.5. Class-by-Class Analysis of the Relationship between Specialization and Tenure, Classes of 1957, 1961, 1967, and 1971

The story for legislative efficiency (not shown) is much the same. Recent careers are characterized by low legislative batting averages in early terms and high averages in later terms. Careers of thirty years ago were the same. The variance introduced by career stage is as large as ever. No flattening can be observed by analyzing the class-by-class contours.

The Legislative Career of Charles Vanik

To make all these aggregated means and relative activity levels slightly more concrete, consider the legislative career of Charles Vanik (D-Ohio). Vanik was first elected to the House in 1954. His career is probably best known for two events. In 1968, after representing Ohio's Twenty-first District (Cleveland's East Side) for fourteen years, redistricting presented him with the prospects of a constituency that was substantially new and primarily black. Vanik wisely perceived his future was no longer in the

Twenty-first, which promptly elected Louis Stokes (D-Ohio), a black who himself has gone on to a lengthy and successful congressional career. Instead, Vanik ran in the Twenty-second District against Frances Bolton, who had been a Republican fixture in the Twenty-second since succeeding her husband to office in 1940. Vanik's bold move was successful in 1968, and he represented the Twenty-second, where his ethnic roots and strong support of Israel played well, until he quietly retired in 1980.

To the extent Vanik's name is familiar beyond Ohio, it is probably due to the second landmark of his career—his sponsorship on the House side of the Jackson-Vanik Amendment prohibiting the granting of most-favored-nation trading status to countries that do not permit reasonably free emigration. Other than these two events, Vanik's House career was not particularly distinctive. Without much fanfare, he worked his way up to be third-ranking majority-party member on Ways and Means and chairman of the Ways and Means Subcommittee on Trade. Thus, there seems to be no reason to believe Vanik's legislative career is misleading in some way, even as there is no reason to believe it is perfectly typical of all modern House careers.

Like most representatives, Vanik became more active over the course of his career. In his first term (the 84th Congress), Vanik gave 66 speeches, sponsored 12 bills, and offered 1 amendment on the floor, figures that approximated the mean for all members of the 84th Congress. Two terms later, Vanik was extremely active, giving 126 speeches (2.15 standard deviations above the mean), introducing 15 bills, and offering 6 floor amendments (2.6 standard deviations above the mean). After the 86th Congress, however, his floor activity lessened for several years until approximately the 91st when his legislative activity picked up again. And, except for declines in the 94th Congress (when Vanik may have been recuperating from the battles over the Jackson-Vanik Amendment) and the 96th Congress (when his retirement decision diminished the motivation to participate in the legislative fray), Vanik's legislative activity remained reasonably high thereafter.

Detailed inspection of his legislative career also reveals that, in standardized terms, Vanik tended to be more active in speech making and amendment offering than in sponsoring legislation, his latter score being the lowest of the three in all but four of his thirteen Congresses. Moreover, the degree to which the three indicators of activity move together is noteworthy. This tendency is apparent with Vanik and with most representatives. While some members specialize in speech making or in bill sponsoring, over time, more often than not, when one measure of raw activity increases, so do the others. It does not seem to be the case that activity surges, say, in bill sponsorship detract from giving speeches and/or offering amendments.

Moving from simple levels of activity to measures of legislative specialization and legislative efficiency, Vanik's legislative career continues to illustrate common patterns. Recall that specialization is simply the percent of a representative's bills that were referred to the same single committee. The increase in the degree to which Vanik was a legislative specialist is striking. As a freshman, only four of his twelve bills went to the same committee (Ways and Means). The other eight fell within the jurisdiction of other committees. By the end of his career, over 90 percent of his bills were going to a single committee (still Ways and Means). In this sense, the variable seems to reflect the known fact that over time Vanik carved out a legislative niche for himself in the area of trade and taxes.

As to legislative efficiency, Vanik received a score of 0 in all but three Congresses (including his last two). It is important to note, however, that such a pattern is not atypical. The operationalization of efficiency simply is the percent of a representative's bills making it out of committee, with double weight given to those bills passing the House. Since most bills never make it out of committee, it is not surprising that in many Congresses, efficiency scores will be 0, just as is the case for ten of Vanik's thirteen Congresses. Even at this, these basic "batting average" measures could be misleading. As has been mentioned, Vanik's greatest legislative achievement was unquestionably his stewardship of the Jackson-Vanik Amendment to the 1974 Trade Bill. Yet the measure of legislative efficiency used here, since it deals only with bills and not with amendments, is oblivious to these events. As a result, Vanik has an efficiency score of 0 in the 93d Congress. These limitations should not be forgotten.

Still, the changes in Vanik's legislative career are readily apparent. He clearly became a more active and focused legislator. No doubt to some extent this was forced upon him as he moved up in seniority on the Ways and Means Committee and assumed chairmanship of one of its subcommittees. Further, there is some indication that Vanik became more efficient in his legislative activity. In his last Congress, twelve of his twenty-four bills made it out of committee, a performance that ranked 1.43 standard deviations above the mean level of legislative efficiency for all members of the 96th Congress. Over-time improvements in legislative specialization and efficiency are the norm for House careers (see figure

5.5), but the changes embodied in Vanik's career appear even greater than those normally produced.

Conclusion

Do senior representatives make disproportionate contributions to the legislative process, as Nelson Polsby and George Will assume? Or, parallel with the findings reported in earlier chapters on electoral support and roll call behavior, and consistent with frequently made claims concerning the death of apprenticeship and the democratization of Congress, has tenure-based differentiation in legislative contribution gone the way of the passenger pigeon? The answer is clear. Senior members are the heart and soul of the legislative side of congressional service. Over the course of their careers, representatives typically become more active in legislation (increments to tenure bring an increasing tendency to speak on the floor, to offer amendments on the floor, and to sponsor legislation) as well as more specialized and more efficient.

More to the point, the slope and contour of the relationship between tenure and legislative activity do not seem to flatten as we move from earlier classes to later classes (as was the case with electoral careers, for example). In fact, perhaps the most surprising aspect of this analysis of legislative activity over careers is that while first-term representatives are consistently the least active members of Congress, relatively speaking, first-termers in more recent Congresses are actually less active than first-termers in earlier Congresses. This is apparent in an increasingly larger negative value of the z-scores for first-termers and in a comparison of first-termers to eighth-termers (see figure 5.2). Apprenticeship as a norm may or may not be dead, but in a strictly behavioral sense, first-term representatives are less active relative to the rest of the membership in the 1980s than they were in the 1960s. This finding is directly at odds with conventional wisdom.

In addition to these simple quantitative measures of legislative activity, variables tapping legislative specialization and efficiency were computed. Legislative specialization is held by many to be an essential component of the modern congressional machine. The results presented in this chapter indicate that senior members are indeed more specialized than their less senior colleagues (see figure 5.4). The relationship is curvilinear with very small increases in specialization coming in the early years of a House career and more rapid increases in specialization coming in the later years. In some respects, it is surprising that specialization is not coming earlier in careers now that positions of influence are coming earlier in careers (see chapter 3), although it should be noted that this trend may be too recent for our data to pick up. The data for the class of 1971 (see figure 5.5), for example, suggest that increases in legislative specialization may be coming a bit earlier in careers than used to be the case.

As will be discussed at greater length in the next chapter, Richard Fenno (1978, 171–211) has invoked the term *expansionist* to describe the early portion of "careers in the *constituency*" and the term *protectionist* to describe the latter portion. With regard to *legislative* careers, the indicator of specialization employed in this chapter suggests that representatives do not spend the first few terms expanding their interests. In the first terms, most members are as legislatively broad as they will ever be. As their careers go on, legislative interests become more and more focused. Given the benefit to the legislative process traditionally thought to derive from specialization (see Matthews 1960), this is powerful evidence of the contribution being made by senior members.

The limited measure of legislative efficiency utilized here follows a pattern similar to that for specialization: very slow growth until late in a career when members tend to become much more adept at getting their bills out of committee and perhaps out of the House itself. Improved efficiency may be due to the development of a better sense of what is and is not possible, or it may be due to better formal positions that usually come along with increased tenure (see chapter 7). Regardless of the reason, the fact remains that most bills making it out of committee and passing on the floor of the House are being shepherded by senior members. And this is not just because they sponsor more bills than their junior colleagues—their success rates are much better too. Moreover, the fact that junior members are less involved in legislation even after the 1970s democratizing reforms suggests that experience itself rather than formal positions held may actually be the crucial variable.

So in three important areas—legislative activity, legislative specialization, and legislative efficiency—senior members dominate. What's more, this dominance is growing rather than shrinking, contrary to most accounts of the modern House. Those advocating congressional term limitations may have some valid arguments supporting their belief, but this chapter highlights the basis of what to my mind is an even more powerful opposing argument: the essential role of veteran representatives in the legislative process. Relatively junior members can be given a subcommittee chairmanship, but it is not nearly so easy to give them an active, focused legislative agenda and the political savvy to enact it. Some things take time and experience, and successful participation in the legislative process appears to be one of these things.

But legislative involvement is only part of the story. Members of Congress do more than introduce bills, give speeches, and cast roll call votes. In addition to careers on Capitol Hill, they also serve careers in their constituencies. In the next chapter, attention shifts to constituency-oriented activities in an attempt to determine the effects of increasing tenure on this important aspect of service in the House.

6 The District Activity Career

Those serving in the House of Representatives are not simply members of Congress; they are also representatives of diverse constituencies. As a result of their having to fill these two fundamentally different roles—one in Washington and one in the district—members are often subjected to powerful conflicting pressures. Congressional scholars, slow to appreciate this situation, for a long while busied themselves studying the minutiae of Washington activity while largely ignoring the basics of activity in the constituencies. Legislating was thought to be synonymous with representing. Thankfully, it is now widely recognized that these perceptions are not true, and there has been a flowering of research on the way members behave in their districts. In fact, the two-distinct-worlds-of-Congress theme has become standard fare, appearing in many American politics textbooks and acting as the organizing principle in a major book on Congress (see Davidson and Oleszek 1989).

While the importance of non-Washington activities was not completely unrecognized before, the publication of Richard F. Fenno, Jr.'s, *Home Style* in 1978 provided the major impetus for students of Congress to start giving more than passing attention to the district-oriented behavior of the nation's legislators. This thrust comported well with the writings of David Mayhew (1974a, 1974b) and Morris Fiorina (1977b, 1989) regarding the emphasis members were believed to be placing on constituency service, advertising, and credit-claiming activities.

Certainly, this two-different-worlds scenario should not be taken too far. Even though the "two worlds" require somewhat different skills, and success in one may not necessarily translate into success in the other, they are clearly related, as the works cited above recognize. Thus, it is primarily for purposes of organization that the focus in this chapter is solely on district-related activities, just as it was solely on legislative activity in the previous two chapters. Then in chapter 7 more direct attention is given to matters such as the relationship between legislative and district activity careers.

Expanding and Protecting

More than the other aspects of congressional careers, change in levels of district activity has already been analyzed with an eye toward career-based change. There is even an overarching conceptualization of how career stage is likely to influence constituency activities. I refer to Fenno's discussion of the expansionist and protectionist phases of the congressional career (1978, 171–211). Fenno's concept is that from the beginning of the congressional career (and even before), individuals are busy trying to build and to extend a base of support. At some unspecified time during the career, either because of reduced energy, reduced need, or both, these expansionist activities begin to wane and the member is in a position to concentrate on protecting the established base rather than expanding this base into previously unsupportive territory. This scenario, an obvious relative of the political life-cycle view, rings true as far as it goes but is more accurately considered a starting point than the final word.

For example, as Fenno points out, some events can jar a member who has already entered the protectionist phase back into an expansionist one. The event most likely to have this kind of effect is an intense electoral scare. One of the most frequently cited examples is the case of Senator Warren Magnuson (D-Wash.) who seemed to give all the signs of being in the protectionist mode when electoral catastrophe nearly befell him in the 1962 election. Magnuson won by a whisker and made significant alterations in his modus operandi. He became an active consumer advocate and environmentalist, and there was much talk of the "new" Warren Magnuson. Issue interests and bases of support were changed appreciably. In the words of Eric Redman, "The 1962 election formed the watershed of Magnuson's career. . . . He began to produce consumer-protection legislation—first in a trickle, then in a torrent. . . . Old cronies and lobbyists spluttered in disbelief, . . . reporters wrote of a 'rekindled' Magnuson, and back home, Republican officials with eyes on a Senate seat became more and more dispirited" (1973, 194–95).

Magnuson responded to electoral pressures by changing his issue agenda and, unavoidably, his relationships with various constituency groups both in Washington state and Washington, D.C. While Magnuson's response to this election may seem more legislative than district oriented, the nature of his district (state) activities was permanently altered by the close call in 1962. Moreover, it is worth stressing that this example involves Senator Magnuson and not Representative Magnuson. A switch in issue agenda is probably a more sensible strategy in the Senate than it is in the House. The reasons? In the House, less publicity is usually generated by issue stances, members have somewhat less issue-agenda flexibility because they have fewer committee assignments, and there are (fading?) expectations that members not flit from issue to issue. Thus, in the House, expansionist yearnings, flamed perhaps by lack of experience or an electoral scare, are much more likely to throw the representative into a frenzy of constituency service/pork barrel–type activities rather than a frenzy of new legislative initiatives. Whether or not this strategy works is another issue entirely, as it is a matter of considerable debate (see Johannes and McAdams 1981a, 1981b; Fiorina 1981). This possibility of reversion to an expansionist phase is just one of many questions surrounding Fenno's perceptions of change in district activity over careers, and this whole set of questions needs empirical testing.

Given the importance of district-oriented activities and given that the emphasis in the previous two chapters was on legislative involvement, attention here will be on more purely constituency-oriented matters. Fenno concentrates on two measures of constituency activity: trips home and tendency to assign staff to offices back in the district rather than in Washington. While these variables capture only a small part of the richness of district activity, they are nonetheless critical aspects of the general concept and are measurable, so they will be employed in this chapter.

Measuring Travel Back to the District

While traveling from Washington back to the district is an undeniably vital aspect of a representative's constituency-oriented activities, there are problems with its operationalization. The most common source of information on trips home is the *Report of the Clerk of the House*, which, for the last few decades, documents any request for reimbursement made by

House offices, including travel to and from the district. What we are left with, then, is a measure of *reimbursed* travel to the district rather than actual travel to the district. In some cases, the figures will be identical, but in other cases, particularly those for representatives whose districts are close to Washington, there may be many more total trips home than reimbursed trips home. This potential source of bias should be borne in mind.

Another major problem with using this variable is that there are so many factors likely to contribute to the explanation of variation in travel home. Distance of the district from Washington, electoral marginality, and whether or not the representative's family resides in Washington or back in the district all are probably involved. Thus, regardless of career stage, some representatives are more likely to return to the home district than others (see Fenno 1978, 35–40; Parker 1986a, 42–44). Finally, the fact that the number of reimbursable trips home was increased so dramatically over time—from 0 in 1963 to 33 beginning in 1977 to a virtually unlimited number in 1979 (unlimited, that is, if a member wanted to allocate his/her entire consolidated office account for travel home rather than office furniture and the like)—is naturally something that cannot be ignored. For a thoughtful discussion of these and related problems, see David Canon's review of Parker's book (1988, 110–12).

While these problems cannot be eliminated, they can be minimized, especially because the nature of the analysis performed here renders them somewhat less acute. My interest is in changes in the tendency of individual representatives to travel home over the course of a career; thus, to the extent a particular representative's likelihood of filing a voucher for a trip home remains roughly constant and to the extent a representative's district remains in the same location relative to Washington, these two data difficulties are much less central. While a representative from Chevy Chase may go home more than a representative from Anchorage, change in the relative proclivity of these two members over their careers should not be influenced systematically by these factors. Movement over careers rather than absolute levels is the key to the analysis reported here.

The expectation, of course, is that representatives' willingness to go back to the district will diminish as the years go by. This may be so for a variety of reasons, including the additional electoral security that is thought to accrue with extended tenure (an accrual that is not taking place very often in more recent careers—see chapter 2) and the assumption by most representatives of additional Washington responsibilities. In short, this expectation follows from the political life-cycle view of congressional careers as well as from Fenno's concept of a movement from expansionist to protectionist career phases.

Somewhat surprisingly, the empirical support for this commonsense expectation, both relating to trips home specifically and district activity more generally, is mixed. Most have found evidence that there is a career cycle to constituency attention. Fenno reports a gamma of −.30 between seniority and trips home and a gamma of −.13 between district staff expenditures and trips home (1978, 37, 43). Albert Cover relates that "senior members are less than half as active as their junior colleagues" insofar as putting out district mailings is concerned (1980, 129). Roger Davidson finds that junior members are more likely to allocate their time to fence-mending activities back home than are senior members (1969, 103). Jon Bond reports that "senior members are less attentive than their more junior colleagues" (1985, 346). And Richard Born concludes that, with regard to utilization of district offices, there is "a rather rapid relaxation in their labors as seniority accumulates" (1982, 357).

But virtually all of these studies are based on cross-sectional data, which, therefore, suffer from the difficulties involved with attempts to draw longitudinal inferences from cross-sectional data. The best longitudinal data base for studying constituency activity, or at least one aspect of it, belongs to Parker. Somewhat disturbingly, however, in his analysis of the number of days members spend back in their districts, Parker finds "no evidence . . . that seniority effects are present: in every cohort, House incumbents increase rather than decrease the amount of time they spend in their congressional districts" (1986a, 81). This finding is consistent with preliminary findings Parker reports elsewhere (1980, 121; 1986b).

Thus, the relationship between additional tenure as a U.S. representative and attention to constituency-oriented activities such as traveling back to the district remains open to question. Is the finding of most scholars that there *is* such a relationship merely the result of testing longitudinal questions with cross-sectional data? Remember, relationships generated when tenure is employed as an independent variable in a cross-sectional analysis could be the result of generational rather than life-cycle effects. This, in fact, seems to be what Parker is arguing on the basis of his longitudinal data. He finds evidence of generational differences even as he dismisses life-cycle effects. In addition to disentangling life-cycle and generational effects, the analyst of reimbursed trips home must battle the sizable and totally unsurprising period effects that are produced by whopping increases in the number of trips home for which members can legally be reimbursed. Parker's null findings with regard to life-cycle effects may be partly a function of how difficult it is to see anything through the glare of these period effects.

What is needed is further use of standardized scores, this time to control the changes caused by secular increases in travel allotments. The question thus becomes, relative to the general tendencies of House members, what is the pattern of a particular representative's travel back to the district? Z-scores can be used to control period effects. Moreover, since our concern is not with explaining variations across representatives in trips home, and since district geographical location relative to Washington is largely stable, the change in the representative's z-score across the career should be a meaningful indicator of how this aspect of district attentiveness changes over the course of a career in the House of Representatives. "Near-in" districts—those in the six states closest to Washington, D.C.—are excluded since they are characterized by substantial unreimbursed travel or, even worse, by fluctuations between reimbursed and unreimbursed travel.

Findings Concerning Travel
Back to the District

As has become customary in this study, I begin by presenting results of the typical career for the entire time period. Unfortunately, for this particular variable the "entire" time period is not all that long. Although the *Report of the Clerk of the House* contains some data on reimbursed trips home in the 1960s, it appears somewhat unreliable and is of questionable utility given the extremely low number of trips home for which reimbursement was a possibility (first 2 and then 4). For this portion of the project, we include data from the first sessions only (to conserve data collection resources) of the 92d through the 99th Congress (1971 through 1985).[1] This means conclusions are based on only eight Congresses and, consequently, will be somewhat more tentative than conclusions regarding the measures of congressional behavior used elsewhere in this work.

This caveat aside, figure 6.1 shows that, on average, as members move through their House careers they tend to travel back to the district less frequently relative to the travel of their colleagues. Members who served in their first Congress from 1971 through 1985 typically went home

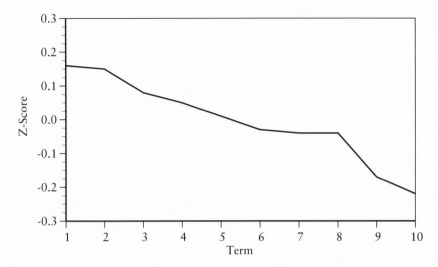

Figure 6.1. Standardized Travel Back to the District in the First Year of Each Congress, by Tenure, 1971–1985

during that first term more than the mean for all representatives in the relevant Congresses (z-score = .16). By their fifth term, representatives were usually at the mean, and after that they went home less than the mean, dropping off most dramatically from the eighth to the ninth terms.

While figure 6.1 is based on figures produced by a standardization of the number of trips back to the district, readers may be interested in the raw data on reimbursed travel. These data are contained in figure 6.2. In addition to providing some sense of the frequency with which members ask for reimbursement for travel from Washington to their districts, this figure demonstrates the growing amount of travel home between 1970 and 1980. During this time, there was indeed a large increase in the mean number of trips home taken by members of the House (other than those in the six closest states). In the first session of the 92d Congress (1971), the mean was 9.2; by the first session of the 96th Congress (1979), this figure had risen to 27.5. But this shift is easily explainable since periodic alterations boosted the maximum number of reimbursed trips home from 12 to 33 during these years (see Parker 1986a, 67).

Beginning in 1980, however, allowances for travel were rolled into consolidated accounts called official expense allowances (see Ornstein, Mann, and Malbin 1987, 154–55). Since then members have been free to

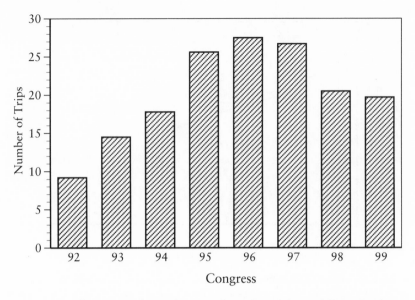

Figure 6.2. Changes in the Mean Number of Reimbursed Trips Back to the District in the First Year of Each Congress, 1971–1985

spend this money on trips home or on equipment, stationery, district offices, computer services, etc. It is interesting to note that shortly after this change, reimbursed travel home began to decline, from 27.5 in the first session of the 96th to 19.7 in the first session of the 99th.[2] It appears that, if members have to sacrifice some other aspect of their operation in order to be reimbursed for traveling back to their districts, they either go home less often or find alternative means of financing their trips. Since previous studies of travel stop with 1980 (see Parker 1986a), this important shift has gone unnoticed.

At any rate, these large changes in the mean number of trips home show why standardization is necessary. If allowances are changed, the number of reimbursed trips home is likely to follow suit. When more travel is allowed on a "use it or lose it" basis, trips go up; but when trips home reduce the funds available for other office activities and needs, funded travel home decreases. If raw data were presented for individual classes, conclusions would be unduly influenced by these rules changes, and it would be difficult to isolate real life-cycle effects. Moreover, we could not determine whether the contours of this aspect of district activity remained stable or whether senior members of more recent Congresses now feel the need to maintain their rigorous travel schedules in contrast to their predecessors who, in their later years, found trips back to the district more onerous, less necessary, or both.

Answering these questions definitively is impossible, given that the data only cover a fifteen-year period. Still, it is possible to speculate on the basis of the information contained in figure 6.3. The figure presents information on four different classes, with varying degrees of overlap. The class of 1959 was in the House for six terms before the time period covered by the data set begins, but from its seventh term to its tenth the tendency to travel back to the district relative to other members serving in the pertinent Congresses dropped briskly. From its fourth term to its tenth, the class of 1965 dropped as well, although not quite as much as the class of 1959. The class of 1971, however, displays a different pattern. Surprisingly, even in its first term, this class traveled back to the district less than the mean of all eligible members of the 92d Congress. But the issue here is not where the class begins but what pattern it follows over the years. This also is a surprise: rather than going home less as it ages, the class of 1971 appears to increase its relative travel. With the exception of its seventh term, this class travels home less (in relative terms) in its first term than any other time. The class of 1977 can only be observed for five terms. It does appear to reduce its district travel, but the decline is quite slight (from z-scores of .25 and .30 in the first two terms to .19 and .12 in the last two).

Data limitations force us to rely too much on the latter portions of careers for the early classes and the early portions of careers for the later classes. If drop-offs in travel home tend generally to be concentrated in the later stages of careers, there is the possibility that the bigger drop for early classes may be due to the shift in the emphasis of the data that are available across classes rather than to an actual shift in the contours of congressional careers. The most that can be said here is that there *appears* to be limited evidence that the degree to which relative behavioral changes are taking place across careers is diminishing.

Naturally, when individual careers rather than class means are analyzed, the story can seem somewhat different. Despite what appears to be a growing tendency to "settle in" to a certain style of activity career, there are those who do change precipitously. Bill Chappell (D-Fla.), before making headlines by being caught in a procurement scandal and by being one of only seven House incumbents defeated in the 1988 elections, dropped from 57 trips home in the first session of the 98th Congress to

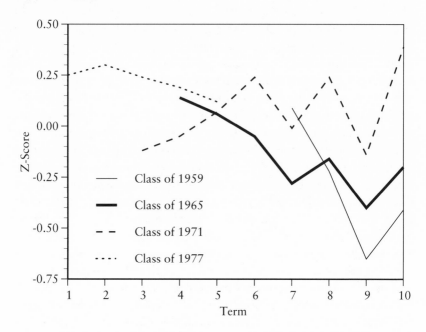

Figure 6.3. Class-by-Class Analysis of the Relationship between
Travel Back to the District and Tenure, Classes of 1959, 1965, 1971,
and 1977

35 trips home in the first session of the 99th (his lowest total since the
changes in the number of reimbursable trips home in 1977). No doubt
the decrease was partially due to the fact that he assumed the chairmanship of the Defense Appropriations Subcommittee upon the death of
Joseph Addabbo (D-N.Y.).

   Representative Mike Synar (D-Okla.) was first elected in 1978, partly
because of a solid Oklahoma pedigree and partly because his opponent,
incumbent Ted Risenhoover (R-Okla.), could not turn aside claims that he
slept in a heart-shaped waterbed and was, more generally, a playboy.
From the beginning, Synar was fond of saying he intended to be a "U.S.
congressman from Oklahoma not an Oklahoma congressman." Still,
during his first three terms, Synar made the grueling trip from Washington to Muskogee with incredible regularity, averaging more than 41
reimbursed trips home per year. But during the 99th Congress, his pattern
changed, and Synar came home "only" 20 times during the first session,
perhaps because his seat was obviously safe by then and/or because he
was heavily involved in committee work (Energy and Commerce, Judiciary).

But some members never feel safe enough, or, alternatively, they like to go home. During the first session of the 98th Congress, Bill Young (R-Fla.) asked for reimbursement for 24 trips home. He then coasted to victory with 80 percent of the vote in the election of 1984. Yet, during the first session of the subsequent Congress (the 99th), Young went home 47 times despite the fact that no serious challenger was on the horizon. Predictably, Young was unopposed in 1986 after the 99th Congress.

A large drop in trips home frequently accompanies a decision to retire voluntarily. One retiree told me this about his final term in the House: "My trips back to the district went way down. There was no reason to go back. My engagement calendar used to be booked up for seven or eight months in advance; after I announced, no one seemed anxious to have me. I stayed in town and found out that Washington was not as bad as I had thought all those years." Another retiree justified his lack of attention to the district by pointing out that "constituents think you leave office as soon as you announce." Representative Gene Snyder (R-Ky.) must have had a similar attitude. After announcing in 1985 that he would be retiring before the 1986 election, Snyder's number of reimbursed trips home dropped from 42 to 17.

Four points need to be made by way of summation. First, traveling back to the district does, to some extent, track with careers. In relative terms, members are more likely to go to their home districts early in their careers than late (see figure 6.1). Previous research has not detected such a pattern largely because it failed to standardize for the sizable period effects that accompanied changes in the reimbursement structure for district travel. Second, the overall tendency of members of the House to travel home declined in absolute terms from 1980 to 1986 (see figure 6.2). Previous research failed to detect this important shift because it did not utilize the most current data. Third, there is some indication that the typical career-based change in travel tendencies has diminished (see figure 6.3). It appears as though variation from early-career travel to late-career travel becomes smaller as the analysis shifts to more contemporary careers. Finally, and least surprisingly, a substantial amount of intriguing individual variation occurs around these mean figures and general conclusions.

Measuring District Staff Allocation

The second aspect of district activity addressed in this chapter involves the decision each member must make concerning how many staff members to assign to a district, rather than Washington, office. As Bruce Cain, John Ferejohn, and Morris Fiorina state, "The decision to locate large numbers of staff in the district rather than in Washington says something about the kind of operation that a member wants to have. Roughly speaking, big district staffs are likely to be active, visible district staffs. Small district staffs probably concentrate more on transmitting requests back to Washington than on looking for new ways in which the congressional office can relate successfully to the constituency" (n.d., 7).

The degree to which a member is willing to sacrifice Washington-based staffers to establish a permanent and visible office presence in the district may be a rough indicator of that member's priorities. As such, we might anticipate that junior representatives in expansionist phases would be more likely to send staffers back to the district than their more senior colleagues, many of whom have presumably entered protectionist phases. In other words, it may be the case that the tendency to assign staff to district offices, like travel home, will be inversely related to tenure. Not only do electoral pressures usually ebb, but Washington responsibilities are likely to increase (although for some members access to committee staffers may compensate for these additional legislative responsibilities).

Previous research on this point is decidedly unsettled. Fenno, in separate 1967 and 1973 cross sections, finds that freshmen sent a slightly greater percentage of their staff back to the district than did nonfreshmen. At the same time, he notes that "of the 149 House members for whom we have data in both years, 32 reduced the percentage of staff personnel in the district during the period, 42 kept it the same, and 75, or 50 percent, increased the percentage of staff in the district" (1978, 208–9). In other words, less than one-third of the members of this group actually reduced district staff presence as their careers advanced. Perhaps six years is not enough for members to enter the protectionist phase or perhaps standardization is needed, but it would appear Fenno's data do not provide strong support for the notion that more senior members will be less inclined to send staff back to the district.

Cain, Ferejohn, and Fiorina analyze staff assignment data for the period from 1959 to 1979. They note that virtually all members over time are sending more staffers back to the district. When they control for electoral margin and previous staff allocation, they find that tenure does have the expected negative relationship with district staff allocations and that it is significant 8 of 10 times (n.d., 31). Unfortunately, despite having data for ten Congresses, they do not engage in any actual longitudinal analyses (except to lag staff assignments), preferring instead to present ten separate cross-sectional regressions. This makes interpretation somewhat more difficult—especially for those interested in life-cycle rather than generational or period change.

Steven Schiff and Steven Smith (1983) proceed in a similar manner. They have staff allocation data for the years 1960, 1968, and 1976. In their multiple regression model, however, they use each year's data in a distinct cross-sectional design. They hypothesize that additional seniority will bring decreasing district staff allocation. This is what they find in the bivariate analysis but not in the multivariate, where they actually report a positive relationship between seniority and sending staffers back to the district (1983, 462). While this may be a function of some unexplained shift in the ordering of values for the seniority variable, the absence of a truly longitudinal design renders it difficult to determine precisely what conclusions are permitted on the topic of career-based changes in district staff allocation.

Findings Concerning District Staff Allocation

Thus, extant research does not enable us to make confident statements about the relationship between tenure and district staff allocation once period effects are taken into consideration. To provide more guidance on this issue, data from the *Congressional Staff Directory* have been collected from 1959 through 1985 (fourteen Congresses) on the total number of personal staffers for each representative as well as the number of those personal staffers who were assigned to district offices.

The explosive growth across this period in district staff presence is readily apparent in figure 6.4. In 1959, the typical House member assigned just under 14 percent of the total number of staffers to the district. By 1985 that figure had risen to over 43 percent. Thus, by the end of the time period, nearly one of every two personal staffers was based in the district rather than in Washington. While noteworthy, this finding generally confirms what observers of the congressional scene have known for some time. For present purposes, one of the more significant messages in figure 6.4 is that before a proper assessment of life-cycle effects can be made, large-scale period effects must be neutralized.

When the usual standardization is performed, we find that, indeed, over the course of a career, members become less likely to send their

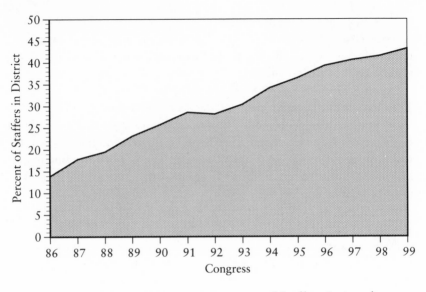

Figure 6.4. Aggregate Changes in Percentage of Staffers Assigned to District Offices, 1959–1985

staffers to the district. Of course, relative statements such as this can be misleading. The percentage of staffers in the district grew for most members as they aged, but the standardization suggests that this growth was not nearly as rapid as the mean growth for all members across this time. Once period effects are controlled, district staff as a percentage of total staff tends to decline with the progression of a career. As figure 6.5 indicates, the decline is not precipitous, ranging only from .06 standard deviations above the mean in the first and second terms to .02 standard deviations below the mean in the seventh and eighth terms.

Yet, probably more than for most of the data sets employed in this study, the overall shifts in staff allocation for all members conceal an important shift in career contours. Moreover, unlike the gradual flattening detected elsewhere in this analysis of congressional careers, the change in career-based staff allocation was relatively sudden and, consequently, can be traced to a particular time. The classes of 1973 and 1975 follow patterns that are distinct from each other, with the former dropping off rapidly in its relative district staff assignments and the latter holding steady or perhaps increasing the relative staff resources devoted to the district. Further, the pattern displayed by the class of 1973 is, for

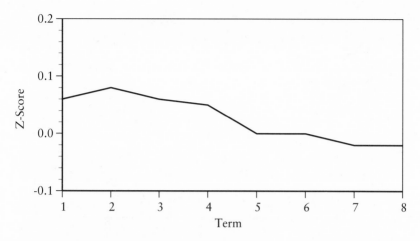

Figure 6.5. Standardized Percentage of Staffers Assigned to District Offices, by Tenure, 1959–1985

the most part, typical of pre-1973 classes, with the only real exception being the class of 1961, which, for reasons I cannot explain, increased its district staff allocation much more rapidly than Congress as a whole. Likewise, the class of 1975 seems to be typical of the classes that follow it, although this conclusion is based upon limited data since few post-1975 classes have had long enough careers to permit accurate readings. With regard to the career-based contours of district staff allocation, and perhaps other factors as well, the Watergate (1975) class seems to have ushered in a new style of career (see Loomis 1988a).

Figure 6.6 presents the two classes that bracket what seems to have been the breakpoint between the old- and new-style career. In the old style, relative district staff allocation dropped fairly sharply as representatives became more senior. In the new-style career, district staff increases over a career are sharp enough that they roughly keep pace with the changes injected by generational replacement. One intriguing feature of many of the individual classes (not shown) is the tendency for relative district staff allocation actually to increase from the first term of a career to the second. Seven of the ten classes initiating their House careers between 1959 and 1977 registered increases in z-scores between the first and second term before declines typically set in for the remainder of the career. Thus, it is not surprising that figure 6.5 indicates a slight increase

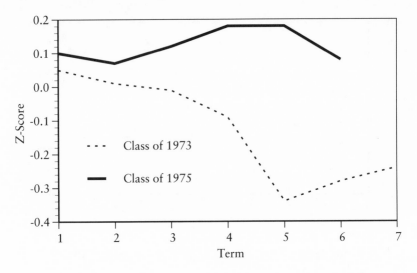

Figure 6.6. Class-by-Class Analysis of the Relationship between District Staff Assignments and Tenure, Classes of 1973 and 1975

from first to second term. Perhaps it takes some members a term to learn the potential value of a strong district staff presence.

Mortality effects are not responsible for the shifting contours of district staff allocation careers. When all eligible class members are included in the computations, as they are in figure 6.6, the N drops for each addition-al term, as members lose or, more likely, retire. For the class of 1973, the numbers look like this: 76 in the first term, 60 in the second, 53 in the third, 41 in the fourth, 34 in the fifth, 26 in the sixth, and 22 in the seventh. For the large Watergate class of 1975, there were 98 in the first, 94 in the second, 78 in the third, 62 in the fourth, 49 in the fifth, and 39 in the sixth. To make sure that this pattern of departures is not biasing the results, I replicated the analysis with only those members who served at least seven terms in the case of the class of 1973 (N = 22) and at least six terms in the case of the class of 1975 (N = 39).

When mortality effects are controlled in this fashion, conclusions re-main identical to those drawn on the basis of figure 6.6: the class of 1973 drops off sharply as it ages while the class of 1975 holds steady. On the basis of these data, it would appear that very recent congressional careers do not contribute to the overall decline in relative district staff allocation depicted in figure 6.5. In fact, these recent careers seem to be one reason the decline for all post-1957 classes is not steeper. As such, we have additional evidence that, once period effects are controlled, life-cycle effects are much more minimal than they used to be.

Another way to grasp what is happening is to focus on the standard deviation around the mean. If the z-scores for more recent classes are flat across careers, this means incumbent members of Congress are sending additional staffers home at a rate roughly commensurate with the increase resulting from membership replacement. This being the case (assuming generational distinctions have not increased), it follows that the standard deviation of district staff allocation within Congresses is less now than it used to be.

The data support this line of thought. Since 1976 or so, the standard deviation around the mean percentage of staffers assigned to the district has fallen by about 60 percent. This standard deviation is now lower than it has been since at least the late 1950s. What this means is that there is now a widely agreed-upon formula for the percentage of staffers in the district: usually about 45 percent of all personal staffers available. Variation from this norm is rare and small. There is a standard operating procedure, and it involves sending almost half of the staff back to district offices.

Being Visible

Why do members of Congress perform district-oriented activities such as assigning staffers to district offices and frequently traveling back to be among constituents? After all, many constituency-oriented activities are at best pedestrian and at worst distasteful. One representative who retired at middle age told me, "I came to Washington to be a member of the greatest legislative body in the world and I ended up being an errand boy." It is a rare member of Congress who actually enjoys constituency service work; this is why nearly all of it is done by staffers. If it is so disliked, why is it such a big part of the modern legislative operation?

Some truth undoubtedly resides in Donald Searing's contention (1985) that legislators do service work partially out of a sense of duty. But the main reason, no doubt, is to make themselves better known among the constituents and to try to make sure that this knowledge is favorable knowledge (see Fiorina 1977a). This increased favorable knowledge likely translates into more votes. Constituency service work provides a great opportunity to score points without risking any (see Cain, Ferejohn, and Fiorina 1987). Using efforts to track down lost veterans' benefits checks as an example of constituency-oriented activities, Fiorina notes, "Some voters will agree with a policy stand, some will disagree. But everyone will applaud the congressman's efforts in behalf of the veterans" (1977b, 180). Similarly, returning to the district frequently would seem to be a relatively safe means of increasing visibility.

In this formulation, then, one of the main goals of district activity is visibility. This being the case, the logical culmination of a chapter on district activity is an investigation of district visibility across a congressional career. Does the visibility of an incumbent—the presumed consequence of much of the constituency-oriented activity addressed in this chapter—vary with career stage? Other things being equal, are senior incumbents more visible back in their districts than junior incumbents, or does their growing Washington focus actually make senior members less visible to the folks back home?[3]

Direct data are not available to address this key aspect of the congressional career. Unfortunately, an insufficient number of representatives have monitored their own visibility carefully, frequently, and over an extended period of time to permit conclusions based on longitudinal data. The best that can be offered would seem to be the cross-sectional data generated by the 1978 National Election Studies (NES) survey of the American public. In this survey, special questions were asked regarding the visibility of incumbents. Moreover, several contextual variables, including the years of service of the relevant incumbent, were added to the survey responses. Finally, in 1978 the congressional district was used as a sampling unit, assuring a reasonable number of respondents in each of a random sample of 108 congressional districts. For all these reasons, the 1978 survey results may provide some sense of the relationship between length of congressional service and visibility among constituents (even though the practice of using tenure as a variable in a cross section generates all of the problems discussed earlier).

Incumbent Recall and Recognition

Two questions in the 1978 survey deal directly with awareness of the incumbent. The first is the traditional survey question regarding the ability of respondents to *recall* the name of the incumbent. The second is the ability of respondents to *recognize* the incumbent's name. The latter is presumed to be quite a bit easier and also to be closer to the task awaiting voters in the voting booth. We know that House incumbents are, on average, more visible than their challengers, but does the visibility of these incumbents increase the longer they serve in the House? Is there some basis in fact for the disconcerting tendency of researchers to treat incumbency as a dichotomous variable, or are there gradations among tenure categories of incumbents as far as visibility in the constituency is concerned?

The 1978 NES survey used 108 congressional districts as the primary sampling units. This procedure makes it possible to aggregate responses to the district level and to utilize some of the many contextual variables added to the data. Those districts in which no incumbent was seeking reelection were removed from the analysis, thereby lowering the number of usable cases from 108 to 95. For each of these districts, the percentage of respondents capable of recalling the name of the incumbent and the percentage of respondents capable of recognizing the name of the incumbent from a list of names was compiled and compared to the tenure of the representative.

Common sense holds that the longer someone has been serving a constituency the more people would be familiar with the person's name. The political life-cycle view leads to the expectation of a positive relationship, but it might append a curvilinear feature with visibility increments decreasing and perhaps even turning negative late in the career when constituency matters have been traded in for Washington activities. On the other hand, the nature of service in the modern House may render tenure categories irrelevant to variations in visibility.

An examination of individual cases offers some support for the general conclusion that visibility tends to increase with tenure. Only one of the ninety-five representatives had his name recalled by all respondents in the district and that was Daniel Flood (D-Pa.) whose thirty total years of House service (twenty-four of them continuous) were not exceeded by any of the other ninety-four representatives whose constituencies were selected as primary sampling units and who ran for reelection in 1978. To be fair, Flood's visibility was enhanced by his waxed mustache, cape, distinctive speech, dramatic flair, and, most notably, by the scandal that surrounded him in 1978, but the general pattern suggests it is likely Flood's extended tenure is at least partially responsible for the high level of visibility he enjoyed among his constituents.

To some extent, this conclusion is also evident when attention is focused on the opposite end of the visibility scale. Of the ten representatives who checked in with the lowest recall levels in the 1978 survey (37 percent or below), six were first elected in 1974 or 1976, within four years of the 1978 survey, and two more were first elected in 1972. The major outlier is Jonathan Bingham (D-N.Y.), who, despite fourteen years of representing his Bronx constituency, had his name recalled by only 29 percent of the respondents in his district. Since the constituents of Clement Zablocki (D-Wis.) and Dan Rostenkowski (D-Ill.) also recalled the names of their representatives at rates less than might have been expected on the basis of the tenure of these individuals, it may be the case that incumbents in urban and especially ethnic urban areas are less likely to find their names on the tips of the tongues of a goodly number of constituents, other things being equal. Be this as it may, eyeballing extremes of the lists does nothing to lead us to reject the notion that the tenure of a representative is related to the tendency of constituents to recall his or her name.

Similar conclusions are drawn if the issue is recognition rather than recall. For example, the three members with the lowest recognition levels in their districts and six of the lowest seven (with Bingham again being the exception) were all elected in 1974 or after. The class of 1975 appears to have achieved visibility beyond what would be predicted simply on the basis of its (as of the election of 1978) four years on the Hill and in the districts. Eight representatives in the sample of ninety-five were recognized by all respondents in the district (compared to only one who was *recalled* by all respondents), and three of these eight were members of the class of 1975. Apparently, the consciously activist and acquisitive stance of this class and the high-octane, media-attuned political styles of a few of its members thrust them into the very visible category much faster than normal.

On the other side of the coin, five members were much less visible than their years in the House would lead us to expect: Bingham, Zablocki, Rostenkowski (remember this was 1978—well before his promotion to chairman of the Ways and Means Committee thrust him into national prominence), Don Edwards (D-Calif.), and Robert McEwen (R-N.Y.). Four of these five represent ethnic urban constituencies, and the fifth (McEwen) is described in the *Almanac of American Politics* as being noticeably "quiet" and as the type of incumbent who "makes few waves" (Barone and Ujifusa 1979, 629). But the larger point is that, in spite of a few atypical cases, tenure seems to influence positively an incumbent's recognizability among constituents.

Challenger Recognition and the Visibility Gap

Earlier, the importance to incumbents of scaring off serious challenges was discussed. It may be that increased tenure plays a role in this as well. In other words, it may be that the longer an incumbent has been around and the more races he or she has won, the less likely it is that a visible, credible challenge will be raised against the incumbent. The strategic-choice vision of Jacobson and Kernell (1983) is in many ways persuasive, although their original emphasis on national variables at the expense of local factors, such as the characteristics of specific incumbents, is something subsequent research needed to correct (Bond 1985; Krasno and Green 1988; and Jacobson 1989 have made a start on this task). Potential candidates ask not only whether it is a good year for, say, Republican challengers generally, as Jacobson and Kernell skillfully point out, but also whether it is a good year for a Republican challenger *in a particular district*. Has the incumbent grown fat and sassy? How did the incumbent do in the last election? Did he run worse than many expected? Does he seem entrenched? Has he been in Congress too long? Has he caught Potomac Fever? Is he vulnerable?

Does a long string of victories for the same incumbent make it less likely a high-visibility challenger will emerge? Is there a relationship between the length of an incumbent's tenure in the House and the visibility of the incumbent's challenger? The 1978 NES data make it possible to address these issues since a question on the ability of respondents to recognize (and rate) the name of the challenger was included. Twenty-one additional districts, those in which the incumbent had no major-party opposition, had to be removed from this portion of the analysis. This leaves 74 districts of the 108 in the original NES sample.

A cursory comparison of incumbent tenure and challenger visibility indicates they are inversely related. For example, the challenger to fifteen-term incumbent Clement Zablocki in 1978 (one Elroy Honadel) was known to only 21 percent of the constituents in Wisconsin's Fourth District (and bear in mind this is ability to recognize; recall rates would be even lower), while the challenger to first-term incumbent Marc Marks (R-

Pa.), former representative Joseph Vigorito, was known to 89 percent of the Twenty-fourth District. There are, of course, examples that do not fit the pattern particularly well, but, on the whole, there seems to be a general tendency for senior incumbents to be confronted with less-visible challengers.

In many ways, however, what is of crucial importance to both challengers and incumbents is not their own or their opponent's raw visibility levels but the *gap* between the visibility of the incumbents and the visibility of the challengers. In fact, of all the findings coming out of the 1978 study on congressional elections, it was this gap that seemed to generate the most excitement. The gap between incumbent and challenger visibility (as measured by the recognize-and-rate question; challenger recall ability was not ascertained) was much greater in the House than in the Senate (see Abramowitz 1980; Hinckley 1980; Mann and Wolfinger 1980). And many thought that this factor explained why Senate races tended to be much more competitive than House races. Poorly known challengers seemed to account for the virtual absence of competition for incumbents in the House. Later research stressed that a bias in the 1978 sample when applied to Senate races was apparently not taken seriously enough when the results of the NES study were interpreted, so the actual size of the difference in the House and Senate recognition gaps is a matter of some debate (see Westlye 1983). But no one disputes the importance of the gap itself as an indicator of challenger-incumbent status and relative position.

What explains variations in the size of the visibility gap across House races represented in the 1978 NES sample? Is the visibility gap between challenger and incumbent positively related to the tenure of the incumbent? The following equation presents information bearing on the answer to these questions.

$$\begin{array}{c} \text{Inc. recognition} \\ \text{minus} \\ \text{Chal. recognition} \end{array} = 28.2 + \underset{(3.99)}{1.57} \text{ (years in House)} + e$$

$$N = 74$$
$$R^2 = .19$$
$$(\ ) = t \text{ ratio}$$

Clearly, the longer a representative has been in the House, the more likely he/she is to have a large advantage in name recognition. The coefficient for tenure is large, is in the expected direction, is statistically significant, and is able by itself to account for nearly one-fifth of the variance in the visibility gap. Each additional year of House tenure increases the visibility gap by over 1.5 percent. Longtime incumbents such as John Conyers (D-Mich.) and Dante Fascell (D-Fla.) had visibility advantages of as much as 9 to 1 over their challengers, while House neophytes such as Marks and Ed Jenkins (D-Ga.) had practically no visibility advantage at all over their challengers. Two-term representative Jim Lloyd (D-Calif.) actually had his name recognized by fewer people than recognized David Dreier, his opponent in 1978. Lloyd's classmate Martha Keys (D-Kans.) found out about the dangers of having a challenger with name recognition approximately equal to the incumbent when she became the only incumbent of the seventy-four in the sample to be defeated in 1978. She was recognized by a meager 11 percent more respondents than Republican opponent Jim Jeffries. The four major outliers (McEwen, Bingham, Edwards, and Augustus Hawkins [D-Calif.]) all come from highly urbanized, ethnic districts.[4]

So the number of years a person has been in the House is related to visibility advantage. Senior incumbents are better known than junior incumbents, and senior incumbents enjoy bigger visibility advantages over their challengers than do junior incumbents. But we have yet to investigate the possibility that the relationship between tenure and visibility advantage is something other than linear. The transition from fifteen-year incumbent to sixteen-year incumbent may bring less in the way of additional visibility advantage than the transition from two-year incumbent to three-year incumbent. Very late in a lengthy congressional career, visibility advantages may even decrease with additional tenure as a result, perhaps, of diminished constituency activity and an improvement in the quality of challengers to the incumbent—a phenomenon somewhat analogous to the initial circling of the vultures. Niemi, Powell, and Bicknell (1986, 191), in fact, report that the relationship between seniority and candidate recognition is curvilinear. However, since their main concern is with other matters, they do not present specific results of a test for curvilinearity.

My analysis does not support this aspect of the life-cycle view of congressional careers. In the case of tenure and the visibility gap, the linear relationship is significant, but deviation from linearity does not occur at a statistically significant level ($p = .59$). A similar conclusion is reached when a curve is specified in the relationship through the use of logarithms. Allowing the line to curve in a manner that would capture decreasing amounts of visibility advantage at higher levels of tenure improves the fit not at all. It would seem the relationship between tenure and visibility gap is, for all intents and purposes, linear.

Many prefer to check for curvilinearity simply by analyzing the scatterplot of the relationship. Partially for this reason, I present in figure 6.7 the plot of the relationship between tenure and incumbent-challenger visibility gap. I have drawn the ordinary-least-squares regression line and labeled some of the outliers and other notable cases to assist readers in making sense of this information. As before, it can be seen that Bingham, McEwen, Zablocki, and a few others have less favorable visibility situations than their tenure would lead us to expect. Others do better than their tenure says they should. Phil Crane (R-Ill.), for example, had served just five terms as of 1978 but possessed the largest advantage over a challenger of any included incumbent—93 percent more respondents knew Crane than knew his challenger. A major reason for this, no doubt, is the fact that Crane had already announced his candidacy for the presidency and was receiving an unusual amount of publicity and recognition as a result. Exceptions like Crane make it clear why we could never hope to capture all the variance in visibility with a single variable like tenure. But the major reason for presenting the scatterplot is to probe for curvilinearity. There would appear to be very little, just as the more systematic tests described above led us to expect. While there are (not surprisingly) more cases toward the left-hand side of the plot, which may give an appearance of curvilinearity (or perhaps heteroscedasticity), actual deviation from linearity is not really visible with the naked eye.

Do Specific Types of Constituency Contact Vary with Career Stage?

Additional analyses were conducted of the relationship between increasing tenure and specific forms of contact with incumbents as reported by respondents in 1978. Possibilities included meeting the incumbent personally, attending a meeting where the incumbent spoke, talking to a member of the incumbent's staff, receiving mail from the incumbent, reading about the incumbent in a newspaper or magazine, hearing the incumbent on the radio, and seeing the incumbent on television. Almost 77 percent of the respondents admitted to some kind of contact with the

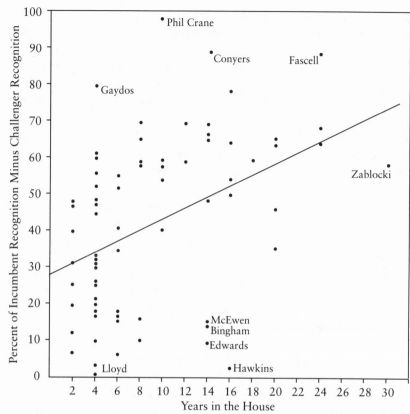

Figure 6.7. Scatterplot of the Relationship between Tenure and the Visibility Gap, 1978 NES Data

incumbent. However, there was wide variation in the nature of this inter-action. *Of those who said they had some contact,* two-thirds had received mail from the incumbent, even more had read about the incumbent in a newspaper or magazine, and 60 percent claimed to have seen the incum-bent on television, but far fewer had heard the incumbent on radio or in person, and only 11 percent of those with some contact and 8 percent of the entire sample said they had talked to a member of the incumbent's staff.

But the question of interest is whether or not the chances of constitu-ents coming into contact with the incumbent or his/her office are in-creased when the incumbent has been in the House for many years. Is there a positive relationship between years of service in the House and these various types of contact between the representative and the represented? Even though contact seems likely to be a cumulative process, the somewhat surprising answer to this question is an only slightly qualified no. Tenure was given the opportunity to explain variance from district to district in the percentage of respondents claiming different kinds of contact with the incumbent representative but failed miserably in this endeavor. Except for a single type of contact, the relationship between tenure and the individual modes of interaction with the incumbent was extremely small, often in the "incorrect" direction, and never even close to achieving statistical significance.

The lone exception was receiving mail from the incumbent's office. For every year of service, an additional 1.8 percent of the constituents claim to have received mail from their elected representative. This relationship is statistically significant but explains only a very small percentage of the total district-to-district variation. All other types of contact—from television appearances to staff contact to reading about the incumbent in the newspaper—were totally unrelated to the number of years the incumbent had spent in the House. It would seem, then, that there is a relationship between tenure and incumbent visibility, but there is not a relationship between tenure and contact with the incumbent. Senior incumbents are better known, but it is not because they are more likely to have come into memorable contact with a goodly number of constituents.

No doubt part of the explanation for this slightly surprising situation stems from problems with the research design we have been forced to employ for this issue. It could be that life-cycle effects are running up against period and generational effects, with the result being that the forces balance themselves out and tenure appears to have no effect at all on most specific modes of contact. In 1978, the senior members were those who had been socialized into the House during a time when there was not as much importance placed on incumbent-generated constituency interaction (see Fiorina 1977b, 54–55, for a discussion of these factors). In relative terms, they probably did even less in 1978 than they did when they first entered, if the earlier portions of this chapter are any indication. Still, they had been around for awhile, and a lot of constituents had some familiarity with them simply as a result of this longevity. Relative newcomers in 1978, on the other hand, were cranking away at a frenetic pace on many constituency-oriented activities. They had been told this was the road to a long legislative life, and they took this advice seriously. Even so, they were new and had not had the time to reach a lot of constituents.

The results of all this may be a wash: the older members' more leisurely pace of constituency activities combined with the extended period over which these activities are performed may roughly equal the younger members' feverish but short-lived activities. Possibilities such as these are the reason we need longitudinal rather than cross-sectional data. Relying on a single batch of cross-sectional data means we can do nothing more than speculate on how generational and life-cycle changes mingle, and this is why individual-level, longitudinal data are so crucial for analyses of congressional careers and congressional behavior more generally.

Conclusion

When forced to draw general conclusions about the typical district activity career during the last several decades, the political life cycle or a movement from expansionist to protectionist phases is clearly evident. In relative terms, extended tenure in the House brings with it declining attention to the district as measured by trips home and the allocation of staffers to district offices. Perhaps this is in keeping with burgeoning Washington responsibilities, electoral security, and/or diminished desire and energy—all contributors to the political life cycle. Tenure does affect congressional activities in anticipated ways.

At the same time, I have tried to convey some sense of the diversity of House careers by referencing several individual cases, some of which follow patterns apparent in the "mean" figures and others of which could not be more different. More important, I have attempted to determine whether the typical career pattern has shifted across the time period. Conclusions on this latter point are limited by the quality and quantity of data available on district activity. It appears as though some shift in patterns has occurred. After controlling for period effects, the degree to which tenure makes a difference in the level of district-oriented activity has declined. With regard to more recent Congresses, there appears to be less variation from early terms to late than was the case with careers in the 1960s and 1970s. In the area of district attention, the political life cycle is less distinct than it used to be.

The last section of this chapter addressed the influence of tenure on the extent to which representatives are known in their districts. Unfortunately, adequate longitudinal data on this matter are not available. As a result, the approach required is the very one I criticized in chapter 1—using cross-sectional data to draw conclusions about the effects of tenure. With this caveat in mind, the findings indicate that increased tenure brings heightened visibility for representatives and an increased gap in the relative visibility of the incumbent and the challenger. Taken together, the home-district situation for a senior incumbent would appear to be a happy one: less relative (though not necessarily absolute) effort is expended than in earlier portions of the career, yet constituent recognition relative to challenger recognition is generally at a much higher level than it was when the member was just beginning a career in the House. The only fly in the ointment would seem to be the suggestion that, if patterns continue to shift as they have, future careers may no longer be marked by late-career relaxations in district-oriented efforts. In recent careers, life-cycle effects have been less apparent.

7 The Integrated Congressional Career

Several times in the preceding pages I have written that some issue or another will be addressed in chapter 7. Now it is time to make good on those promises. Such statements were usually made in reference to the potential interaction of various independent variables. These issues were left until now because previous chapters were concerned almost exclusively with bivariate relationships; that is, with the effects of increasing House tenure on electoral success, on formal positions held, and on legislative and constituency activity. But it is possible that factors other than tenure also affect these variables, and it is even likely that these competing variables could alter the nature of the relationship between tenure and the various dependent variables.

To cite a specific example, it was evident in chapter 6 that constituency attention decreases (in relative terms) with additional House tenure. On average, senior members pay less attention to their constituencies than do junior representatives. So far I have given little attention to the question of why tenure matters. What is it about more senior members that causes them to pay less attention to their constituencies? Is it that they lack a compelling motivation since their electoral situation is sometimes more secure than that of many junior members? Is it that senior members frequently are legislatively active and therefore have less time to go home? Or is it that senior members are less likely to pay attention to constituents because, well, simply because they are senior?

A Career-Based Model
of Congressional Behavior

To answer these important questions, variables must be brought together in a single model rather than isolated in distinct chapters. The basic model from which we will work in the pages to come is presented in figure 7.1. There are ten possible arrows in the model: four of them—the ones emanating from House term—have been addressed in previous chapters, but the six arrows that do not begin with tenure have not been discussed. Two of these (the dotted lines) represent links with little theoretical justification. It is unclear whether electoral security would increase or decrease legislative involvement, and it would seem that if formal position is going to influence constituency attention it would be through legislative involvement rather than directly. Thus, these links will not figure prominently in the presentation to follow.[1] But many of the remaining arrows represent relationships vital to the understanding of congressional behavior. Do representatives under electoral stress respond by increasing their constituency attention? What about the effects of formal House positions? Do they increase legislative involvement? Is there a trade-off between legislative and constituency activities?

Figure 7.1 also contains the hypothesized direction of the various relationships. Tenure (House term) is expected to exert a positive effect on electoral support, formal position, and legislative activity but a negative effect on constituency attention (more tenure brings less attention). Electoral success is predicted to decrease constituency attention. Formal positions should lead to more legislative involvement. And there should be a trade-off between constituency attention and legislative involvement.

Determining whether or not these hypothesized relationships square with reality requires several procedural and methodological alterations. First, a new data set was structured around members of the House who started their House careers from 1955 through 1973 and who served at least eight terms (members of the class of 1973 were included if they served seven terms [the maximum possible by 1986]). Two hundred and five individuals met these restrictions. After employing the procedures described in previous chapters, I transcribed each representative's standardized scores for all of the analyzed variables in a master data file. Theoretically, then, information would be available on the tenure, electoral support, formal positions, constituency activity, and legislative activity for these 205 members during every term of service (up to and including their twelfth).

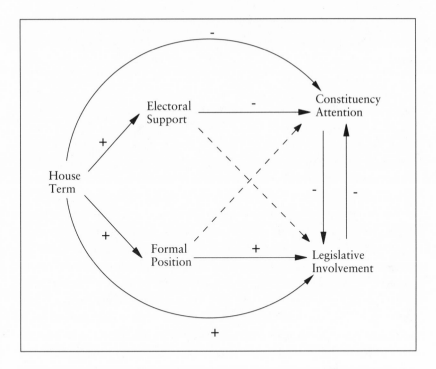

Figure 7.1. Expected Relationships of the Variables in the Integrated Model of Congressional Careers

In reality, we have less information than this because data are not available for all measures and for all individuals during the entire 1955–86 time period. For example, information on trips home was collected only from 1970 on and only from those members not representing a district that was close to the District of Columbia. Moreover, information on formal positions was recorded only for Democrats because the minority status of House Republicans since 1955 prohibited them from serving as committee or subcommittee chairs. These exclusions become important because in a typical multivariate model, information on all variables is required. Thus, estimations of coefficients for the complete model will be based on 51 representatives rather than all 205. The N will be much more than that, of course, because each term of each eligible representative is treated as a separate case.

The model would be easier to estimate were it not for the nonrecursive qualities introduced by the double arrow between constituency attention and legislative involvement. At all other junctures, the arrows move from left to right. Since it is theoretically sensible to hypothesize that constituency attention inversely affects legislative involvement and that legislative involvement inversely affects constituency attention, an estimation bias would result if each were used to predict the other or if the two arrows were omitted. Consequently, I employed two-stage least squares (2-SLS) rather than ordinary least squares. In this procedure, the remaining independent variables are used to predict constituency attention and (separately) legislative involvement. Along with the other variables, this predicted variable is then used in the second stage to explain variation in constituency attention. (For a discussion of two-stage least squares, see Asher 1976, 59–61.)

The variables themselves have been described in previous chapters and should be familiar by now, with two exceptions. Legislative involvement is a combination of the index of legislative activity, the measure of specialization, and the measure of legislative efficiency (all standardized by Congress and all described in chapter 5). Constituency attention is a combination of travel home and the percentage of staffers assigned to district rather than Washington offices (again both standardized). However, travel home has now been adjusted for the distance of the representative's home state from Washington. The states closest to Washington were excluded, states in the near South and Northeast were scored 0, states in the near Midwest and far South were coded 1, states in the Plains were coded 2, and states in the far West were coded 3. The constituency-attention variable, then, is actually a combination of staffers back in the district and the residual of a regression of trips home on distance from Washington (effort to travel home). This correction was unnecessary in chapter 6 when the issue was *change* in travel home over the course of a career. In this chapter, data run across careers but also across members, so distance from Washington must be taken into account.

Bivariate Relationships

Before turning to findings based on the complete model, it may be worthwhile to present the bivariate relationships. This practice would serve as a review of those links involving the connection of increasing House tenure to the variables discussed in previous chapters (electoral support, formal positions, legislative involvement, and constituency attention). It would provide some sense of the uncontrolled relationships between electoral

Table 7.1. Simple Correlations of Variables in the Integrated Model

Variables	R	N	Sign. Level
Tenure-electoral success	.17	1,983	.01
Tenure-formal position	.54	1,182	.01
Tenure-constituency attention	−.17	927	.01
Tenure-legislative involvement	.38	1,477	.01
Electoral support-constituency attention	.03	924	.43
Formal position-legislative involvement	.32	940	.01
Constituency atten.-legislative involvement	−.10	729	.01

Source: Computed by the author.

support and constituency activities, between formal positions and legislative activities, and between constituency and legislative activities. It would allow comparisons to be made between controlled and uncontrolled relationships. Finally, it would allow the maximum number of cases to be used in estimating each relationship whereas the complete model will require information on all variables before any case can be included in the regression.

Table 7.1 presents the simple correlation for the specified relationships along with the N and the level of statistical significance of each relationship. As can be seen, all the relationships save one are in the expected direction, and all the correlation coefficients save the same one are statistically significant. The problem child is the connection between electoral support and constituency attention. When no other factors are controlled, it is *not* the case that increasing electoral support brings decreasing attention to constituents.

Beyond this relationship, everything appears to be consistent with theory and with the findings of previous chapters. Increasing tenure in the House is usually accompanied by some increase in electoral support, by improved formal positions in the House, by diminished attention to constituent matters, and by increased attention to legislative concerns. Improved formal positions usually come in conjunction with heightened legislative involvement, and there appears to be a trade-off between legislative involvement and constituency attention.

The varying number of cases on which the correlations are based reflects the previously discussed exclusions that were made for certain computations. Members of the minority party do not have scores for formal House positions; terms in which members introduced fewer than four bills do not have the composite index for legislative involvement; and terms coming before 1970 do not have the overall index for constituency attention. Thus, a correlation such as that between legislative involvement and constituency attention only applies to legislatively active members serving after 1970.

Estimating the Complete Model

But uncontrolled correlation coefficients tell only a small part of the story. The key issue in this chapter is the extent to which the relationship of increasing tenure to a particular aspect of congressional life is real and the extent to which it is reduced by the addition of other relevant variables. In figure 7.2, 2-SLS standardized regression coefficients have been inserted into the model along with an indication of whether or not they achieve statistical significance at the .05 level (one-tail test).

It would appear from figure 7.2 that many of the bivariate relationships described in earlier chapters and summarized in table 7.1 hold up even with controls. As was determined in chapter 3, there is a strong positive relationship between increasing tenure in the House and the quality and quantity of formal positions members hold. This is no surprise. There is not, however, a corresponding relationship between increasing tenure and electoral support. This relationship is actually slightly negative, although it is not statistically significant. Part of the reason for the lack of a relationship between tenure and electoral support is the fact that in estimating the complete model, only those representatives with constituency attention scores were included and only those serving after 1970 possess constituency-attention scores. Recall from chapter 2 that the relationship between increasing tenure and electoral support used to be strong and direct but that in more recent years the relationship has vanished. Since cases for the complete model are drawn from these later years, it is easy to understand why the coefficient is insignificant. (The relationship between tenure and electoral support for all 205 representatives, while small, is positive and significant at .17—see table 7.1.)[2]

Somewhat surprisingly the intermediate variables of formal position

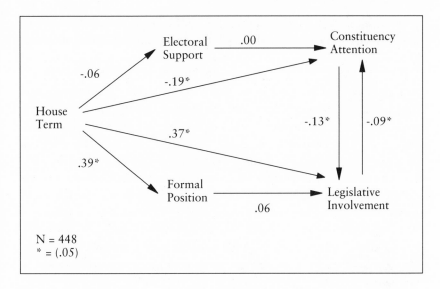

Figure 7.2. Two-Stage Least Squares Estimates of the Integrated Model

and electoral support have very little effect on the behavioral variables of legislative involvement and constituency attention once other variables in the equation are held constant. The connection between electoral support and constituency attention could not be weaker, and, once tenure is controlled, formal position does not have a significant effect on legislative involvement. Along with the previously explained sign reversal of the tenure–electoral support coefficient, the weakness of the relationship between formal position and legislative involvement is probably the biggest change from the simple bivariate correlations (table 7.1) to the controlled regression coefficients (figure 7.2). Formal position and legislative involvement are highly correlated, but when other factors, notably tenure, are controlled, the relationship all but disappears. In other words, to a large extent, the relationship between formal position and legislative involvement is spurious and is really due to the influence of tenure on both variables.

Some observers may have expected that the introduction of controls for formal position would reduce the influence of tenure on legislative involvement, but this is not the case. The tenure–legislative involvement connection remains rock solid after controls. These results suggest that two ten-term House veterans could both be expected to be legislatively involved even if one had a committee chairmanship and the other did not. Conversely, formal position, if it is not accompanied by extended tenure, may not be enough to generate substantial legislative involvement.

It might be anticipated that increased electoral support, other things being equal, would cause a representative to pay less attention to constituency matters. Figure 7.2 provides no support for this line of thought. Contrary to expectations, electoral support is uncorrelated with constituency attention. Instead, what comes through loudly and clearly is the direct influence of tenure on the behavioral variables even when the indirect effects of tenure through formal position and electoral support are allowed to operate separately. For the most part, these indirect effects add very little in the way of ability to explain variation in constituency attention and legislative involvement. For example, while there is a reasonably strong direct relationship between tenure and constituency attention $(-.19)$, the indirect relationship of tenure through electoral support is nonexistent $(-.06 \times .00 = .00)$.

Likewise, the effects of tenure on legislative involvement are direct $(.37)$, not indirect through formal positions $(.39 \times .06 = .02)$. Increasing tenure improves legislative involvement not because senior members tend to have better formal positions within the House (these formal positions do not independently generate sizable improvements in legislative involvement when other factors are controlled), but because of the less-tangible factors associated with extended exposure to the inner legislative workings of the body.

The trade-off between constituency attention and legislative involvement is apparent. Whichever way the arrow runs, the coefficient is negative and statistically significant. Even after controlling for tenure, formal position, and electoral security, it is difficult for a representative simultaneously to pay a great deal of attention to the constituency and to be highly involved in legislative matters. Constituency attention detracts from legislative involvement, and legislative involvement reduces constituency attention quite apart from these other factors.

Summarizing the findings to this point, the previously delineated effects of tenure on legislative involvement and constituency attention do not vanish when electoral support and formal position are introduced. Even when these factors are controlled, increasing House tenure brings reduced attention to constituents and, especially, increased involvement in legislation. On the other hand, once tenure is controlled, electoral support and formal position have generally weak and unstable effects on constituency attention and legislative involvement, respectively. The results presented so far in this chapter make it difficult to deny that increasing House tenure has an important independent effect on legislative and constituency activity.

Lags and Leads

Employing data on individual members at several stages of their careers amounts to a pooled time-series design. Analyzing these data in a cross-sectional fashion is revealing but does not begin to tap the information contained in the numbers. For example, many scholars have wondered about the proper causal order for these variables. Do legislative involvement and constituency attention at $t - 1$ affect electoral support or perhaps formal position at t? The results just presented show that electoral support performs poorly as an independent variable. Maybe it is actually the consequence of behavior in the term before. After all, one of the widely accepted explanations for the increase in the mean electoral support for House incumbents in the mid-1960s is that representatives of late have been working harder at servicing constituents (see Fiorina 1977a, 1977b). Is there evidence of this at the individual level? Similarly, are formal positions at t at all the consequence of behaviors the term before? Is quality legislative involvement able to generate more rapid acquisition of formal positions? This seems unlikely, but it is possible.

In figure 7.2 the lag was automatic since elections and position assignment for a given Congress are generally completed by the time legislative and constituency activities begin. To answer the questions posed in the preceding paragraph, however, legislative and constituency behavior in, say, the 98th Congress must be used to predict electoral results and leadership selection in the 99th. Thus, I have lagged legislative involvement and constituency attention in an effort to determine their effects on electoral support and the receipt of formal positions in the House.

The simple bivariate correlation of constituency attention $(t - 1)$ and electoral support (t) is .06 (N = 860), which is significant at the .10 level. Modest though it may be, this finding is suggestive. Both in the bivariate specification (table 7.1) and in the more complete model (figure 7.2), the connection between electoral security and constituency attention was weak and statistically insignificant. When constituency attention *precedes* the election, however, a glimmer of a relationship appears. The bivariate coefficient has doubled in size from table 7.1 (albeit only to .06) and now achieves at least a permissive significance level. In addition, the sign is what was expected; that is, more constituency attention is related to higher vote share in the next election. While extreme caution needs to be exercised in making even rough comparisons of bivariate coefficients, these results suggest that there may be more to the notion that constituency attention can help attract support in ensuing elections (see Fiorina 1977a, 1977b) than to the notion that electorally marginal members will be particularly attentive to their constituency.[3]

With regard to the relationship between formal position and legislative involvement, the correlation when position precedes involvement is .32 (see table 7.1); when involvement precedes position, it drops to .23. Thus, it would appear that, as might be expected, position leads to involvement more than involvement leads to committee or party position.

Dummy Variables

As James Stimson notes in his helpful discussion of pooled time-series data, ordinary least squares (the same would apply to two-stage least squares) "simply ignores the pooled structure of the data. . . . Each case is treated as independent of all others, not as part of a set of related observations" (1985, 918). Consequently, the time-honored nemeses of regression—autocorrelation and heteroscedasticity—will likely be more serious problems than usual unless between-unit variation is quite small relative to over-time variation.

In this case the units are the individual representatives and time is the multiple terms for which we have data on these representatives. As such, it can be said unequivocally that substantial between-unit variation exists. I have been emphasizing the very real behavioral consequences of career stage, but let there be no mistaking the fact that these over-time changes are quite modest when compared to the variation across individual representatives. As a result, the coefficients in figure 7.2, based as they are on standard regression procedures, are likely biased and inconsistent "as they become in effect proxies for omitted intercept terms" (Stimson 1985, 920).

The most intuitive of the three solutions proposed by Stimson for this problematic situation is to include dummy variables for each unit (representative), which is the approach adopted in this section. In order to maximize degrees of freedom, we must select units that have reasonably complete data, since each unit will have a dummy variable regardless of how much information we have over time for that unit. This means we must restrict this data base to Democrats (they will then have scores for the formal-position variable) whose careers run well past 1970 and whose districts are not too near the District of Columbia (they will then have scores for constituency attention) and who were at least minimally active legislators (they will then have scores for legislative involvement). Twenty-five individuals meet these requirements. Dummy variables were created for each of these individuals, then the procedures described in conjunction with figure 7.2 (2-SLS regression) were replicated except that twenty-four of the twenty-five dummies were also included. The results are presented in figure 7.3.

Since the dummy variables were used as control variables for purposes of obtaining more-accurate and less-biased coefficients, I do not present them in the figure.[4] The dummies themselves reveal little more than what can be gleaned from the raw data: some members, regardless of career stage, electoral situation, or formal position, pay much more attention to constituents and are more legislatively involved than others. We learn that people like John Breaux (D-La.), Pat Schroeder (D-Colo.), and to some extent Kika de la Garza (D-Tex.) were legislatively involved and that people like Jack Brinkley (D-Ga.), Bill Chappell (D-Fla.), and Glenn Anderson (D-Calif.) were attentive to constituents. Overall, there appears to be much more individual variation in constituency attention than in legislative involvement. Eleven of the twenty-four dummy coefficients are statistically significant when constituency attention is the dependent variable, and only two of the twenty-four are significant when legislative involvement is the dependent variable. Beyond this, however, little reason exists for discoursing on the dummy coefficients. The major purpose here is to determine what these between-unit controls do to the coefficients for tenure, formal position, and electoral support.

According to figure 7.3, these controls (perhaps in combination with the more-limited data base) do have some impact on the coefficients, although much of the basic message remains unchanged. The effect of increasing House tenure on legislative involvement is apparent again with this formulation. In fact, the impact of tenure is greater in figure 7.3 than in figure 7.2. Increasing tenure does not improve legislative involvement because of indirect effects through formal positions. While increasing tenure clearly brings better formal positions (.51), these positions do not

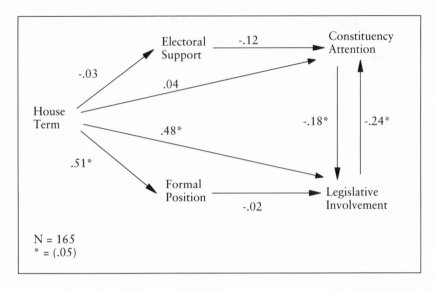

Figure 7.3. Two-Stage Least Square Estimates of the Integrated Model, Controlling for Between-Unit Variation

have an independent effect on legislative involvement once the effects of increasing tenure are taken into consideration (.51 × −.02 = −.01).

In general, the effects of the intermediate variables—electoral support and formal position—continue to be weak and insignificant, just as they were in figure 7.2. The connection between formal position and legislative involvement shrinks to virtual nonexistence. On the other hand, the inverse impact of electoral support on constituency attention strengthens somewhat when between-unit variation is controlled. In figure 7.3 the path coefficient is −.12, although with the reduced N it just misses achieving statistical significance at the .10 level.

The trade-off between legislative involvement and constituency attention is strengthened by the formulation leading to figure 7.3. The coefficient for the impact of constituency attention on legislative involvement is −.18, and the impact of the legislative-involvement instrument on constituency attention is even more notable. Apparently, substantial constituency attention frequently hinders legislative involvement just as substantial legislative involvement makes it more difficult to shower constituents with attention.

The biggest change from figure 7.2 to figure 7.3 is the diminished influence of tenure on constituency attention. Without the dummy variables, the direct impact is −.19, significant at the .05 level. With between-unit variation controlled, the direct impact is only .04. This coefficient is small, in the unexpected direction, and statistically insignificant. In fact, it might be said more broadly that this model casts some doubt on the degree to which constituency attention can be explained from these particular variables. While House tenure is intimately connected to formal position and to legislative involvement, it is only weakly connected to electoral support and perhaps to constituency attention. The remaining relationships in the model are modest at best when individual variation is controlled.

Individual Careers

I conclude this chapter with a brief look at the congressional careers of three individual representatives, as portrayed in the variables employed in this study. In many respects, sufficient data exist to treat cases individually. For each representative we have information on at least seven and up to twelve contiguous data points, and this information covers many aspects of congressional careers—from activities to positions to electoral support. The selection of specific representatives for this special treatment is governed again by the classes and characteristics for which we have more complete data. I have tried to select individuals with dissimilar career paths. Les Aspin's (D-Wis.) career has been well publicized and borders on the meteoric. He obtained a major-committee chairmanship (Armed Services) after only seven terms in the House. Frank Annunzio's (D-Ill.) House career was much more low profile even though he eventually became chairman of the House Administration Committee and of an important subcommittee (Consumer Affairs) of the Banking, Finance, and Urban Affairs Committee. Finally, James Corman (D-Calif.) represents an earlier career, having first been elected in 1960.

Les Aspin

Les Aspin (D-Wis.) was assigned to the Armed Services Committee as soon as he entered the House in 1971. He also served briefly on the District of Columbia, Government Operations, and Budget committees, but the major landmark of his career occurred in 1985, when, largely as a result of Armed Services chair Melvin Price's (D-Ill.) health problems and general frailty, a new committee leader was deemed necessary. Aspin was selected despite the fact that four other Democrats on the committee had more seniority. Two years later, many of Aspin's supporters, particularly liberals, were not pleased with his leadership of the committee on such matters as continued funding of the MX missile system and backing for the Nicaraguan Contras. Attempts to unseat Aspin were unsuccessful, but not by much.

How is Aspin's career captured in more systematic data? Legislatively, the changes are notable. In his first term (92d Congress), Aspin sponsored twenty-seven bills, but his legislative interests were unfocused and unpersuasive. Of the twenty-seven bills, eleven were referred to Ways and Means, eight to Energy and Commerce (as it is called now), five to Judiciary, and one each to Administration, Armed Services, and Interior. None of the bills made it out of committee. By the 99th Congress, Aspin's first as chairman of the full Armed Services Committee (he had chaired a subcommittee in the 98th), Aspin's raw quantity of bills was down, but his indices of specialization and efficiency were way up. He sponsored fifteen bills, fourteen of which went to his own Armed Services Committee. Moreover, four of these fifteen made it out of committee *and* out of the House (actually one was tabled in lieu of a nearly identical Senate bill). Relative to most members this is an impressive record of efficiency (1.4 standard deviations above the mean for the 99th Congress). Much of his improvement came between the 98th and 99th Congresses, with his assumption of the committee chairmanship.

On other counts, Aspin's changes are less noticeable. He never was big on speech making or the offering of amendments, compiling totals that ranked him well below average in all Congresses except the 99th, when his duties as chairman required him to speak frequently on the floor. Aspin's roll call behavior is worth some attention, especially in light of all the talk about whether he is a hawk or a dove or a chameleon. Aspin's (attendance-corrected) conservative coalition score for the first term of his career was only 8.6 percent, ranking him 1.47 standard deviations below the mean. In other words, he was among the more liberal members of the House. By his sixth term, however, Aspin had moderated substantially. In the 97th Congress, Aspin supported the conservative coalition 43.6 percent of the time it surfaced (and Aspin voted), which made his voting record only slightly more liberal than the mean in that Congress. This is where his record stayed in the 98th and the 99th. There was no detectable shift to the right in his roll call scores after he became chair of Armed Services. His party-unity scores actually went up from the 98th to the 99th. Perhaps those surprised by his ideological leanings as chairman were overly influenced by his early record, or perhaps there is some truth to the claim that he made misleading statements in his efforts to acquire the chairmanship.

As far as other aspects of Aspin's career are concerned, stability has been the dominant feature. Electorally, his district is not the safest in the world. He was held to around 56 percent of the vote in 1978, 1980, 1984, and 1988, all reasonably good years for Republicans, but he is usually in the low 60-percent range, and after ten straight victories his seat is probably secure. Perhaps this is part of the reason Aspin does not bestow an inordinate amount of attention on his constituents. He travels back to the district less (sixteen times in 1985; twelve times in 1983) than the norm, and he assigns fewer staffers (usually five or six) to the district than most. His level of constituency attention, however, does not appear to have declined much with increased tenure, and there is no indication of a precipitous decline in conjunction with his assumption of the heavy legislative burdens of the chairmanship.

Frank Annunzio

Frank Annunzio's (D-Ill.) career was anything but meteoric. After he served as a Chicago official for the United Steel Workers and subsequently drew the attention of Richard J. Daley, the machine asked Annunzio to run for Congress in 1964. He did and he won easily. Electorally, Annunzio's main problem came in 1971 when an adverse redistricting caused him to move from the near West Side to the northwest corner of the city. However, after winning the 1972 race with only 53 percent, he was safe until 1990 and his embarrassing association with the Savings and Loan debacle.

In Washington, Annunzio busied himself on the Banking Committee and established a record that usually, but certainly not always, pleased his political patron saints in organized labor and in the Daley machine. Even though he became chairman of the House Administration Committee in 1985, his main source of influence and interest has been the chairmanship of the Consumer Affairs Subcommittee of the Banking Committee (acquired in 1975). As with Aspin, a comparison of first term to last (for which we have data) reveals the evolution of a legislator. In the 89th

Congress Annunzio sponsored eleven bills, none of which came close to making it out of committee. Moreover, these bills were quite diverse. Four were referred to Banking, two to Veterans, and one each to Judiciary, Energy, Armed Services, Public Works, and Administration. Twenty years later, Annunzio sponsored almost the same number of bills (twelve), but this time eight of them not only made it out of committee but were passed on the floor of the House, and eleven of these twelve had been referred to Banking. By the 99th Congress, Annunzio was an efficient and specialized legislator.

Ideologically, Annunzio's record is similar to Aspin's. He began as a strong liberal, as evidenced by a record of support for the conservative coalition that was 1.3 standard deviations below the mean. After three terms of increasing support for this so-called coalition, Annunzio leveled off, still more liberal than the mean but less liberal than most northern Democrats. But in attention to constituents Annunzio's record is more reflective of typical patterns than is Aspin's. The influence of Annunzio's close call in 1972 may be apparent. After this race, Annunzio increased his travel home as well as his record of attendance at roll calls. A few terms later, as the evidence made it clear that his seat was safe, both travel home and the tendency to assign staffers back to the district dropped off rapidly. In 1985 he went home only fourteen times compared to thirty-one times in 1975, and in the 99th Congress only two of his staffers were assigned to a Chicago office, far below what was normal for members of Congress at that time.

James Corman

Some students of American politics may remember James Corman (D-Calif.) for the publicity resulting from the decision of his former wife (Patti Lear Corman, daughter of the inventor of the Lear Jet) to seek her own seat in the House of Representatives. Over her husband's strenuous objections, she twice challenged Barry Goldwater, Jr. in what was then California's Twentieth District. This disagreement over appropriate career goals and strategies apparently contributed to the breakup of the marriage. A more intriguing aspect of Corman's association with the House of Representatives is that he had the rare privilege of serving under two legendary committee chairmen—first Emanuel Celler and later Wilbur Mills.

Corman now speaks glowingly of both individuals. Of Celler he told me, "I wouldn't have considered missing one of Manny's committee meetings. They were too much fun, and they contained too much information. They were like seminars, and he was the master teacher." Celler allowed Corman to play an important role in the shaping of the 1964 Civil Rights Act. Despite Corman's lack of congressional experience at the time and despite the fact that he was not on the actual subcommittee involved with the markup, Celler was able to establish Corman as someone whom both the conservative southerners and the ardent civil rights advocates could at least tolerate.

And it is clear that Corman holds Mills's career in high regard and regrets its ignominious conclusion. As a young representative on the Ways and Means Committee, Corman had attempted to shift an exemption to a tax credit. The move went down in flames as his proposal received only four votes out of the entire committee membership. After the room had apparently cleared, a despondent Corman was startled to find Chairman Mills standing over him. Mills gave him a pat on the back and said, "Don't feel bad, I tried exactly the same thing when I first came on this committee and had the same result."

Corman must have learned something about the legislative process from these two. The nine bills he sponsored in his first term went to six different committees and, like his tax credit, failed to advance out of committee. But in his last term, he sponsored thirty-nine bills and all but three went to a single committee—Ways and Means. Seven of them passed the committee *and* received majority support on the House floor.

When it came to roll call voting, unlike Aspin and Annunzio, Corman never lost one scintilla of his liberal convictions. He entered the House opposing the conservative coalition more than 90 percent of the time, and he left the House opposing it more than 90 percent of the time. His district was never particularly secure, as might be expected of a liberal from his particular portion of southern California, and he was defeated in 1980. The data indicate that Corman slowed down prior to this election. His travel home dropped from .5 standard deviations above the mean in the 95th Congress (an astounding figure for someone representing a West Coast district) to .75 standard deviations below the mean in the 96th Congress, and his roll call participation also dropped to well below the mean in the 96th Congress.

These factors may or may not have contributed to his very narrow defeat in a strong year for Republicans, but his activity patterns in the 96th Congress could be construed as those of a representative who has "gone Washington." Corman was clearly involved up to his neck in Ways and Means legislation, and he was not doing some of the things that impress constituents such as making the red-eye flights between Washington and Los Angeles and riding the Capitol subway between his office and floor votes.

Conclusion

What then can be said as a result of this effort to integrate the many parts of the congressional career? Most importantly, it can be said that career stage matters and that it matters not just because of an association with electoral support or formal positions held. As members progress through a career in the House, they usually become less attentive to constituents and more involved with legislation. This is the case even when increasing tenure does not bring the representative a more electorally secure district and a more favorable positional base within the House.

The direct relationships between increasing tenure and the behavioral indicators employed here were typically the strongest. This basic conclusion held up in a variety of specifications, from uncontrolled bivariate correlations to a more completely specified two-stage-least-squares technique, and from procedures that treat the pooled data as a cross section to those that are more truly longitudinal. Increasing tenure has a substantial independent effect on congressional behavior. Since the variables have been standardized for mean activity levels in each Congress and since we have looked at many cohorts, we can be confident that the effects are not period or generational. They are indeed life-cycle effects.

Simply being in the institution for extended periods of time brings changes in legislative involvement presumably because of an improved understanding of the legislative process, of what is possible and what is not, of the value of specialization, and of the importance of being active. Similarly, extended tenure directly and inversely affects constituency attention because increased legislative involvement requires it, because energies abate, because a reputation has been established, and perhaps because even representatives who have been marginal in several consecutive elections begin to expect that they may continue to be reelected.

Less centrally, improved positions obviously do go along with increased tenure, but these positions, in turn, have a surprisingly modest effect on legislative involvement. An improved electoral situation, however, is no longer a perquisite of increased tenure, and electoral safety or insecurity has little to do with constituency attention. Finally, constituency attention and legislative involvement, even when all other variables in the model are held constant, are inversely related to each other. Those members who are active with the constituency usually have to make legislative sacrifices, and those who are very legislatively involved find it difficult to devote resources to constituents.

8 Conclusion:
Gary Myers
Left Too Soon

Gary Myers (R-Pa.) was elected in 1974 when he beat incumbent Frank Clark (D-Pa.) by, among other things, calling attention to Clark's incessant junketeering. In many ways, Myers's victory was stunning. After all, 1974 was not a year in which a lot of Republicans were able to defeat Democratic incumbents. Moreover, Pennsylvania's Twenty-fifth District (the hilly steel-mill country north of Pittsburgh) is not exactly Republican territory. For the most part, the district is a labor stronghold, populated by ethnic blue-collar workers who like a voting record similar to that compiled by Frank Clark—economically liberal and socially conservative.

But Myers won with 54 percent of the vote and in the process displayed energy, intelligence, tenacity, and an ability to take full advantage of each of the many mistakes Clark had made. In 1976 Myers refused to accept Political Action Committee money, spurned big fund-raisers, spent less than $40,000, and still expanded his vote share to 57 percent. Myers did not always vote the way the unions would have liked, but his moderate Republican voting record was a reasonable match with the residents of the district, alongside of whom he had worked for many years. Indications are that Myers could have made this a safe seat by doing all the things representatives know they need to do these days.

But Myers did not have the stomach for it, and he decided against seeking reelection in 1978. Instead, he returned to being a foreman at the steel mill. When I visited with him several years ago, he was obviously proud of the fact that he had been able to convince his bosses to facilitate my interview by adding an extra half-hour to his lunch break. He met me in the cafeteria area, wearing a hard hat and steel-toed shoes and clutching his lunch pail. No mahogany paneling, potted palms, and overstuffed furniture here. No bluster about how the people of the district loved him or what an important person he had been back in Washington. I venture to say there will never be a Gary Myers Memorial Library in Butler, Pennsylvania, or anywhere else. He would not stand for it.

Myers is simply an utterly sensible human being who, after working tirelessly to get to Congress and after serving as best he could for four years, came to the conclusion that he did not want to spend his career there. Now he is the odd man out. For the most part his coworkers at the mill have difficulty coming to grips with what Myers has done and where he has been. And certainly no one in Washington—then or now—has the foggiest notion of why someone would voluntarily leave the U.S. House of Representatives to punch the time clock as foreman at a western Pennsylvania steel mill. To be sure, none of this matters to Gary Myers. He never craved special treatment, and he never received it (the mill agreed to hold a job for him while he was in Washington but nothing more—no moving up the pay scale or the seniority scale). In fact, he has little tolerance for those who do demand special treatment, and this may be a large part of the reason he was uncomfortable in Washington. He is, by a wide margin, the most extraordinary member of Congress I have met.

"Typical" Careers and Term Limitations

No doubt the truncated House career of Gary Myers could be used to illustrate a large number of points about the modern Congress. For example, Myers's premature departure may suggest that the wrong kind of individual is encouraged to run for (see Fowler and McClure 1989) and to stay in Congress these days. This is not a new thought. Several congressional observers have claimed that the only people to survive and to prosper in the modern Congress are the frequently air-headed, blow-dry, John-Kennedy-look-alike members, whose only agenda is self-promotion. Real people, it is alleged, do not want to be a part of all the artificiality and posturing. The merits of this critique aside, my purpose in describing the career of Gary Myers is to introduce what I feel is a needed counterbalance to the belief that virtually all members of Congress have been serving since shortly after the Jurassic period.

The mean number of years served by the 435 members of the House in the 101st Congress was just over eleven, and the median terms served was five. Fifty-five percent of the membership in the 101st was elected in 1980 or after (see also Swift 1989). By historical standards, modern House careers are long, but in many other respects, they could be viewed as fairly short. The length of the typical congressional career, for example, is not out of line with the length of careers in many other developed national legislatures. Congressional commentators frequently emphasize lengthy careers, thereby leaving a slightly inaccurate impression. My own presentation in the preceding pages may contribute to this view since it has featured figures displaying the contours of eight-term, ten-term, and twelve-term House careers. While I hope readers understand why this was done, I hope they also understand that fifteen-, twenty-, and twenty-five-year House careers are not the norm. Eighty-five percent of the current membership has *not* served ten terms in the House. In length at least the congressional career of Gary Myers is far more typical than the career of Emanuel Celler.

One of the refrains of this study has been that before valid opinions can be formed on issues such as mandatory term limitations for members, it is necessary to understand what changes occur during a career. Forced congressional rotation may sound farfetched, but it is a powerful concept in many parts of the political system. As mentioned earlier, the general idea has the support of influential people and groups, including Ralph Nader's network and the National Federation of Independent Businesses, it has been widely (and increasingly) discussed in the popular press, and, most importantly, it receives overwhelming approval from the American public as a whole. According to a Gallup poll conducted in late 1989, 70 percent of Americans "favor curtailing the number of years a person can serve in Congress." Relatedly, 65 percent of the public favor a mandatory retirement age for members of Congress ("Most Want to Limit Time" 1990).

Further, unless turnover increases markedly in the next few elections (and there is a small chance that it may as a result of redistricting in 1992), it seems safe to say that the drumbeat for reform will become louder. The most serious obstacle is the membership itself, which, not surprisingly, opposes term limitations by approximately a 2 to 1 margin. In fact, the only surprise is that 33 percent actually support the idea (support in the Senate is even higher—43 percent favor term limitations). Thus, the proposal to place mandatory limits on congressional service is not an out-of-the-mainstream idea. It receives broad and growing support in a variety of places and has even become law for some state legislatures. Is a limitation on the number of years a person could serve in Congress a good idea or a bad idea? A brief summary of the main findings of this study should set the stage for the answer to this question.

Things change for members of Congress as their careers progress. The usual pattern as postwar members have acquired additional tenure is for them to become electorally safer, to assume better formal House positions, to participate less in roll calls, to otherwise moderate or maintain their roll call voting patterns, to become less attentive to constituents, to become more active in purely legislative matters, and to become more legislatively specialized and efficient. The situations and activities of senior members are usually quite different from what they were when these senior members were junior.

But these contours themselves have shifted over the years. Recent careers are no longer characterized by improving electoral security; after the first three or four terms, the acquisition of quality formal positions is not as strongly related to tenure; the decline in constituency attention over careers is not nearly as precipitous as it used to be; and early-career roll call behavior is now a more accurate predictor of late-career roll call behavior than was the case years ago. The suspicions raised in chapter 1 about the political life cycle being replaced by an essentially unvarying stint in Congress receive quite a bit of support from the data. At several points, one appropriate conclusion is that, given the increasingly undistinguished contours of careers, there may not be the kind of professional growth we would like to see when many of our national legislators spend year after year in the House. If the story ended here, it seems to me, support would be provided for the term limiters. What is the harm of banning extended tenure if senior members are just like junior members?

But this somewhat pessimistic conclusion is not entirely warranted. With regard to one major cluster of variables, the data did *not* indicate a flattening of career contours with the passage of the decades. In fact, these variables seemed to demonstrate that career-based differentiation was actually increasing. I refer to legislative involvement. The conclusion that the differences in the legislative contribution of junior and senior members have grown is startling, as conventional wisdom on career-based change probably offered the clearest expectations in regard to these very activities. The demise of the apprenticeship norm was supposed to have made all members roughly equal in their likelihood of sponsoring bills and amendments and generally being involved in the legislative process. Instead, the findings presented in chapter 5 demonstrate that there is now even more variation in legislative involvement from early-career stages to late than there was thirty years ago. The learning process is particularly evident in our measures of the key variables legislative specialization and efficiency.[1]

What this means, of course, is that requiring representatives to leave after a set number of years would likely result in a devastating loss of legislative acumen, expertise, and activity. With no other area of congressional activity is the learning curve as evident as it is with legislative activity. Moreover, the results of chapter 7 make it obvious that simply doling out formal positions to the junior members who remain after the senior members have been exiled will in no way take up the legislative slack created by these forced departures. Even when formal positions are held constant, increasing tenure is strongly and positively related to legislative activity as well as to legislative specialization and efficiency. Tenure in and of itself helps members to be focused and successful legislative players, and this situation has definitely not gone into abeyance in the 1980s.[2]

For these reasons, my conclusion is that mandatory term limitations for members of Congress is a bad idea. I say this not as an apologist for Congress; it needs reform. For what it is worth, I worry about the lack of competition in congressional elections, about members inventing ways to circumnavigate ethics codes, about the role of money in the process, about superficiality replacing legislating, and about shameless pork-barrel politics in a time of massive budget deficits. I feel we need to initiate public financing of congressional elections along with a range of other reforms. But these reforms should not include mandatory term limitations. Attaining a more competitive and open legislative process does not need to come at the expense of those representatives making the biggest legislative contribution. We need their legislative experience.

In some respects, the conclusion that imposing term limitations would remove experienced legislators is virtually definitional. How could it be otherwise? But the specifics of what would be lost were unclear since never before have we had systematic data on precise longitudinal variations in the contributions and activities of several classes of representatives. Moreover, many descriptions of the modern House hold that there is no reason to expect senior members to be much different than junior members, what with the demise of the apprenticeship norm and the general democratization of the body in terms of resource distribution and political opportunities. The distinctive legislative role of senior members in the 1980s House was anything but a foregone conclusion, particularly when juxtaposed with other aspects of the congressional career that, in the 1980s, are totally unrelated to tenure.

The Nature of Modern
Congressional Service

But determining whether or not it is wise to limit congressional terms is just one benefit of the broad look at modern congressional careers I have tried to present here. Careerism in general is such a big part of modern congressional service that it is difficult to understand one without understanding the other. In addition to the findings relating to term limitations, this broader inspection has generated several noteworthy conclusions.[3]

First, other things being equal, senior representatives are not now any more secure than they were at the beginning of their careers. Conclusions to the contrary are likely the result of a failure to appreciate the very real effects of attrition (differential mortality) and/or a failure to recognize the changing shape of modern electoral careers. Second, representatives now acquire formal House positions earlier in their careers than they used to. This may seem like mere confirmation of conventional wisdom, but previous empirical research seldom supported conventional theory (and was based on designs that did not separate the effects of real contour shifts from effects generated simply by the proliferation of party and committee positions). Third, as careers unfold, representatives' roll call behavior becomes less liberal, less extreme, less supportive of the party, and just less (that is, participation goes down). Fourth, legislative involvement, here defined as a combination of legislative activity, legislative specialization, and legislative efficiency, increases with tenure. Moreover, contrary to all the talk about diminished apprenticeship, the increase in legislative involvement has become more abrupt rather than less in the 1980s. Fifth, representatives travel home less now than they did ten years ago, presumably because office allotments were consolidated. Even in relative terms, however, tenure is associated with declining travel home and attention to the district. Finally and more generally, the political life-cycle view does not fit modern careers on a number of counts. I find little evidence of the curvilinear patterns so prevalent in the life-cycle view, and many of the connections hypothesized by this view of congressional careers do not emerge from a multivariate analysis. Changes in constituency attention and legislative involvement, for example, are not due to changes in electoral support and formal positions nearly so much as they are due to increasing tenure.

Putting all these findings together (and drawing some inferences from them) leads to the following picture of the modern congressional career. New members now set up shop quickly in terms of their constituency-oriented operations. Polls, political parties, seminars, management guides, focus groups, seasoned staffers, delegation colleagues, and common sense all help new members to learn very early how to organize and to initiate a smoothly running constituency operation. This operation becomes routinized almost immediately, with standard trips home, standard response letters, and standard procedures for dealing with constituent requests. This is not to say no learning curve exists in matters pertaining to the constituency. Certainly Fenno's work exposes the artistry with which some members are able to work the district, or, more accurately, the many different districts, usually changing styles while often not changing messages (1978, 157–60). Such skills cannot be taught in a seminar and are probably developed and refined over the years. But this kind of personal interaction is only a part of the congressional office's constituency-oriented activities and is largely unmeasurable. Much less variation exists in other aspects of constituency matters—both across members and for the same member over time—than there used to be. The routinized career, it seems to me, predominates in the area of measurable constituency activities. A formula exists, and most members follow it. Career stasis has captured the parts of the congressional career that are most amenable to a kind of machinelike bureaucratic operation.

With regard to legislative activity, career stage still makes a great difference, as has already been discussed at length. But lest we be too complacent, it is possible that the routinization currently characterizing some aspects of the House career will spread. Constituency/electoral concerns have a way of gobbling up legislative/policy concerns. Constituency service used to be thought of as a policy matter. An elderly representative who retired in 1978 captured this notion when he said, "You learn more about the job by doing constituent service work than anything else. It shows you where the loopholes and cracks in the legislation are. It tells you whether or not the legislation is doing what it is supposed to do" (Hibbing 1982a, 54). Although many members would probably deny this, and although I am sure there is the occasional incident to the contrary, I doubt that constituency service activities and legislative agendas/actions are intimately related anymore. The sheer volume and perceived electoral importance of constituency service have caused congressional offices to become much more mechanistic in this regard.

At times it appears the same fate is befalling formal positions in the House. More and more they are used as constituent-impressing newsletter fodder—the congressional equivalent of résumé filler. Less and less they serve as true bases for concerted legislative action. Many subcommittee chairs put the subcommittee through its paces, hoping to attract some media attention along the way. Then, when it comes time to cut the real legislative deal, they watch from the sidelines as Appropriations or Ways and Means make the key decisions (see Ehrenhalt 1986, 2136–37). No doubt I have overstated the case, as many subcommittees are capable of making lasting public policy changes, but the fact remains that what seems legislative is not always legislative. It could be said further that elections now rarely turn on policy matters, not even the simplistic policy element contributed by the partisan-swing pattern of years gone by. Today scandals, stylistic missteps, and personal embarrassments are more likely to spell defeat than are perceived partisan responsibilities for policy failures (see Bauer and Hibbing 1989).

Equally disturbing is the increasing ability of early-career roll call activity to predict late-career roll call activity. This suggests that while the focus and crafting of legislation may still improve with the passing of the years, modern members may feel increasingly constrained in their roll call behavior. The unblinking observation and ubiquitous, simple-minded vote-scale calculations of interest groups, combined with the willingness of challengers to pull any and every vote from the files, probably work to discourage ideological shifts of all but the most subtle varieties. In the modern environment, cries of "flip-flop" cannot be countered by a statement such as, "Yes, after reading and reflecting, I have decided my earlier position was not correct." As a result, the aforementioned continuing career-based effects visible in legislative activities do not seem to apply to roll call voting.

The good news is that the findings presented in this study indicate learning and professional growth are still evident in some important parts of the legislative career. The bad news is that just because this was true in the 1980s does not mean it will be so in the 1990s. The trends do not seem favorable. Countless pressures are pushing members in the direction of static careers in which past procedures become a formulaic substitute for careful thought and reflection on current situations. Stability itself is not always bad, but it is bad in the case of an institution that is supposed to be responsive to changing public moods and concerns. The bureaucratization of Congress is a danger to its ability to be sensitive to these changes; not bureaucratization in the sense of burgeoning staffs but in the sense of an increase in the number of members who are too risk-averse to use their imagination, information, and experience. (If it is in fact the desire on the part of members for extended congressional careers that fosters such a regimented approach, the advocates of term limitations may find their ranks growing.)

Political scientists are often blamed for not appreciating the artistry of congressional politics and politicians, for trying to quantify that which defies quantification. But the truth is that the behavior of many, but certainly not all, members of the modern Congress only serves to encourage our tendencies in this regard. Under the guise of "entrepreneurial politics" or a "problem-solving approach to representation" they often downplay their positions on the major issues of the day. I venture to say that most students of Congress would gladly exchange explanatory capabilities for an influx of representatives who are willing to make congressional service something other than the political equivalent of painting by the numbers.

Notes

Chapter 1

1. Somewhat surprisingly, since about 1970 there has been a decrease in the average length of stay in the House. Mean years of service reached a peak of 12 in the 92d Congress but declined to less than 9 by the 99th Congress. The precise meaning of this reversal of the long-standing trend toward longer and longer careers in the House is difficult to say, (especially since in the last three Congresses mean years of service increased again) but it is clearly at odds with notions that continuous and monotonic institutionalization has permanently beset the body.

2. Gary Jacobson (1987a) has even argued that since electoral inconsistency increased at about the same time as the average share of the vote for House incumbents increased, the net effect may have been very little change. In other words, Jacobson believes incumbents are objectively no safer than they used to be because a large margin of victory is just as likely to be followed by electoral defeat as was a smaller margin of victory years ago. See Bauer and Hibbing (1989) for a different view of the evidence bearing on this point.

3. Parker (1986b) has attempted to determine if a trade-off exists between formal position and attention to constituents. But even here, it may be assumed that the relationship between power on the Hill and constituency attention has changed from a strong negative relationship in the 1950s and 1960s to a much weaker correlation in recent years (since all members do a lot of constituency service, there is little variation in one of the variables). This concept is not tested by Parker, although there is something intriguing in the findings he reports. It appears as though committee leaders lag behind the mean amount of constituency service work for all members in the early years but approach the mean in later years. If substantiated, this result would be consistent with the idea that there has been a shift away from the political life cycle.

Chapter 2

1. Moreover, the academic "models" vary widely and produce a disconcertingly heterogeneous set of predictions for any given election year. Also, the

standard errors of most of the regressions equations in this area are very large and should encourage us to be cautious about the accuracy of resultant predictions. For further evidence on the local politics side of the argument, see Ehrenhalt (1984, 2979). For information on partitioning the influences of national and local forces, see Katz (1973); Stokes (1973); Claggett, Flanigan, and Zingale (1984); and Vertz, Frendreis, and Gibson (1987).

2. Throughout this chapter, both share of the vote and percentage victorious will be used as measures of incumbent security. In the case of an individual career, however, percentage victorious makes little sense, so Celler's electoral career is only viewed according to the share of the vote he received at different stages.

3. The number of cases naturally decreases as we move toward higher levels of tenure. It should be recognized that means at the top of the tenure scale are correspondingly less stable. The following are the N's from the first through the twentieth reelection bids in order: 1,478, 1,171, 984, 800, 677, 549, 359, 290, 221, 172, 141, 117, 75, 56, 33, 25, 21, 17, 14.

4. Mean N's for figure 2.5, from first to fifteenth term, are 380, 291, 240, 202, 170, 146, 109, 91, 73, 66, 41, 32, 28, 19, 14.

5. This type of partisan correction was unnecessary in the analyses reported earlier in this chapter since the rationale for the partisan correction is diminished by the averaging together of data from several classes—classes that are generally quite diverse as far as partisan composition is concerned.

6. When single classes are studied, the analysis is not able to extend as far into careers. Average N's for the four classes presented in figure 2.9 by tenure level are 81, 65, 43, 42, 31, 27, 26, 15.

7. All three coefficients are statistically significant at the .05 level; N = 14, 16, and 14, respectively. These results are somewhat at odds with Jacobson's finding of greater variability from one election to the next.

Chapter 3

1. Actually the figures reported here represent Landrum's corrected party-support scores, which are calculated by the following commonly employed formula:

corrected party support = [party support/(party support + party opposition)] × 100.

This correction takes into account the fact that failure to vote on included issues lowers party-support scores.

2. See Polsby, Gallaher, and Rundquist (1969) for specific data on changes in the tendency to obey the seniority rule.

3. There are obvious problems with this threefold classification—problems most readily evident when one considers the policy and constituency committee category. Substantial differences exist in the clout of the Energy and Commerce Committee as opposed to the Merchant Marine Committee, yet respondents were forced to treat them equally. Unfortunately, the alternative was to ask our respondents to give distinct ratings to twenty-two separate committee chair positions and twenty-two separate subcommittee chair positions (or hundreds of individual subcommittee chair positions). Since this strategy is unworkable, the three-category option and its accompanying oversimplification seemed the most sensible. Of course, the use of three different categories of committees and subcommittees represents a substantial improvement over previous efforts, which generally do no more than take note of the number of individuals holding subcommittee chairs regardless of whether they are subcommittees of prestige committees or of less desirable committees.

4. The Rules Committee has occasionally used two subcommittees, and since 1974 the Ways and Means Committee has been forced to have subcommittees. These entities were treated in the same fashion as subcommittees of policy and constituency committees.

5. According to the procedures employed here, a member was given only one score per committee. If a representative held two subcommittee chairs on the same committee, for example, he/she was given credit for only one. Further, no member was given more than 100 points even though combinations of committee and party assignments on occasion would have put members over 100.

6. It should be noted that the skewness statistic is statistically significant at the .01 level for all sixteen Congresses, indicating that the odds of that degree of deviation from the normal distribution occurring by chance are extremely small.

7. The procedures used in this chapter have not captured change in the House resulting from the shifting nature of the positions themselves. Obviously, this kind of thing happens. For example, the Rules Committee and, therefore, its chairmanship are less a source of independent power than was the case in the sixties, prior to the reforms that made the committee essentially an "arm of the Democratic leadership" (see Oppenheimer 1977). Alan Ehrenhalt argues persuasively that ordinary members of prestige committees like Appropriations and Ways and Means have gained in importance relative to subcommittee chairs of policy and constituency committees (1986, 2131–38).

8. Actually, Delaney had served one previous term early in the 1940s. Mayhew presents Delaney's much-discussed Rules Committee vote against the 1961 Federal Aid to Education Bill as an exercise in courage since it took many members off the hook by saving them from having to cast a floor vote. In truth, Delaney, a staunch Roman Catholic from the most Irish district in New York, had a long record of opposition to bills he felt would not have been beneficial to parochial schools.

9. The initial class in the study—1955—also is an exception, presumably because the Democrats had just become the majority party again after a brief stint in the wilderness. Because of the atypical nature of the class of 1955, some of the conclusions in Stubben and Hibbing (1987), which were largely based on a preliminary analysis of the classes of 1955 and 1971, are not as generalizable as we had hoped.

10. It makes little sense to analyze classes more recent than 1975 since they have not served enough terms. Even the class of 1975 cannot be viewed out to the full eight terms used for the other classes in figures 3.2 and 3.3.

Chapter 4

1. Conservative coalition support scores correlate quite strongly with other measures of ideology (see Poole 1981). The data start with 1957 since conservative coalition scores were not recorded prior to that date.

2. The figures reported are the average of the standard deviation for the various classes at each career stage, weighted by the number of members of that class reaching that particular career stage.

Chapter 5

1. Rohde (1988, 140) actually argues that members' perceptions and expectations are more important to study than behavior patterns. Obviously, however, if the members say they think an apprenticeship norm is good but behave as if the apprenticeship norm is bad, what they say they think is of minimal consequence.

2. Results were also computed using a "two highest committee" procedure. This was the approach favored by Matthews (1960, 275). Conclusions were very similar when this approach was adopted, reflecting the fact that one procedure produces figures that correlate fairly highly with the other (.83).

3. To reduce coding demands, only the first sessions of six of the sixteen Congresses (89th–94th) were included. This should not create any systematic bias in the kinds of conclusions drawn since the relative activity of members will be similar regardless of whether one year or two years of information is collected. Still, to the extent that certain members or classes were either more or less likely than others to concentrate their legislative activities in the first rather than the second session, some distortion could result. Finally, some irregularities may exist in the manner in which the *Congressional Record* index records information on amendment introduction in the recent (97th, 98th, and 99th) Congresses. These indices have not been aggregated over entire terms yet. There appear to be lapses and double countings in the indices, which, as of now, cover (usually) three-week

periods. There is no reason to assume these irregularities alter the relative activity levels of certain classes or members. However, they would raise questions if these sources were used to compute mean activity levels for the entire membership of those few Congresses.

4. See Pedhazur (1982, 426–30) for a description of the appropriate technique.

5. This potential trade-off between legislative activity and attention to constituents/reelection will be addressed directly in chapter 7.

6. Or perhaps, as the quote suggests, the real changes have come in the committee participation of first-term members rather than in floor participation.

7. As before, results were obtained for all sixteen classes. Presentation of results for all classes would not appreciably alter the conclusions drawn.

8. These basic messages are not altered when mortality effects are controlled. The analysis just discussed was replicated on only those members who served more than seven terms. For space reasons, I will not present the results in graphic form, but by all appearances, general conclusions are not affected by the exclusion of those members who spent shorter periods of time in the House.

9. Detailed analyses of legislative efficiency by class are not provided because of the interaction of small N's and the distorted distributions resulting from so many values of 0.

Chapter 6

1. Even though the data involve travel undertaken during only the first term of a Congress, some vouchers for this travel may have been filed well after the travel was actually undertaken. Consequently, the *Report of the Clerk* was searched for the year in which travel was undertaken as well as in the six months after the travel was taken. A few requests may have been logged after this six-month period, but (on the basis of some spot checks) the number appears to be very small, and there is no reason to believe their omission would create any systematic bias.

2. It is possible that the reapportionment of 1982, by creating more seats in the far-distant Southwest portion of the country and fewer seats in the Northeast, may have contributed marginally to the decrease in reimbursed travel to the home district.

3. Of course, Fiorina (1977a, 1989) argues that the *content* of information about the incumbent may be more important than the percentage of constituents who are able to recognize or to recall the name of their representative. This is a more difficult concept to glean from survey data, although the questions about the nature of contact with the incumbent (addressed shortly) speak to this issue somewhat more directly.

4. The case of Hawkins is an unusual one. Probably because of its memorable

nature, the name of Hawkins's challenger in 1978 (Uriah Fields) was recognized by all respondents in the district even though Fields received only 15 percent of the vote in 1978. It is obviously impossible for an incumbent to have a sizable visibility advantage over a challenger if that challenger has perfect recognition; thus, it is unsurprising that Hawkins had a smaller gap than his years in the House would lead us to predict.

Chapter 7

1. However, they do figure in indirectly. In order to estimate two-stage-least-squares models, the system needs to be identified. This means at least one variable must be influencing constituency attention but not legislative involvement while at least one other variable must be influencing legislative involvement but not constituency attention. Thus, the absence of a theoretical connection between electoral support and legislative involvement and between formal positions and constituency attention makes it possible to estimate the model.

2. The analyses involving electoral support were also replicated with a restriction to only those representatives who were always faced with major-party opposition in general elections as well as to only nonsouthern representatives. Neither of these exclusions modified coefficients or conclusions significantly.

3. In addition to these experimentations with lags and leads, I also investigated the possibility that variables computed by first-differencing would be more powerful. For example, it may be that a decline in electoral support from one election to the next would be a better indicator of the need for concern than a variable based simply on share of the vote in the last election. For the most part, however, analyses based on first-differencing procedures yielded disappointing results.

4. These procedures reduced the degrees of freedom to 137.

Chapter 8

1. One concern of some readers may be the effects of the standardization procedures employed so generously in this research. Computing z-scores changes the issue at hand but does not change the conclusions generated. Instead of talking about whether senior members go home less than when they were junior, the issue becomes whether they go home less in relation to their colleagues in that particular Congress. While standardized scores have been utilized more than the raw scores, because I feel they are more appropriate given various procedural and institutional changes that have occurred, actual values are meaningful too. Fortunately, if raw values are substituted, the messages emphasized in this final chapter would not need to be altered. Election results have become flatter in

actual and in standardized terms; the results for formal position careers were presented both ways (see figures 3.2 and 3.3); roll call behavior is similar with uncorrected and corrected data (although with uncorrected data the career-based decline in participation is naturally smaller); and legislative involvement increases with tenure in absolute as well as relative terms. The only shift in conclusions necessitated by a reliance on absolute data applies to constituency attention. Even though in relative terms senior members pay less attention to their districts as they grow older, in absolute terms they have paid more attention. This particularly reflects the sharp increase in the practice of sending staffers back to the district, which has occurred since the early 1960s, but when life-cycle effects are isolated from these period effects, the career-based decline is evident.

2. Another possible concern is simply the magnitude of the career-based movements of which so much has been made here. In discussing shifts in z-scores, Verba and Nie (1972) convert each standard deviation into 100 parts so that a shift of .02 standard deviations becomes a shift of 2. Such a transformation seems unnecessary since it does not affect the actual size of the movement. While small fractions of standard deviations may not seem like much, they frequently represent shifts across several dozen representatives (see the normal distribution chart of any statistics book). For shifts of this magnitude to occur just because of career-stage effects seems noteworthy.

3. What has been provided here is only the beginning of that which can profitably be mined from a career-based perspective. A wide variety of additional variables remain to be scrutinized from the vantage point afforded by changes over careers. The availability of financial data beginning around 1974 will soon make possible the study of fund-raising careers (standardized for period effects, no doubt). Committee activity has been largely ignored here. Given its importance, much more needs to be done on how it changes over the course of a career. Use of the franking privilege may vary with tenure. Success in pork-barrel politics may be related to tenure (see Wilson 1986, 59). And the list could go on and on.

References

Abram, Michael, and Joseph Cooper. 1968. "The Rise of Seniority in the House of Representatives." *Polity* 1:52–85.

Abramowitz, Alan I. 1980. "A Comparison of Voting for U.S. Senator and Representative in 1978." *American Political Science Review* 74:633–40.

Abramson, Paul R. 1979. "Comment: On the Relationship between Age and Party Identification." *Political Methodology* 6:447–55.

Alford, John R., and David W. Brady. 1989. "Personal and Partisan Advantage in U.S. Congressional Elections, 1846–1986." In *Congress Reconsidered*, 4th ed., ed. Lawrence C. Dodd and Bruce I. Oppenheimer. Washington, D.C.: Congressional Quarterly.

Alford, John R., and John R. Hibbing. 1981. "Increased Incumbency Advantage in the House." *Journal of Politics* 43:1042–61.

Asher, Herbert B. 1973. "The Learning of Legislative Norms." *American Political Science Review* 63:496–508.

———. 1975. "The Changing Status of the Freshman Representative." In *Congress in Change*, ed. Norman J. Ornstein. New York: Praeger.

———. 1976. *Causal Modeling*. Beverly Hills, Calif.: Sage.

Asher, Herbert B., and Herbert F. Weisberg. 1978. "Voting Change in Congress: Some Dynamic Perspectives on an Evolutionary Process." *American Journal of Political Science* 22:391–425.

Bach, Stanley, and Steven S. Smith. 1988. *Managing Uncertainty in the House of Representatives*. Washington, D.C.: Brookings.

Barber, James David. 1965. *The Lawmakers*. New Haven, Conn.: Yale University Press.

Barone, Michael, and Grant Ujifusa. 1979. *Almanac of American Politics*. New York: E. P. Dutton.

———. 1981. *Almanac of American Politics*. New York: Barone.

Bauer, Monica, and John R. Hibbing. 1989. "Which Incumbents Lose in House Elections: A Response to Jacobson's 'The Marginals Never Vanished.'" *American Journal of Political Science* 33:262–71.

Beck, Paul Allen, and M. Kent Jennings. 1979. "Political Periods and Political Participation." *American Political Science Review* 73:737–50.

194   References

Bond, Jon R. 1985. "Dimensions of District Attention over Time." *American Journal of Political Science* 29:330–47.

Born, Richard. 1979. "Generational Replacement and the Growth of Incumbent Reelection Margins in the U.S. House." *American Political Science Review* 73:811–17.

———. 1982. "Perquisite Employment in the U.S. House of Representatives." *American Politics Quarterly* 10:347–62.

Brady, David W. 1988. *Critical Elections and Congressional Policy Making.* Stanford, Calif.: Stanford University Press.

Brady, David W., and Naomi Lynn. 1973. "Switched-Seat Congressional Districts: Their Effect on Party Voting and Public Policy." *American Journal of Political Science* 17:528–43.

Brady, David W., and Joseph Stewart. 1982. "Congressional Party Realignment and Transformation of Public Policy in Three Realignment Eras." *American Journal of Political Science* 26:333–60.

Bullock, Charles S. 1972. "House Careerists: Changing Patterns of Longevity and Attrition." *American Political Science Review* 66:1295–1300.

Bullock, Charles S., and Burdett Loomis. 1985. "The Changing Congressional Career." In *Congress Reconsidered,* 3d ed., ed. Lawrence C. Dodd and Bruce I. Oppenheimer. Washington, D.C.: Congressional Quarterly.

Burnham, Walter Dean. 1975. "Insulation and Responsiveness in Congressional Elections." *Political Science Quarterly* 90:411–35.

Cain, Bruce E., John A. Ferejohn, and Morris P. Fiorina. N.d. "Allocation of Personal Staffs by Members of the House of Representatives, 1959–1979." Unpublished paper, Stanford University, Stanford, Calif.

———. 1987. *The Personal Vote.* Cambridge: Harvard University Press.

Campbell, Angus, Philip Converse, Warren Miller, and Donald Stokes. 1960. *The American Voter.* New York: John Wiley and Sons.

Canon, David T. 1988. "Book Review of Glenn Parker's *Homeward Bound.*" *Congress and the Presidency* 15:110–12.

———. 1989. "The Institutionalization of Leadership in the U.S. Congress." *Legislative Studies Quarterly* 14:415–44.

———. 1990. *Actors, Athletes, and Astronauts: Political Amateurs in the United States Congress.* Chicago: University of Chicago Press.

Cherryholmes, Cleo H., and Michael J. Shapiro. 1969. *Representatives and Roll Calls.* Indianapolis, Ind.: Bobbs-Merrill.

Claggett, William, William Flanigan, and Nancy Zingale. 1984. "Nationalization of the American Electorate." *American Political Science Review* 78:77–91.

Clausen, Aage. 1973. *How Congressmen Decide.* New York: St. Martin's.

Clem, Alan. 1977. "Do Representatives Increase in Conservatism as They Increase in Seniority?" *Journal of Politics* 39:193–200.

Collie, Melissa P. 1981. "Incumbency, Electoral Safety, and Turnover in the House of Representatives, 1952–1976." *American Political Science Review* 75:119–32.

———. 1984. "Voting Behavior in Legislatures." *Legislative Studies Quarterly* 9:3–50.

"Congress: Leaders in Peril." 1980. *Newsweek* 29 (September): 26–29.

Congressional Quarterly. 1986. *Congressional Quarterly Almanac, 1985.* Washington, D.C.: Congressional Quarterly.

Converse, Philip E. 1964. "The Nature of Belief Systems in Mass Publics." In *Ideology and Discontent*, ed. David E. Apter. New York: Free Press.

Cook, Rhodes. 1989a. "Is Competition in Elections Becoming Obsolete?" *Congressional Quarterly Weekly Report* 47:1060–65.

———. 1989b. "The Reagan Years and Vin Weber." *Congressional Quarterly Weekly Report* 47:3466.

Cooper, Joseph. 1970. *The Origins of Standing Committees and the Development of the Modern House.* Houston: Rice University Publications.

Cooper, Joseph, and David W. Brady. 1981a. "Institutional Context and Leadership Style: The House from Cannon to Rayburn." *American Political Science Review* 75:411–26.

———. 1981b. "Toward a Diachronic Analysis of Congress." *American Political Science Review* 75:988–1003.

Cover, Albert D. 1980. "Contacting Congressional Constituents: Some Patterns of Perquisite Use." *American Journal of Political Science* 24:125–35.

Cover, Albert D., and David R. Mayhew. 1981. "Congressional Dynamics and the Decline of Competitive Congressional Elections." In *Congress Reconsidered*, 2d ed., ed. Lawrence C. Dodd and Bruce I. Oppenheimer. Washington, D.C.: Congressional Quarterly.

Davidson, Roger H. 1969. *The Role of the Congressman.* New York: Pegasus.

Davidson, Roger H., and Walter J. Oleszek. 1989. *Congress and Its Members.* Washington, D.C.: Congressional Quarterly.

Dodd, Lawrence C. 1983. "The Calculus of Legislative Change." Paper presented at the annual meeting of the Midwest Political Science Association, April, Chicago.

———. 1986. "A Theory of Congressional Cycles: Solving the Puzzle of Change." In *Congress and Policy Change*, ed. Gerald C. Wright, Leroy N. Rieselbach, and Lawrence C. Dodd. New York: Agathon.

Dodd, Lawrence C., and Bruce I. Oppenheimer. 1977. "The House in Transition." In *Congress Reconsidered*, ed. Lawrence C. Dodd and Bruce I. Oppenheimer. New York: Praeger.

———. 1981. "The House in Transition: Change and Consolidation." In *Congress Reconsidered*, 2d ed., ed. Lawrence C. Dodd and Bruce I. Oppenheimer. Washington, D.C.: Congressional Quarterly.

Dometrius, Nelson C., and Lee Sigelman. 1989. "Costs, Benefits, and Careers in the U.S. House of Representatives: A Developmental Approach." Paper presented at the annual meeting of the Southern Political Science Association, November, Memphis, Tenn.

Ehrenhalt, Alan. 1984. "GOP Finds All Politics is Local—After All." *Congressional Quarterly Weekly Report* 42:2979.

———. 1986. "Media, Power Shifts Dominate O'Neill's House." *Congressional Quarterly Weekly Report* 44:2131–38.

———. 1987. "Influence on the Hill: Having It and Using It." *Congressional Quarterly Weekly Report* 45:3–4.

Erikson, Robert S. 1971. "The Advantage of Incumbency in Congressional Elections." *Polity* 3:395–405.

———. 1976. "Is There Such a Thing as a Safe Seat?" *Polity* 9:623–32.

Erikson, Robert S., and Gerald C. Wright. 1985. "Voters, Candidates, and Issues in Congressional Elections." In *Congress Reconsidered*, 3d ed., ed. Lawrence C. Dodd and Bruce I. Oppenheimer. Washington, D.C.: Congressional Quarterly.

Fenno, Richard F., Jr. 1973. *Congressmen in Committees*. Boston: Little, Brown.

———. 1978. *Home Style*. Boston: Little, Brown.

———. 1982. *The United States Senate: A Bicameral Perspective*. Washington, D.C.: American Enterprise Institute.

Ferejohn, John A. 1977. "On the Decline of Competition in Congressional Elections." *American Political Science Review* 71:166–76.

Fiorina, Morris P. 1974. *Representatives, Roll Calls, and Constituencies*. Lexington, Mass.: D. C. Heath.

———. 1977a. "The Case of the Vanishing Marginals: The Bureaucracy Did It." *American Political Science Review* 71:177–84.

———. 1977b. *Congress: Keystone of the Washington Establishment*. New Haven, Conn.: Yale University Press.

———. 1981. "Some Problems in Studying the Effects of Resource Allocation in Congressional Elections." *American Journal of Political Science* 25:543–67.

———. 1989. *Congress: Keystone of the Washington Establishment*. 2d ed. New Haven, Conn.: Yale University Press.

Fiorina, Morris P., David W. Rohde, and Peter Wissel. 1975. "Historical Change in House Turnover." In *Congress in Change*, ed. Norman J. Ornstein. New York: Praeger.

Fowler, Linda L., and Robert D. McClure. 1989. *Political Ambition: Who Decides to Run for Congress*. New Haven, Conn.: Yale University Press.

Frantzich, Stephen E. 1979. "Who Makes Our Laws? The Legislative Effectiveness of Members of the U.S. Congress." *Legislative Studies Quarterly* 4:409–28.

Garand, James C., and Donald R. Gross. 1984. "Change in the Vote Margins for Congressional Elections: A Specification of Historical Trends." *American Political Science Review* 78:17–30.

Glenn, Norval D. 1976. "Cohort Analyses' Futile Quest: Statistical Attempts to Separate Age, Period, and Cohort Effects." *American Sociological Review* 41:900–904.

Hammond, Thomas H., and Jane M. Fraser. 1983a. "Baselines for Evaluating Explanations of Coalition Behavior in Congress." *Journal of Politics* 45:635–56.

———. 1983b. "Null Hypothesis Models in Legislative Studies." *Journal of Politics* 45:672–74.

Hibbing, John R. 1982a. *Choosing to Leave.* Washington, D.C.: University Press of America.

———. 1982b. "Voluntary Retirement from the U.S. House: Who Quits?" *American Journal of Political Science* 26:467–84.

Hibbing, John R., and John R. Alford. 1981. "The Electoral Impact of Economic Conditions." *American Journal of Political Science* 25:423–39.

Hibbing, John R., and John G. Peters. 1990. *The Nature of the United States Senate.* Berkeley, Calif.: Institute of Governmental Studies Press.

Hibbing, John R., and Sue Thomas. 1990. "The Modern United States Senate: What Is Accorded Respect?" *Journal of Politics* 52:126–45.

Hinckley, Barbara. 1970. "Incumbency and Presidential Vote in Senate Elections: Defining Parameters of Subpresidential Voting." *American Political Science Review* 64:836–42.

———. 1971. *The Seniority System in Congress.* Bloomington: Indiana University Press.

———. 1976. "Seniority 1975: Old Theories Confront New Facts." *British Journal of Political Science* 6:383–99.

———. 1980. "The American Voter in Congressional Elections." *American Political Science Review* 74:641–50.

Hook, Janet. 1986. "House Democrats, Republicans Begin Committee Assignments." *Congressional Quarterly Weekly Report* 44:3073.

———. 1987. "Bitterness Lingers from GOP Assignments." *Congressional Quarterly Weekly Report* 45:961.

———. 1988. "The Education of Minnesota's Vin Weber." *Congressional Quarterly Weekly Report* 46:2264.

———. 1990. "New Drive to Limit Tenure Revives an Old Proposal." *Congressional Quarterly Weekly Report* 48:567–69.

Huntington, Samuel P. 1965. "Congressional Responses to the Twentieth Century." In *Congress and America's Future,* ed. David B. Truman. Englewood Cliffs, N.J.: Prentice-Hall.

Jacobson, Gary C. 1983. *The Politics of Congressional Elections.* Boston: Little, Brown.

――――. 1987a. "The Marginals Never Vanished: Incumbency and Competition in Elections to the U.S. House of Representatives, 1952–1982." *American Journal of Political Science* 31:126–41.

――――. 1987b. *The Politics of Congressional Elections.* 2d ed. Boston: Little, Brown.

――――. 1989. "Strategic Politicians and the Dynamics of U.S. House Elections, 1946–1986." *American Political Science Review* 83:773–94.

Jacobson, Gary C., and Samuel Kernell. 1983. *Strategy and Choice in Congressional Elections.* New Haven, Conn.: Yale University Press.

Jennings, M. Kent. 1979. "Another Look at the Life Cycle and Political Participation." *American Journal of Political Science* 73:755–71.

Jennings, M. Kent, and Gregory B. Markus. 1984. "Partisan Orientations over the Long Haul: Results from the Three-Wave Political Socialization Panel Study." *American Political Science Review* 78:1000–1018.

――――. 1988. "Political Involvement in the Later Years: A Longitudinal Survey." *American Journal of Political Science* 32:302–16.

Jewell, Malcolm E., and Samuel C. Patterson. 1986. *The Legislative Process in the United States.* 4th ed. New York: Random House.

Johannes, John R., and John C. McAdams. 1981a. "The Congressional Incumbency Effect: Is It Casework, Policy Compatibility, or Something Else?" *American Journal of Political Science* 25:512–42.

――――. 1981b. "Does Casework Matter?: A Reply to Professor Fiorina." *American Journal of Political Science* 25:581–604.

Katz, Richard S. 1973. "The Attribution of Variance in Electoral Returns: An Alternative Measurement Technique." *American Political Science Review* 67:817–28.

Kernell, Samuel. 1977. "Toward Understanding Nineteenth-Century Congressional Careers." *American Journal of Political Science* 21:669–93.

――――. 1978. "Explaining Presidential Popularity." *American Political Science Review* 72:506–22.

Kingdon, John W. 1981. *Congressmen's Voting Decisions.* 2d ed. New York: Harper and Row.

Kostroski, Warren Lee. 1978. "The Effect of Number of Terms on the Reelection of Senators, 1920–1970." *Journal of Politics* 40:488–97.

Kramer, Gerald H. 1971. "Short-Term Fluctuations in U.S. Voting Behavior, 1896–1964." *American Political Science Review* 65:131–43.

Krasno, Jonathan S., and Donald Philip Green. 1988. "Preempting Quality Challengers in House Elections." *Journal of Politics* 50:920–36.

Kurtz, Karl. 1972. "Elections and the House of Representatives." Ph.D. diss., Washington University, St. Louis, Mo.

Langbein, Laura I., and Lee Sigelman. 1989. "Show Horses, Work Horses, and Dead Horses." *American Politics Quarterly* 17:80–95.

Lewis-Beck, Michael S., and Tom W. Rice. 1984. "Forecasting U.S. House Elections." *Legislative Studies Quarterly* 9:475–90.

Loewenberg, Gerhard. 1971. *Modern Parliaments: Change or Decline?* Chicago: Aldine-Atherton.

Loomis, Burdett A. 1984. "Congressional Careers and Party Leadership in the Contemporary House of Representatives." *American Journal of Political Science* 28:180–202.

———. 1988a. *The New American Politician.* New York: Basic Books.

———. 1988b. "Political Skills and Proximate Goals: Career Development in the House of Representatives." Paper presented at the annual meeting of the American Political Science Association, September, Washington, D.C.

McClosky, Herbert. 1958. "Conservatism and Personality." *American Political Science Review* 52:27–45.

MacRae, Duncan, Jr. 1958. *Dimensions of Congressional Voting.* Berkeley: University of California Press.

Mann, Thomas E. 1978. *Unsafe at Any Margin: Interpreting Congressional Elections.* Washington, D.C.: American Enterprise Institute.

———. 1981. "Elections and Change in Congress." In *The New Congress*, ed. Thomas E. Mann and Norman J. Ornstein. Washington, D.C.: American Enterprise Institute.

Mann, Thomas E., and Raymond E. Wolfinger. 1980. "Candidates and Parties in Congressional Elections." *American Political Science Review* 74:617–32.

Markus, Gregory B. 1983. "Dynamic Modelling of Cohort Change: The Case of Political Partisanship." *American Journal of Political Science* 27:717–39.

Matthews, Donald R. 1960. *U.S. Senators and Their World.* Chapel Hill: University of North Carolina Press.

Matthews, Donald R., and James A. Stimson. 1975. *Yeas and Nays.* New York: John Wiley.

Mayhew, David R. 1966. *Party Loyalty among Congressmen.* Cambridge: Harvard University Press.

———. 1974a. *Congress: The Electoral Connection.* New Haven, Conn.: Yale University Press.

———. 1974b. "Congressional Elections: The Case of the Vanishing Marginals." *Polity* 6:295–317.

Mezey, Michael L. 1981. "Apprenticeship and Participation in the House of Representatives." Paper presented at the annual meeting of the Midwest Political Science Association, April, Cincinnati, Ohio.

Mezey, Michael L., and Robert W. Gaudry. 1979. "The Changing Pattern of Freshman Behavior in the House of Representatives." Paper presented at the annual meeting of the Southern Political Science Association, November, Gatlinburg, Tenn.

Moore, Michael, and Sue Thomas. 1989. "Correlates of Legislative Effectiveness in the United States Senate." Unpublished paper, University of Nebraska, Lincoln.

"Most Want to Limit Time in Congress." 1990. *Lincoln Star*, 12 January, 2.

Mueller, John E. 1973. *War, Presidents, and Public Opinion.* New York: John Wiley and Sons.

Niemi, Richard G., Lynda W. Powell, and Patricia L. Bicknell. 1986. "The Effects of Congruity between Community and District on Salience of U.S. House Candidates." *Legislative Studies Quarterly* 11:187–202.

Olson, David M., and Cynthia T. Nonidez. 1972. "Measures of Legislative Performance in the U.S. House of Representatives." *American Journal of Political Science* 16:269–77.

O'Neill, Thomas P. 1988. *Man of the House.* Boston: G. K. Hall.

Oppenheimer, Bruce I. 1977. "The Rules Committee: New Arm of Leadership in a Decentralized House." In *Congress Reconsidered*, ed. Lawrence C. Dodd and Bruce I. Oppenheimer. New York: Praeger.

Ornstein, Norman J., Thomas E. Mann, and Michael J. Malbin. 1987. *Vital Statistics on Congress, 1987–1988.* Washington, D.C.: American Enterprise Institute.

———. 1990. *Vital Statistics on Congress, 1989–1990.* Washington, D.C.: American Enterprise Institute.

Ornstein, Norman J., Robert L. Peabody, and David W. Rohde. 1989. "Change in the Senate: Toward the 1990s." In *Congress Reconsidered*, 4th ed., ed. Lawrence C. Dodd and Bruce I. Oppenheimer. Washington, D.C.: Congressional Quarterly.

Parker, Glenn R. 1980. "Sources of Change in Congressional District Attention." *American Journal of Political Science* 24:115–24.

———. 1986a. *Homeward Bound: Explaining Changes in Congressional Behavior.* Pittsburgh: University of Pittsburgh Press.

———. 1986b. "Is There a Political Life Cycle in the House of Representatives?" *Legislative Studies Quarterly* 11:375–92.

Payne, James L. 1980. "Show Horses and Work Horses in the United States House of Representatives." *Polity* 12:428–56.

Peabody, Robert L. 1976. *Leadership in Congress.* Boston: Little, Brown.

Pedhazur, Elazar J. 1982. *Multiple Regression in Behavioral Research.* 2d ed. New York: Holt, Reinhart, and Winston.

Polsby, Nelson W. 1968. "The Institutionalization of the U.S. House of Representatives." *American Political Science Review* 62:144–68.

Polsby, Nelson W., Miriam Gallaher, and Barry Rundquist. 1969. "The Growth of the Seniority System in the U.S. House of Representatives." *American Political Science Review* 63:787–807.

Poole, Keith T. 1981. "Dimensions of Interest Group Evaluation of the U.S. Senate, 1969–1978." *American Journal of Political Science* 25:49–67.

Poole, Keith T., and R. Steven Daniels. 1985. "Ideology, Party, and Voting in the U.S. Congress, 1959–1980." *American Political Science Review* 79:373–99.

Poole, Keith T., and Howard Rosenthal. 1985. "A Spatial Model for Legislative Roll Call Analysis." *American Journal of Political Science* 29:357–84.

Price, H. Douglas. 1971. "The Congressional Career: Then and Now." In *Congressional Behavior*, ed. Nelson W. Polsby. New York: Random House.

———. 1975. "Congress and the Evolution of Legislative Professionalism." In *Congress in Change*, ed. Norman J. Ornstein. New York: Praeger.

———. 1977. "Careers and Committees in the American Congress." In *The History of Parliamentary Behavior*, ed. William O. Aydelotte. Princeton, N.J.: Princeton University Press.

Pritchard, Anita. 1986. "An Evaluation of CQ Presidential Support Scores." *American Journal of Political Science* 30:480–95.

Redman, Eric. 1973. *The Dance of Legislation*. New York: Simon and Schuster.

Rice, Stuart A. 1928. *Quantitative Methods in Politics*. New York: Knopf.

Ripley, Randall B. 1988. *Congress: Process and Policy*. New York: W. W. Norton.

Rohde, David W. 1988. "Studying Congressional Norms: Concepts and Evidence." *Congress and the Presidency* 15:139–46.

———. 1989. "Democratic Party Leadership, Agenda Control, and the Resurgence of Partisanship in the House." Paper presented at the annual meeting of the American Political Science Association, September, Atlanta.

Rovner, Julie. 1988. "Turnover in Congress Hits an All-Time Low." *Congressional Quarterly Weekly Report* 46:3362–65.

Schiff, Steven H., and Steven S. Smith. 1983. "Generational Change and the Allocation of Staff in the U.S. Congress." *Legislative Studies Quarterly* 8:457–68.

Schneider, Jerrold E. 1979. *Ideological Coalitions in Congress*. Westport, Conn.: Greenwood Press.

Schneider, William. 1989. "JFK's Children: The Class of 1974." *Atlantic Monthly* 263 (March): 35–59.

Schneier, Edward V. 1988. "Norms and Folkways in Congress: How Much Has Actually Changed?" *Congress and the Presidency* 15:117–38.

Searing, Donald. 1985. "Comment on Cain, Ferejohn, and Fiorina." *American Political Science Review* 79:1174–75.

Shaffer, Samuel. 1980. *On and Off the Floor*. New York: Newsweek Books.

Shannon, Wayne. 1968. *Party, Constituency, and Congressional Voting*. Baton Rouge: Louisiana State University Press.

Shepsle, Kenneth A. 1978. *The Giant Jigsaw Puzzle*. Chicago: University of Chicago Press.

————. 1987. "Representation and Governance: The Great Legislative Trade-off." Paper presented at the Constitutional Bicentennial Conference, May, Dartmouth College, Hanover, N.H.

Shively, W. Phillips. 1979a. "Rejoinder to Abramson." *Political Methodology* 6:457–61.

————. 1979b. "The Relationship between Age and Party Identification: A Cohort Analysis." *Political Methodology* 6:437–46.

Sinclair, Barbara Deckard. 1976. "Political Upheaval and Congressional Voting." *Journal of Politics* 38:326–45.

————. 1983. *Majority Leadership in the U.S. House.* Baltimore: Johns Hopkins University Press.

————. 1986. "Senate Styles and Senate Decision-Making, 1955–1980." *Journal of Politics* 48:877–908.

Smith, Steven S. 1986. "Revolution in the House: Why Don't We Do It on the Floor." Brookings Discussion Paper No. 5, Brookings Institution, Washington, D.C.

Smith, Steven S., and Christopher J. Deering. 1984. *Committees in Congress.* Washington, D.C.: Congressional Quarterly.

Stimson, James A. 1985. "Regression in Space and Time: A Statistical Essay." *American Journal of Political Science* 29:914–47.

Stokes, Donald E. 1973. "Comment: On the Measurement of Electoral Dynamics." *American Political Science Review* 67:829–31.

Strate, John, Charles J. Parrish, Charles D. Elder, and Coit Ford III. 1989. "Life Span Civic Development and Voting Participation." *American Political Science Review* 83:443–64.

Struble, Robert, Jr. 1980. "House Turnover and the Principle of Rotation." *Political Science Quarterly* 94:649–67.

Stubben, Jerry, and John R. Hibbing. 1987. "The Prestige of Formal Positions in the Modern U.S. House of Representatives." Paper presented at the annual meeting of the Midwest Political Science Association, April, Chicago.

Swift, Al. 1989. "The 'Permanent Congress' Is a Myth." *Washington Post National Weekly Edition* 6 (June 26–July 2): 29.

Tobin, Maurice B. 1986. *Hidden Power: The Seniority System and Other Customs of Congress.* New York: Greenwood Press.

Tufte, Edward R. 1975. "Determinants of the Outcome of Midterm Congressional Elections." *American Political Science Review* 69:812–26.

————. 1978. *Political Control of the Economy.* Princeton, N.J.: Princeton University Press.

Turner, Julius (with Edward Schneier). 1970. *Party and Constituency.* Rev. ed. Baltimore: Johns Hopkins University Press.

Van Doren, Peter M. 1990. "Can We Learn the Causes of Congressional Decisions from Roll-Call Data?" *Legislative Studies Quarterly* 15:311–40.

Verba, Sidney, and Norman H. Nie. 1972. *Participation in America: Political Democracy and Social Equality.* New York: Harper and Row.

Vertz, Laura L., John P. Frendreis, and James L. Gibson. 1987. "Nationalization of the Electorate in the United States." *American Political Science Review* 81:961–66.

Weisberg, Herbert F. 1983. "Alternative Baseline Models and Their Implications for Understanding Coalition Behavior in Congress." *Journal of Politics* 45:657–71.

Westlye, Mark C. 1983. "Competitiveness of Senate Seats and Voting Behavior in Senate Elections." *American Journal of Political Science* 27:253–83.

Will, George. 1990. "Limiting Congressional Terms Just Won't Wash." *Lincoln Star*, 8 January, 14.

Williams, Robin M., Jr. 1968. "The Concept of Norms." In vol. 10 of *International Encyclopedia of the Social Sciences*, ed. David L. Sills. New York: Macmillan.

Wilson, Rick K. 1986. "What Was It Worth to Be on a Committee in the U.S. House, 1889 to 1913?" *Legislative Studies Quarterly* 11:47–64.

Wittmer, T. Richard. 1964. "The Aging of the House." *Political Science Quarterly* 79:526–41.

Index